REVOLUTIONARIES

www.royalcollins.com

REVOLUT

ONARIES

THE **BLOOD** OF THE MARTYRS WHO GAVE BIRTH TO NEW CHINA

He Jianming

REVOLUTIONARIES:

The Blood of the Martyrs Who Gave Birth to New China

HE JIANMING

First published in 2022 by Royal Collins Publishing Group Inc.
Groupe Publication Royal Collins Inc.
BKM Royalcollins Publishers Private Limited

Headquarters: 550-555 boul. René-Lévesque O Montréal (Québec) H2Z1B1 Canada
India office: 805 Hemkunt House, 8th Floor, Rajendra Place, New Delhi 110 008

© Copyright 2020 by He Jianming
Originally published in China as《革命者》
Translated with the permission of the author and the Shanghai Literature
& Art Publishing House

All rights reserved. Without limiting the rights under copyright reserved above, no part of this publication may be reproduced, stored in or introduced into a retrieval system, or transmitted in any form or by any means (electronic, mechanical, photocopying, recording or otherwise), without the prior written permission of both the copyright owner and the above publisher of this book.

ISBN: 978-1-4878-0910-2

To find out more about our publications, please visit www.royalcollins.com.

*We are grateful for the financial assistance of B&R Book Program
in the publication of this book.*

PROLOGUE

Singers of October 1st

TRUE, JUST A FEW MONTHS BEFORE THE FOUNDING OF THE People's Republic of China, and only ten days away from the liberation of Shanghai, your son sacrificed his life—becoming one of the last martyrs who shed blood and died gloriously for the birth of the country...

He died a hero. As an audit officer at the Central Bank of the Kuomintang Government, as soon as he discovered that Chiang Kai-shek urged Tang Enbo of Shanghai to smuggle the last batch of gold from the treasury to Taiwan five times in a row, he notified the Shanghai underground party organization promptly, while uniting and leading the staff of the Central Bank to suppress the last madness of the reactionaries...

"They have transported four million taels of gold, almost emptied the treasury. We have to stop them and save the last bit..."

"Indeed, we swear to guard the life-saving money of millions of people in Shanghai!"

It has been six days since the battle to liberate Shanghai broke out. At night, when your son and the bank clerks were plotting a collective uprising at full stretch, dozens of heavily armed secret agents broke in: "Freeze! Get'em all!"

They tortured him in the basement with all sorts of excruciations: "Confess! How much information did you leak to the communists?"

Prologue

His skin was ripped, bleeding, his eyes wide open, he scowled at them, "It is hardly a secret, the smuggling of gold and silver from the treasury, is it?"

"A Harvard graduate, and your father is a senior of our party. President Chiang would appreciate that you come to Taiwan with us. You should know better and ditch the Communist Party. Siding with them is anything but promising." A senior Kuomintang official deigned to play the good cop.

He sneered: "A dying regime, to an island, do you hear yourselves?" Then, he raised his blood-filled head at the secret agent, and persuaded, "Last chance to switch ships. Come to the light."

"Shut his crazy mouth. Shut it! Now!" The head of the secret agents shouted furiously, and his minions attacked your son.

"Since he cannot be persuaded, leave him in Shanghai!" Tang commanded Mao Sen, the head of the secret agents, who came to report.

"Alive?" Mao Sen was struck by a sudden chill as he thought of you.

"President Chiang has ordered them to be killed." Tang Enbo sneered, "Leave a corpse."

"Understood."

The sound of gunshots on the outskirts was approaching the Bund. In the middle of the night, rescue operations were underway.

"Get up!" At the same time, the Kuomintang agents dragged your son up from a pool of blood.

"What do you want?" He woke up from the coma, resisting, trying to kick them with his legs.

"Well, look at those legs! Break'em!" In the chaotic noise, his legs were immediately fractured. He fell back into a coma. They dragged him out of the basement to a clump of grass and threw him carelessly into a previously dug pit.

The enemies buried him alive.

When that happened, you were in Beijing discussing with Mao Zedong, Zhu De, and Zhou Enlai about forming the Central People's Government of the People's Republic.

Six days after the liberation of Shanghai, you noticed the news in *Ta Kung Pao* about the murder of martyrs who guarded the bank: "Murderous enemies buried patriots alive."

Singers of October 1st

Thirteen bodies excavated from the Nanshi secret service agency yesterday
Nanshi Chezhan Road, No. 190 is the secret service agency of the
Ministry of National Defense of the Kuomintang Government. Before the
People's Liberation Army freed Shanghai, arrested patriots were sent there
every day to be killed. As the city was liberated, the People's Liberation Army
took over this murderous den. The agents had fled, leaving behind only an old
concierge to guard the gate. Yesterday, the nasty stench in the open space of
the backyard drew the attention of People's Liberation Army, who started to
dig by the wall in the southwest corner and unearthed the body of a victim.

When you read this, you could hardly breathe. The report continued: as soon as your daughter-in-law heard the tragic news—

She rushed there immediately and identified the corpse. The murder of the
deceased was extremely brutal. His hands were tied behind his back with
hemp rope, his head was covered with cloth, and his body was covered in
blood, indicating torture when he was alive. It is believed that he was buried
alive, and the bottom of the pit was covered with lime. Because the mud in
the two spots near the northwest wall and the middle of the north was loose,
it was doubted that there must be corpses underneath. Workmen were hired
to dig. Down less than three feet, three dead bodies were found one after
another, murdered in the same cruelty, and four feet down the mud in the
middle of the north were piled with corpses. One by one, they were hoisted
from the soil by the workmen with a rope. There were nine in total, and with
the first four, thirteen killed.

Your heart ached, so painful that you could no longer read more. Your boy and the other twelve martyrs were tormented by the secret agents with utmost brutality. It was too much to bear.

"The bodies are naked, some with broken heads, some broken feet." And the report disclosed clearly that the body with a broken right foot was identified by your daughter-in-law, the second son you were so proud of.

My boy! You died so miserably!

Tragically and magnificently!

You held the *Ta Kung Pao* newspaper, old tears soaking the picture of

Prologue

the blurry naked body at the excavation site.

You were drowning in grief and fury.

However, you had to bury this grief and fury deep in your heart at the moment, and devote yourself to the great cause of assisting Mao Zedong and other Chinese communists in the founding of the country.

You were a typical old intellectual, but also a passionate revolutionary. Building a people's republic where the people rule was your lifelong pursuit. As a Shanghai native, you followed Sun Yat-sen when you were young, holding the banner of "Education to Save the Nation," and founded Pudong Elementary School, Pudong Middle School, and the famous Chinese Vocational School. You were the leader of the Democratic National Construction Association, participating in the formation of the Central People's Government of various parties, led by the Chinese Communist Party.

October 1, 1949, was a great day.

Before that, you participated in the first Chinese People's Political Consultative Conference, where matters concerning the establishment of the PRC were decided. As an important member of the decision-making of this historic cause, you were filled with great excitement, when looking at the new realm under the leadership of the Communist Party of China.

"Indeed, we are excited. Today, we, under the leadership of the Communist Party and Chairman Mao, are honored to announce the great opening of the Chinese People's Political Consultative Conference."

"We are going to build the People's Republic of China on the eastern continent."

This was the heartfelt words of a revolutionary who longed for national rejuvenation, independence, freedom and happiness, and has fought for those all his life. Your speech at the National Committee of the Chinese People's Political Consultative Conference was eloquent, loud and clear, and poetic, cheering up everyone present, even the leaders of the Communist Party of China such as Mao Zedong, Zhu De, Zhou Enlai were attentive, listening to every word you uttered:

"Indeed, the new nation will be beautiful and great."

"Indeed, the new nation will be independent, democratic, peaceful, united, and prosperous."

Singers of October 1st

"Indeed, the new nation will be fueled by the common program of the Chinese People's Political Consultative Conference."

October 1st was finally upon us, the birthday of a great new nation that the Chinese have been longing for hundreds of years. It was a grand holiday for the 400 million Chinese, and a day of special significance to you. You were born on October 1, 1878, in a poor family of scholars in Chuansha County in Shanghai.

The midwife joked your father that you were a chubby boy. He laughed and gave you a resounding first name Yanpei–meaning to remind you constantly that wherever you go, never forget your Chinese origin.

At the grand celebration of the birth of PRC, you stood beside Chairman Mao on the Tiananmen Gate tower, watching the crowds cheering and red flags on the square. You were elated as if the blood in your whole body was burning.

"Comrades! The Central People's Government of the People's Republic of China is established today!" With Chairman Mao's solemn declaration, a great amount of pride and joy washed over you, overwhelming.

History is a textbook, and we are all students who have benefited, one new era after another is formed, developed, and advanced as guided by this textbook, you thought to yourself.

The parade of the founding ceremony commenced. In the sound of majestic melody, groups of People's Liberation Army officers and soldiers who survived the hard-fought wars and the brightly dressed teams of workers, farmers, businessmen, and students marched forward cheering through Tiananmen Square, inspected by Chairman Mao and other founding fathers. Cheers and shouts of slogans, accompanied by the sound of national flags waving in the wind, echoed across the sky.

"Long live Chairman Mao!"

"Long live the people!"

"Long live the Communist Party!

"Long live the motherland!"

Together, the square and the gate tower responded with roars, the voice of 400 million Chinese people, and the voice of leaders of the Chinese Communists. It was a magnificent moment, in which Huang Yanpei was completely captivated.

Prologue

"Birthday! My birthday! The People's Republic of China's birthday!" At first, those were silent words inside his heart, but he couldn't help uttering them out loud.

Chairman Mao smiled at him; Zhu De did the same.

Zhou Enlai stretched out his hand to him; Soong Ching Ling smiled and opened her arms to him.

"Happy Birthday!"

"Happy Birthday!"

"Happy Birthday!"

...

Huang Yanpei, who was in his 70s, did not see it coming. It was a humane episode in the founding ceremony. Huang blushed and replied in Shanghai dialect, "I could not be happier, thank you all."

At the end of that day, he confessed to an old friend, in tears: "I have followed Mr. Sun Yat-sen for decades. This is exactly the day that we have been longing for, isn't it?"

"Indeed, my friend." The friend confirmed.

The founding ceremony did not end until nearly ten o'clock that night. When Huang returned home, he was no less excited, looking up to the east outside the window, and he felt the urge to compose poetry:

Underneath the five-star flag
We sing the national anthem
To the country, a new name is given
People's Republic of China

...

It's people's government
It's people's armed forces
It's people's country
On Tiananmen Square
300,000 people present at the founding ceremony
The red flag symbolizes the loyalty
To defend the nation
To love the people

...

Singers of October 1st

> *Sacrifices are made for the revolution*
> *By the heroes*
> *Immortal they are*
> *Guarding the gate of the new nation*

As soon as the poem was finished, it was already a rosy dawn.

"Why the tears?" His wife was astonished as she gently put on him the coat.

"Let's go see our son!" He put on his coat, ready to leave.

"Back to Shanghai?"

"No, to Tiananmen Square."

After he arrived at the square, he observed hundreds of people from a distance around the newly built Monument to the People's Heroes offering flowers, saluting, or gazing with respect.

Excited again, he composed another short poem—

> *Every time we walk through Tiananmen Square*
> *We think of thousands of heroes*
> *Who sacrificed themselves for the country and the people*
> *One of them is you*

"Son, this is for you, and for the thousands of heroes who did the same as you."

I read the story in the Shanghai Longhua Revolutionary Martyrs Memorial Hall of Huang Yanpei's Singers of October 1st and the death of his son Huang Jingwu ten days before Shanghai's liberation. And it was a reading experience that has had a long-lasting effect because my heart has not calmed down ever since. Those words composed by such a friend of the Communist Party of China for his son burn eternally in my heart, so I began to explore the heroic epics of the martyrs.

In the process, I was stunned to discover that in the history of the Chinese revolution, Shanghai, where the Communist Party of China was born and the early organs of Central Committee of the Communist Party of China were located, witnessed countless struggles and fights of the

Prologue

revolutionaries, who since 1921 have shed a river of blood for the liberation of the city and the founding of new China.

I was also shocked to find that Shanghai was, in addition to the birthplace of the Communist Party of China and the seat of the early organs of Central Committee of the Communist Party of China, where the Jiangsu Provincial Committee of the Communist Party of China was located, which fought the harshest battles against Kuomintang Nanjing government. For the multiple roles of Shanghai, the number of Chinese Communists who sacrificed their lives in Shanghai under the White Terror was particularly large, especially among those high-ranking officials in the party. Over half of the martyrs who died in Nanjing Yuhuatai were working for the underground party in Shanghai.

Therefore, since the Qing Ming Festival in 2014, I have been tracing the footsteps of the martyrs in Shanghai and Nanjing, among other places, and vow to complete such a work that shines with the light of the Communist Manifesto and the character of the Communists:

REVOLUTIONARIES

Table of Contents

PROLOGUE

Singers of October 1st / v

CHAPTER ONE

The First Blood / 3

CHAPTER TWO

Flames of War on Nanjing Road / 33

CHAPTER THREE

Shanghai University: A Crucible for Revolution / 65

CHAPTER FOUR

1927, the Year Dyed Red by the Blood of Communists... / 113

CHAPTER FIVE

The Higher the Position, the Greater the Risk of Death—No Regrets / 143

CHAPTER SIX

Intrigues, Defectors, Wrong Routes: the Reign of Terror / 173

CHAPTER SEVEN

The Flower of Life Blooms / 207

Table of Contents

CHAPTER EIGHT

Youth Comes Gently, Leaves Too Soon... / 231

CHAPTER NINE

My Love, Roses of Blood / 255

CHAPTER TEN

Family Note, Last Note and Final Cry, the Eternal Wave... / 295

REVOLUTIONARIES

CHAPTER ONE

The First Blood

Who shed thousands of hectares of blood, cleansing the filth of this world?
Who ignited the fire in the heart, burning the sins of mankind?
My friends, who sacrificed for justice, a glorious death indeed,
Which I hope becomes the fuse, detonating the bombs of the revolution,
Marching forward in the sunlight.

THE AUTHOR OF THIS POEM IS GUO BOHE, AN UNFAMILIAR NAME. Even in the Shanghai Longhua Revolutionary Martyrs Memorial Hall, there is merely some brief introduction of him if one searches carefully. And I believe that if I hadn't accidentally came across one of his poems, maybe I would never remember his name.

There are exhibits of the heroic deeds of over 3,000 martyrs in two revolutionary martyrs memorial halls, Longhua in Shanghai and Yuhuatai in Nanjing. However, we may have merely heard of dozens of them. And this book aims to make hundreds of their names known and remembered.

This indignant poem was written for one of his classmates, Huang Ren, the first young communist I saw at the Martyrs Memorial Hall, who died in Shanghai, only 20 years old. In October 1924, Shanghai business and academic circles held a rally to commemorate the 13th anniversary of the Revolution of 1911. He was thrown off a seven-foot high platform by a group of thugs employed by the Kuomintang rightists and was violently punched and kicked. Qu Qiubai and others rushed to the hospital where he was taken as soon as they heard the news, but the doctors failed to save the young revolutionary.

The memorial service for Huang was hosted by Chen Wangdao. Yun Daiying, Qu Qiubai, and He Bingyi took to the stage to give speeches, denouncing the criminal actions of the reactionaries. Compared with the few well-known early revolutionary youth leaders of the Communist Party, the name of Guo Bohe is known to almost no one. But around 1924, he was a well-known revolutionary and the Chairman of the National Student Union Congress. Four years older than his classmate and friend Huang Ren, Guo was a native of Nanxi, Sichuan. His father was a *xiucai* (one who passed the imperial examination at the county level in the Ming and Qing dynasties), thus his family was well-off nobility. Since childhood, Guo sympathized with the suffering masses and could not stand the dark forces of the old society. When he turned 16 years old, he fervently denounced the oppression of imperialism and feudalism in China at the memorial of General Cai E. In 1922, with the dream of saving the country, he came to Shanghai to study and seek truth, where he often attended the lectures of Chen Duxiu, Qu Qiubai, and Yun Daiying, and befriended his progressive classmates Huang Ren, Liu Hua, and Li Shuoxun, who together founded the Civilian World Society and launched the progressive magazine *Civilian World*. For his progressive thinking and dedication to student work, Guo was soon elected as the Chairman school's Student Union. It was at the rally Guo held and hosted that Huang was beaten to death. Guo was also one of 15 victims, beaten and injured when the spies attacked them and was brutally imprisoned in a cell. Upon release, he learned the tragic news of the death of his classmate and friend Huang and immediately mobilized the students to fight. He personally drafted the manuscript to the All-China Federation of Students. Guo made a solemn vow in front of Huang's body.

For you
I shall scream
I shall mourn
I shall finish your unfinished revolutionary missions
We shall be more enthusiastic, more diligent than ever
We shall stand on the front line of the revolution

The First Blood

> *Comrade Huang, who died before us*
> *Give us some strength*
> *We shall march forward on your blood*

This is the voice of the revolutionaries. This is the revolutionary spirit of that era. In less than three years, on June 26, 1927, Guo, who served as the Minister of Organization of the Jiangsu Provincial Committee of the Communist Party of China (CPC), along with Chen Duxiu's son Chen Yannian, and Huang Jingxi, were arrested by reactionaries at 104, Hengfengli, Shanyin Road, Hongkou District, Shanghai. A few days later, he was shot and killed at the age of 27.

He died in 1927, when the Great Revolution failed. It was a year when tens of thousands of communists and revolutionaries like him were killed.

Regarding Huang's demise, he was the first early youth member of the Chinese Communist Party to be killed on the streets of Shanghai, which immediately ignited outrage throughout the city and even the country. Chen Duxiu, the standard bearer of the May Fourth Movement, who had extensive influence among the youth and the people at that time, at once published an article condemning the counter-revolutionary atrocities. Various progressive newspapers in Shanghai reported the tragic death of Huang, excoriating the crimes of the reactionary hooligans. The All-China Students' Federation and Shanghai universities broadcast the tragic news across country. For a time, the Huang Ren tragedy put the entire society in shock. As the Republic of China Daily supplement *Awakening* put it, the death of martyr Huang has aroused enormous grief and indignation among the youth; this was expanding his circle, making the voice of revolution heard loud and clear among them and at every forgotten corner of the society.

Two months after the tragedy, from January 11 to 22, 1925, the Fourth National Congress of the CPC took place in Shanghai. In the three years since the First National Congress in 1921, the number of party members has increased from over 50 at the beginning to 994. In the meantime, as the *Awakening* pointed out, the sacrifice of young student Huang Ren has awakened countless progressive youth and intellectuals to join the revolutionary torrent led by the CPC. As China's largest city, Shanghai was

Revolutionaries

where workers and students gathered the most. Naturally, there were more party members and revolutionaries than any other place. By the time the Fourth National Congress of the Party was held, Shanghai had grown into the center of the national revolution.

The storm of revolution was brewing in this great eastern city.

This was related to the historical trend at home and abroad back then, and of course to the birth and rise of the CPC in this very city.

It is necessary to mention some crucial historical shots here.

The first shot was on the eve of the birth of the CPC: at the end of the nineteenth century, a group of intellectuals from the Society for the Diffusion of Christian and General Knowledge Among the Chinese (SDCK) gathered to discuss a book, *The History of Socialism,* commissioned by the British missionary Timothy Richard. It introduced Marx, the originator of the doctrine of socialism and the communist doctrine that were emerging in Europe, and labeled him the most famous and authoritative figure in the history of socialism; he and his friend Engels were widely believed to lead the scientific and revolutionary socialist faction, which has representatives in all civilized countries, and everyone regarded it the most powerful new faction in socialism.

"China is a great country, once the most powerful in the world. Today, even the Japanese pirates dare to invade. We shall never tolerate it. It's time that this new faction should rise and make a change." In 1894, the SDCK founded by the British missionaries aimed to replace the old ideas of China with the new ones of the West. The truth is that it was colonialism and enslavement in disguise that hindered the future of China. However, the SDCK had also blended some new doctrines such as socialism and communism. In this way, Marx and his concepts of socialism and communism made a debut in Shanghai, China. From February to April 1899, the *Global Magazine* sponsored by the SDCK in Shanghai serialized an article entitled *Big Classmates,* calling him the famous leader of the working class.

In the 20th century, Marx and his socialist and communist doctrines have gradually become a special light among the many roads of salvation explored on the Shanghai docks. Some progressive newspapers in Shanghai at the time regarded socialism and communism as bright and magnificent

The First Blood

like the budding of a spring flower, soon to sweep the world. It was also at this time that a group of young intellectuals in pursuit of national independence and liberation took their initial impressions of Marx, of socialism and communism across the sea to Europe and the United States to study for the truth and national salvation. Among them, there were pioneers of the Chinese communist movement such as Chen Duxiu, Li Da, Li Hanjun, Chen Wangdao, as well as revolutionaries who fought side by side with the CPC like Lu Xun, and those who later became a KMT theorist like Dai Jitao.

In November 1917, the Russian October Revolution broke out, feeding China with Marxism-Leninism. Revolutionaries who pursued national salvation and truth were therefore inspired, proud and incandescent, for a good fight. Li Dazhao in the north was the first to raise the banner of Marxism, shouting that the October Revolution was the dawn of a new civilization in the world. He publicly proclaimed and advocated that the revolution of the working class would be the world-wide trend, all exploiting classes, warlords, and foreign aggressive forces would be swallowed in the torrent and wither like autumn leaves one by one, and all the laborers and farmers would act together to create a brand new world where communism thrives.

At the end of 1918, in the chilly wind of a pier on the Huangpu River a young man away from his home for years, carrying a diploma from the Civil Engineering Department of the Tokyo Imperial University and two large cloth bags, set foot on the Bund. He was called Li Hanjun, one of the representatives of the First Congress of the CPC.

Li was more fluent in Japanese than Mandarin because he had studied in Japan with his brother since early childhood. Years of Japanese training and studies made him behave more like a Japanese boy. However, this young Chinese who was deeply influenced by Japanese education showed little interest in civil engineering, which his father urged him to do. Instead, he was fascinated with Marxism in college, and slowly became a disseminator of Marxism and communism. There was not even one book on civil engineering in the two cloth bags he brought back from Japan. They were all Marxist books in English, German, and Japanese.

Back then, there were two big fish in the Chinese intellectual circles in Shanghai, Cai Yuanpei and Dai Jitao. Cai represented the revolutionary faction of saving the country through education, while Dai advocated a new propaganda faction of socialism. Dai lived in Yuyangli, a place that attracted many revolutionary intellectuals in favor of Marxism and communism. Eight months later, Chen Duxiu joined them there and commenced with fellow comrades the preparation for the establishment of the CPC. It has therefore become the office for the early Communist Party of China and where the preparation to build the Chinese Communist Youth League took place.

"Hanjun, come meet a fellow from Hubei." One day, Zhan Dabei, an alternate member of the KMT Central Committee and representative of the KMT government in Shanghai, introduced Li Hanjun to an honest-looking man. "This is Dong Biwu."

"Nice to meet you." The handshake led to a friendship between these two men, who would become confidants and comrades. They both attended the first National Congress of the CPC two years later.

From the day they made acquaintances, Li explained the Russian October Revolution and Marxism to Dong Biwu and Zhan Dabei every day, and showed them the progressive magazines *Dawn, Transformation,* and *New Wave* that he brought back from Japan. Both Dong and Zhan used to follow Sun Yat-sen, but they began to worship Marxism and believe in communism because of Li. Several years later, Dong confided in the wife of a famous American journalist Edgar Snow that he embarked on the revolutionary road of communism because of Li and called Li his Marxism teacher.

Zhan Dabei, three years old than Li, was already a pioneer of the anti-Yuan Shih-kai movement of Hubei and even of the nation before they met. During the period of cooperation between the KMT and the Communist Party, Zhan participated in the drafting of the Manifesto on the Reorganization of the Chinese KMT, which in fact incorporates many ideas of communism. In 1926, he accompanied the Northern Expedition to Wuhan and served as a member of the Hubei Provincial Government Affairs Committee and acting director of the Department of Finance. On December 16, 1927, as he was having a discussion with Li at home, a team of KMT agents broke in, arrested them, and took them to the Public

The First Blood

Security Bureau of the Wuhan National Government. The reactionary agents, without initiating any interrogation, executed them on the bank of Huangxiao River on Zhongshan Avenue with the charge of conspiracy with the Communist Party. The two Hubei revolutionaries were butchered. Half an hour before the arrest, Zhan urged his wife Chen Xihui to warn Dong, who took refuge in a friend's house on Nanxiao Road in the Japanese Concession, to evacuate promptly, given that the current situation was tense. His last words saved Dong's life. Zhan's wife took the risk to find the place in the Japanese Concession and informed the landlord of the danger, so that Dong could timely disguise himself as a cook, boarded a steamer, and fled to Shanghai.

Now let's flash back to those years after Li and Dong made their acquaintance at Zhan's residence:

Earlier, an important figure in Shanghai was invited by Cai Yuanpei to teach at Peking University. It was Chen Duxiu.

At the request of Cai, when Chen Duxiu left for Beijing, he took away a copy of *New Youth*, which had cast a great influence in promoting Marxism and communism in Shanghai. Li Hanjun, who had just returned to China, was determined to act as a Chinese propagandist for Marxism, co-founded *Weekly Review* with Dai Jitao and Shen Xuanlu, thus joining the torrent of Chinese progressive forces at that time.

Dai Jitao and Shen Xuanlu, who worked with Li, were prominent figures among radical intellectuals in Shanghai. In his early years, Dai followed Sun Yat-sen as a member of the Chinese Revolutionary League. He was good at theory, rather interested in Marxism at the beginning, and made some efforts promoting it. However, he developed his personal Dai-ism that deviated from authentic Marxism. Subsequently, he devoted himself to serving Chiang Kai-shek as the director of the Political Department of the Whampoa Military Academy, where he earned the nickname Chiang's shadow writer and KMT theoretician. In February 1949, seeing that the Chinese Communists he had used to fight side by side defeated the KMT, the mortified theoretician committed suicide.

Shen Xuanlu was no less notorious. Not only did he edit and publish *New Youth* with Chen Duxiu, but he was also a member of the Shanghai Marxist Research Association and participated in the formation of the

CPC. Shen was the Speaker of Zhejiang Province as early as 1916, and served as the commander-in-chief of the Zhejiang Student Army during the Northern Expedition. Next, having getting acquainted with Chen Duxiu and other advanced intellectuals in Shanghai, he converted to communism. In addition to his contribution to the formation of the CPC, he also helped draft the *Program of the CPC*. Shen had a change of beliefs, divorced himself from the CPC, and joined the KMT. While serving as the director of KMT's Zhejiang Provincial Party Headquarters, he ordered the arrest of over 1,800 revolutionaries from Zhejiang, a large number of communists were shot to death. He betrayed the revolution, a sinner. In 1928, he was assassinated. Nobody knows who the killer was.

This was what happened later.

When Li Hanjun returned to Shanghai, Chen Duxiu was in Beijing. Under the wing of Cai Yuanpei, Chen joined hands with comrade Li Dazhao. With the help of Deng Zhongxia, Zhang Guotao, and a group of talented and incandescent youth from Hunan, including Mao Zedong, Chen's reputation and influence in Beijing continued to grow.

Then World War I ended, a major event for China and the world. As one of the victorious Entente countries, China was waiting for the return of Qingdao, which Germany occupied before the war. Naturally, Chen was advocating justice to triumph over power.

On January 18, 1919, the Paris Peace Conference was convened, where the issue of a peace treaty with Germany was discussed. However, the Conference was mostly controlled by the five powers of Britain, France, the United States, Italy, and Japan, who totally ignored the solemn protests and demands of the Chinese representatives and decided to transfer all the German privileges of Qingdao and Shandong to Japan. It was a humiliation to China.

Therefore, the moment the results of the Paris Peace Conference spread to China, on May 2, led by student leaders Deng Zhongxia and others, over two thousand protesters rallied at Peking University. Immediately, people from all walks of life in Beijing responded and protested against the traitorous authorities and foreign embassies and institutions in China. Chen Duxiu published articles in newspapers, calling on the Chinese to wake up and fight resolutely against the traitorous government and imperialist

The First Blood

forces. On May 4, over 3,000 students from more than a dozen schools in Beijing marched in the streets, flags held high, and gathered in Tiananmen Square from all directions, shouting slogans like *Resist the power outside, eliminate the traitors inside! Return Qingdao! Abolish Article 21! Never sign at the Paris Peace Conference!*

The great May Fourth Movement astonished the world.

Immediately, the student movement in Beijing ignited the country and more took place across the territory. The theme of the movement went beyond anti-imperialist and anti-comprador governments to opposing feudalism and old culture. At the forefront of the movement were young students and intellectuals. There was no doubt that Chen Duxiu and Li Dazhao, who were in the center of the May Fourth Movement, became heroes among them at that time.

Chen's active nature and sharp writing also influenced the movement. On the night of June 11, in a white hat and suit, he had something in his pocket: mimeographed leaflets of the *Beijing Citizens Declaration* he wrote in both Chinese and English. The secret agents had long had their eyes on him. As he distributed the leaflets, they immediately arrested and imprisoned him.

The imprisonment of the hero of the May Fourth Movement naturally shocked the nation again. Even Sun Yat-sen pressured the Beiyang government to release him. With public help, Chen, after being imprisoned for 98 days, was eventually released on September 16, 1919. To celebrate, *New Youth* published vernacular poems by intellectual leaders such as Liu Bannong, Hu Shi, Li Dazhao, and Shen Yinmo. Li Dazhao's poem reads:

We are delighted that you are released.
No prison or horror can bend you.
We are delighted that you are released.
The youth are living the words you uttered, out of the lab and into the prison,
and vice versa.

The great stormy movement and days of imprisonment built Chen a more profound prestige among the progressive forces of the Chinese revolution.

He therefore changed from a democrat to a Marxist and had a clearer attitude towards the revolution and its leadership. When he secretly left Beijing, he issued a declaration *To Beijing Workers*, which explained that the labor world he was talking about refers to the people with no property that feed on their labor entirely; they make up the proletarian working class. And he chanted, *when the revolution time comes, we must fight the devil!*

It was bitter cold in Shanghai in early 1920. Snow covered both banks of the Huangpu River, and Yuyangli in the French Concession was all white.

"I am bathed in warmth when I am next to you, like by the fireplace." He scooted on the snow and arrived at 2 Yuyangli, Huanlong Road. Once he saw Li Hanjun and Chen Wangdao, he took off his coat, shook hands with both of them, and talked incandescently. Chen was a person with endless passion. He sat down to discuss a major matter with them.

"The October Revolution triumphed. We have to do one thing, establish our own political party. I had already had a discussion about it with Mr. Li Dazhao before leaving Beijing. And I am here in Shanghai because I believe we can make this great cause together!"

Chen Duxiu didn't waste a second before elaborating his visions and tasks.

"To establish a political party, we must first be ideologically ready. Now the ideas and dissemination of socialism and Marxism are rather chaotic. There should be an authoritative position to spread the real Marxism," Chen Wangdao pointed out.

Li Hanjun added: "I agree. To do that, we must first thoroughly study Marxism, so that we will not lose our way. I suggest that we should imitate Japan, establish a Marxism research association first and translate the key work *The Communist Manifesto* of Marx and Engels as soon as possible."

Chen Duxiu nodded frequently to their opinions. "That's quite true. The formation of a political party must rely on ready theories." He spoke as he paced around in the room. Suddenly, he stopped and suggested, "So, the prior task is to translate *The Communist Manifesto* and publish it in Hanjun's *Weekly Review*. Next, we establish a Marxism Research Association to prepare for the establishment of our own proletarian party.

The First Blood

In the meantime, I will move, as soon as possible, *New Youth* from Beijing to Shanghai and make it the official newspaper of the new political party."

"I totally second that. Let's act immediately." Li Hanjun and Chen Wangdao expressed their support in unison.

Next, Li Hanjun gave Chen Wangdao an English version of *The Communist Manifesto* and a Japanese version he had brought back from Japan. Both Chen Duxiu and Li Hanjun agreed that it was a good idea because Chen Wangdao was better at Japanese and English than they were.

"The translation of Marx's classics must be accurate, word for word. Wangdao is the perfect man for that." Chen Duxiu clasped his hands, "Please! The sooner the better! Better leave Shanghai and find somewhere secluded to do it."

Chen Wangdao grimaced: "Looks like I have to return to my hometown, Yiwu, except it will also a trouble for you to find me."

"Great!" Li Hanjun was pumped, "A page of *Weekly Review* is available for you at any time."

Chen Duxiu waved his hand: "Not only in your newspaper. We should publish a separate book. Let all Chinese revolutionaries and progressive youth have one copy!"

Li Hanjun and Chen Wangdao exchanged a smile. They believed in the path to take more than ever.

I never intended to give any ink to the third shot, but I have been to Yiwu several times and was too impressed with the idea that the truth tastes sweet, which lured me to visit the hometown where he finished the translation. His story is deeply unforgettable...

It takes a tad more than an hour on high-speed train from Shanghai to Yiwu, a small county in Zhejiang. However, a hundred years ago, the trip was one day long. From Yiwu to Chen Wangdao's hometown Fenshuitang, it would take two days, because there was no road at all for any vehicles. Travelers had to tramp over hill and dale.

His father was a rich man locally, and farsighted that he insisted sending his two sons to Japan to study, which helped him grow into the revolutionary and educator he was, dedicating most of his life to teaching in Fudan University in Shanghai.

In the early spring of 1920, he took two copies of *The Communist Manifesto* in foreign languages, braved the freezing wind and snow, and returned to his hometown. In contrast to the metropolis Shanghai, where the flames of revolution were burning fiercely, it was bleak and serene here.

To better concentrate, he merely put a table in a room with firewood at home and began the translation.

"Rong'er, it's freezing here. Move to the attic. Warmer there." While delivering the meal, his mother called him by his pet name, laid a thick cotton blanket on his legs, nagging with love.

"No worries. It's quiet here, I need it quiet!" He was fully committed to the translation work of the book into foreign languages, which his mother understood not even one word.

"These sweet rice dumplings are so yummy! When I ate pickled cabbage in Japan, I immediately thought of the rice dumplings you made. Incomparable." He grabbed the red bean dumplings his mother brought him, commenting as he gorged on them.

"Glad you like it. I can make them every day." She picked up the reed leaves he had dropped, quietly exited the wood hut and shut the door.

Translation may be tedious to some, but not to Chen Wangdao. *The Communist Manifesto* by Karl Marx and Friedrich Engels, like a flame kindled in the mountains shrouded in the dark, shone bright in his eyes, inspiring him enormously: it turned out that the world has already prepared the perfect prescription to save mankind and the Chinese nation.

Listen, the sound is thunderous, deafening:

A spectre is haunting Europe—the spectre of Communism. All the Powers of old Europe have entered into a holly alliance to exorcise this spectre: Pope and Czar, Metternich and Guizot, French Radicals and German Police-spies.

Where is the party in opposition that has not been decried as communistic by its opponents in power? Where the Opposition that has not hurled back the branding reproach of Communism, against the more advanced opposition parties, as well as against its reactionary adversaries?

Listen, the sound is thunderous, clarifying:

The First Blood

Two things result from this fact.

1. Communism is already acknowledged by all European Powers to be itself a Power.

2. It is high time that communists should openly, in the face of the whole world, publish their views, their aims, their tendencies, and meet this nursery tale of the Spectre of Communism with a manifesto of the party itself.

True, proletariats in the world lose only their chains, but earn the world!

This is the future of the world, of China!

Chen Wangdao was thrilled again and again. Excited, he read *The Communist Manifesto* aloud in English or Japanese. His voice escaped the wood hut and echoed in the valley of his hometown. Even though his mother and fellow villagers did not understand a word, they believed the young man with foreign education must be doing something important. Once in a while, they would sneak to the door of the wood hut, attempted a few glimpses, and tiptoed away with a smile, "Leave him alone."

The kind mountain folks calmed him so that he could concentrate on his own translation, fascinated by the world presented by Marx and Engels in the texts, as if he were there witnessing the bloody battles in France in 1870.

In the Franco-Prussian War of the European Hegemony, the French army suffered a crushing defeat. In September, the Paris Revolution overthrew the Second Empire and the Third Republic rose. One hundred thousand Prussian troops were approaching Paris; the workers in the French capital fought courageously. However, the Third Republic was more terrified of the workers' armed forces than the Prussian army. Having suppressed the two armed uprisings of the people of Paris, it signed an armistice agreement with Prussia.

In February 1871, the French traitor Adophe Thiers organized a new government and kept implementing the policy of betraying national interests and opposing the proletariats. In the early morning of March 18, the Thiers government deployed troops to attack the cannon square in Montmartre Heights in an attempt to disarm the workers. Under the leadership of the Central Committee of the National Guard, Paris workers defeated the government forces, staged an armed uprising, and took over the Paris city government. On March 28, the newly elected member of the commune, Henri Joseph Ranvier, solemnly announced: "I declare the establishment of the commune in the name of the people!" The first proletarian regime in history was born.

However, the Paris Commune made a fatal mistake: it did not seize the day and eliminate the remnants of the Thiers government. As a result, Thiers regrouped the armed forces and colluded with the Prussian army to invade the city of Paris on May 21. Having sustained a week of fierce battle, in the early morning of May 28, the soldiers of the Paris Commune ran out of ammunition and food, the last 147 members massacred by government troops under the wall of the northeast corner of the Patrice Lachaise Cemetery. The streets of Paris were blood-stained, a horrifying scene.

Arise, ye prisoners of starvation!
Arise, ye wretched of the earth!
For justice thunders condemnation:
A better world's in birth!
No more tradition's chains shall bind us;
Arise, ye slaves, no more in thrall!
The earth shall rise on new foundations:
We have been naught, we shall be all!
'Tis the final conflict;
Let each stand in his place.
The International working class
Shall be the human race!

This is a poem written by Eugène Edine Pottier, a member of the Paris Commune and one of the leaders of the commune. It was later composed into an anthem for international proletarian revolutionaries: *L'Internationale.*

At the moment, this Chinese youth in Yiwu was alternately reading aloud the masterpiece of this French revolutionary poet in his proficient English and fluent Japanese, fully immersed in indignation and passion.

The workers of Paris and their commune will always be venerated as

The First Blood

the glorious pioneers of the new society. The heroes have always been engraved in the great heart of the working class, said Karl Marx.

While translating, he was prudently grasping *The Communist Manifesto* written by Marx and Engels, consolidating his belief that it is the light of truth for mankind and for China to rid the shackles of the old world. As a result, this young man from Yiwu forgot everything around him, completely committed to the translation.

At this moment, his mother came in with a rice bowl, a few rice dumplings, and a saucer of brown sugar. Seeing her son concentrating on the work, she knew better than to disturb him and tiptoed out and gently shut the door. "Alas, a bookworm!" The mother sighed softly as she exited and returned do housework in the house about fifty or sixty meters away from the wood hut.

It often rains in early spring in the south of the Yangtze River. On both sides of the wood hut were big houses of the neighbors, from whose eaves rain dripped and coincidentally on the small half of the roof of the wood hut. The water ticking was noisy enough, but lost in the grand revolutionary passion and literature translation, he was never aware of the rain outside at all. When he was hungry, he subconsciously reached out to grab the zongzi on the table without looking at it. He unwrapped the reed leaves with the fingers of his left hand, habitually dipped it in the saucer a tad of brown sugar and stuffed it into his mouth, chewing on the delicious rice dumpling that mother had prepared specially for him, moist and sweet. And so, the work and meal were taken care of simultaneously.

"Rong'er, is the sugar enough?" It was mother's voice. She stood outside the door asking, for fear of any disturbance.

"Yes, it's pretty sweet." The son replied.

She asked no more and went back to the courtyard to work. Towards the evening, she gently opened the wood hut door and went in to clean up the dishes. Why was the brown sugar still full? She found it peculiar, so she inspected the man still immersed in writing. "Why is your mouth all black?"

"Huh?" He raised his head.

"Yikes! It's all ink." Mother cried, "How did that happened?"

He wiped his mouth, looked at it, and laughed hysterically: "I must have mistaken the ink as brown sugar."

"Look at you!" Mother gave him a distressed look, and grumbled, "You bookworm. Ink is not sugar. This book has messed you up."

He laughed: "I'm perfectly sane. Zongzi and brown sugar are sweet, and so is my book."

This conversation between mother and son of the Chen family and the story of him mistaking ink as sugar when translating *The Communist Manifesto* were spread subsequently, hence the idea truth tastes sweet.

As soon as the translation was complete, he immediately returned to Shanghai and handed over the Chinese manuscript to Li Hanjun and Chen Duxiu, who proofread it word by word. Chen Duxiu sang praises of the translation, but when it came to publishing, he was a tad embarrassed to be short of money.

Li Hanjun devoted himself to promoting Marxism as soon as he returned to the motherland. The magazine *Weekly Review* he started with friends had been losing money, hardly making ends meet. The translation Chen Wangdao dedicated himself to for several months voluntarily was unable to be published for the lack of cash for printing.

Chen Duxiu, a professor who had not collected a paycheck for months, helplessly shrugged, teasing himself that it was a tragedy that money should get in the way.

At this time, Bolsheviks led by Lenin sent a representative, Grigori Naumovich Voitinsky, to assist China to form the Communist Party.

The first stop Voitinsky made was Beijing. He first met Li Dazhao, who was working at the Peking University Library and introduced him the Russian October Revolution and their socialist system. Li Dazhao familiarized him with China's revolutionary status and the process and nature of the May Fourth Movement. Also, he introduced Deng Zhongxia, Zhang Guotao, Liu Renjing, Luo Zhanglong and other progressive students to Voitinsky. In the following days, they held multiple meetings and discussions at the newly-built red library of Peking University to jointly plan the formation of the CPC.

Following Li Dazhao's suggestion, Voitinsky visited Shanghai and couldn't wait to meet Chen Duxiu, an influential representative of the progressive intellectual circles at that time.

The First Blood

"We have nothing except our words and writing." Chen Duxiu was delighted about the arrival of Voitinsky. Excited, he went straightforward, bring up his money shortage to publish the translated *Communist Manifesto*.

"We will finance it." Voitinsky promised.

"Great! It seems that revolution can't just rely on slogans. Money is essential, too." Chen Duxiu was overjoyed. He immediately contacted Li Hanjun: "Find a reliable publishing house and print it!"

Shortly, the first Chinese edition of *The Communist Manifesto* came out in Shanghai, like a beam of sunlight shining through the mist, dispelling the haze that hung over those searching for light in the dark. It was interesting that maybe because of the rush of time, on the cover of the first edition of *The Communist Manifesto*, the title was misprinted like *The 'Comnumist' Manifesto, with two Chinese characters reversed.* This flawed version is collected in the Historical Archives and the Shanghai Library. It allows us to feel the eagerness and poor working conditions of the revolutionaries who sought truth at that time. The entire publishing might be done by just one person, in secret and short of money.

The mistake was promptly corrected. The advent of a Marx classic readable to ordinary Chinese has greatly encouraged the followers of Marxism in Shanghai and across the country. From the Manifesto, they learned what is real proletarian revolution, what is real socialism, and what is the lofty ideal of communism.

Next, Marxists represented by Chen Duxiu and Li Dazhao pioneered many great historical events and feats of the Chinese revolution, such as the establishment of the first Marxism Research Association in Shanghai, with members including Chen Duxiu, Li Da, Li Hanjun, Chen Wangdao, Shen Yanbing (pen name of writer Mao Dun), Shao Lizi, etc.; the establishment of the first early Communist Party organization with Chen Duxiu as the secretary, who later served as the director of the Guangdong Provincial Department of Education and appointed Li Hanjun in charge of the organization, and Li Da and Chen Wangdao, etc. as the backbone.

Subsequently, as instructed by Chen Duxiu, Li Hanjun and others communicated with Marxism research groups in Beijing, Changsha, Wuhan, Shandong and other places in the name of the Shanghai Communist Group, actively preparing to build the early organizations of the CPC.

Revolutionaries

"Whether to name it Social Party or what?" Chen Duxiu, indecisive about the name, consulted with Li Dazhao in Beijing.

"Cai Hesen sent a letter, suggesting it be called the Communist Party."

What happened next is nothing we did not know: On July 23, 1921, the First National Congress of the CPC was held in Shanghai in secret. The precise address was 106 Wangzhi Road (now 76 Xingye Road). The house was the residence of Li Hanjun and his brother Li Shucheng, commonly known as the Li Mansion.

Thereafter, the great history of China opened a new page. Representatives from various places attended the conference, including Li Da and Li Hanjun from Shanghai, Zhang Guotao and Liu Renjing from Beijing, Mao Zedong and He Shuheng from Changsha, Dong Biwu and Chen Tanqiu from Wuhan, Wang Jinmei and Deng Enming from Jinan, Chen Gongbo from Guangzhou, Zhou Fohai from Japan and Bao Huiseng on behalf of Chen Duxiu, 13 in total. Chen Duxiu and Li Dazhao, who should have been present, were absent because of their special identity and the need for confidentiality. The representative of the Beijing group, Deng Zhongxia, who had to attend the annual meeting of the Youth China Association, was replaced by Liu Renjing.

Among the representatives who attended the First National Congress of the CPC, Li Hanjun, He Shuheng, Chen Tanqiu, Wang Jinmei, and Deng Enming were all revolutionary martyrs who died heroically.

It only took four years to go from the First National Congress of the CPC to the second, the third, and the fourth. In these four years, China and the world were caught in violent turbulence; the CPC was at a stage of continuous exploration and understanding. Especially the first Congress of the Communist Parties and national revolutionary groups in the Far East held in Moscow in January 1922, shortly after the First National Congress of the CPC, had an enormous impact on the revolutionary direction of CPC in the early days of its founding. The conference called upon the oppressed nations of the East to rise up and embark on a national democratic revolution against imperialism and feudalism. Lenin personally received Zhang Guotao, the representative of the CPC, Zhang Qiubai, the representative of the Kuomintang, and Deng Pei, the representative of the railway workers. He not only required a revolution, but also inquired about

The First Blood

the possibility of cooperation between the CPC and Kuomintang.

Zhang Guotao immediately reported to Chen Duxiu and the CPC Central Committee upon his return to China. Consequently, Lenin's theory of nations, colonies, and united fronts played a direct role in the subsequent formulation of the CPC's revolutionary program. In early May 1922, the First National Labor Conference and the First National Congress of the Chinese Socialist Youth League convened in Guangzhou by the leaders of the CPC pinpointed that among our many enemies, imperialism and the warlords of the country were the archenemies, that only when they are eliminated will we gain a bit of freedom, and even publicly proposed slogans for political actions, *Down with imperialism, Down with the warlords.*

In fact, under the guidance of Voitinsky, within a few days after the First National Congress of the CPC, the first revolutionary organization of the working class, the Secretariat of the Chinese Labor Union, was established. It is the labor movement and trade union organization established under the leadership of the CPC. Zhang Guotao served as the director. By 1922, Deng Zhongxia took over his position, with Li Lisan and Liu Shaoqi as his deputy. Since both Marx and Lenin believed that the communist movement must be led by the proletariat, whose vanguard is the working class, the CPC attached great importance to the primary force of the revolution, the working class, since its own founding.

The Second National Congress of the CPC lasted from July 16 to 23, 1922. Hosted by Chen Duxiu, it made three major accomplishments after the founding of the party. The first is to have determined the party's maximum and minimum programs; anti-imperialist and anti-feudal democratic revolution program at the time was its minimum program; organizing the proletariat and establishing a political dictatorship of workers and peasants by the means of class struggle to eradicate the private property system and gradually reach a communist society is the maximum program. The party's goals were clarified as to eliminate civil strife, take down warlords, and build domestic peace; overthrow the oppression of international imperialism and achieve complete independence of the Chinese nation; and unify China as a true democratic republic. The second accomplishment is that a democratic joint front policy was proposed. It was mainly to establish a united front with the Kuomintang led by Sun Yat-sen. In the early days of the founding of the CPC, the Communist International required it to participate in reforming the Kuomintang, and this became a major resolution of the Third National Congress of the CPC. In addition, as Sun Yat-sen proposed the slogan, *Unite with Russia and the CPC, Help Farmers and Workers,* and actively invited CPC members to help with the reorganization of the Kuomintang, many famous CPC leaders, including Mao Zedong, joined the Kuomintang in their personal capacity. This was after the Third National Congress of the CPC. The third accomplishment was of great significance, the formulation of the Constitution of the CPC.

After the sacrifice of 20-year-old student Huang Ren, the social situation in Shanghai was more representative of the situation in China at that time.

Within the country: there was warlords' melee. Outside the country: foreigners oppressed the Chinese. Both were unbearable.

At the Shanghai Library, I noticed a palm-sized book published a century ago. It astonished me. Apart from seeing such a tiny book for the first time, I was even more surprised by the title *The Way Out for Shanghai Citizens,* so I copied the first a few paragraphs:

> *The citizens of Shanghai are suffering. Since the price of rice has soared, it has become more of a struggle for us common folks to survive. As prosperous and glamourous as Shanghai appears, it is just a living hell for millions of us, businessmen, workers, laborers, and the destitute.*
>
> *What happened to this city? Why is it that most of us are so indigent, our lives precarious, but Jiangsu and Zhejiang are still titled rich and prosperous districts, and Shanghai the country's No. 1 thriving society? We businessmen worked relentlessly throughout our lives, yet in recent years, all industries have regressed, debts have accumulated, business is lost, and we are at the edge of bankruptcy. What is the reason? We workers earn a living with labor, exchange blood and sweat for a little wage, yet in recent years, everything has become expensive and survival is hard, and we suffer abuses, beatings, and dismissal from factory owners and employers. Business is halted once demanded, encouraging repeated strikes, and the number of the unemployed is increasing. What is the reason? We laborers and the destitute are experiencing worse living conditions. Labor is sold for nothing, not even*

The First Blood

a meal. There is no place to make a living in this enormous and beautiful city. We sleep on the street. In winter, it is freezing and there is nothing to keep us warm, in the summer, there is no shelter to escape the heat. We die either of starvation, or of sickness; in Shanghai, of the more than two million residents, most indigent suffer similarly. What is the reason? What can be done? Poor citizens!

The only explanation is that the Chinese have not yet become independent, that the Chinese are still ruled, trampled, exploited, and oppressed by foreigners and warlords, bureaucrats and compradors who collude with one another. Over one million citizens of Shanghai are ruled by merely thousands of foreigners and hundreds of Chinese warlords, bureaucrats and compradors. They have hired patrols, detectives, and policemen to besiege us layer by layer. They impose all kinds of forced donations and taxes over and over again. The Ministry of Industry of the imperialists in the concession charges more than 1,240,500 taels of silver each year; warlords and government offices in the southern and northern parts of Shanghai levy as many as several hundred kinds of taxes and donations, and the number keeps going up, sucking our blood. But what else do we have besides our lives?

...

These textual records elucidate the picture of Shanghai a hundred years ago, confirming that revolutionary direction of the CPC at that time was more correct, that is, anti-imperialism and against the warlords. The life of the people was miserable. Ethnic conflicts and struggles required most urgent solutions in the turbulent China of the time.

Twenty-year-old Huang Ren was a young soldier who gave his life in the urban revolutionary struggles. His sacrifice appalled the equally young CPC and progressive intellectuals—the revolution is an uncompromising and brutal fight, and death is inevitable. However, in order to establish a new China, it was a glorious and respectful sacrifice.

Around the Fourth National Congress of the CPC, China was in extreme turbulence. Sun Yat-sen travelled north, as invited by Feng Yuxiang, to discuss affairs of national interest but unfortunately died of illness in Beijing. His demise encouraged the warlords to become more rampant, the imperialist powers took this opportunity to intensify oppression of China.

Revolutionaries

The life in the city was suffocating the working people. Even small business owners who used to make a living with their hands failed to maintain basic production and survival. At this time, China, especially Shanghai, was at the darkest hour. A revolutionary storm was brewing.

Imperialism is a monster that has broken into the homes of the common people. Rebelling is the only way out. Progressive magazines such as *Awakening* and *Workers* published articles lashing out at the situation. The fuse of a fight was ignited, the oppressed workers and citizens could no longer tolerate it.

A young worker who was working in a Japanese yarn mill described it:

At the time, I was living in Baoxing Lane, Baoshan Road, Zhabei. I witnessed some female workers of a silk factory in Yokohama Bridge forced to steal sesame seed buns and sweet potatoes from the stalls across the bridge; caught by the foreman, they were immediately whipped and kicked.

There is also a glass factory owned by the Japanese on West Baoxing Road. It was surrounded by bamboo fences on all sides and roofed with a few iron sheets. A dozen Chinese workers, naked, surrounded the stove, holding glass tubes in their hands, blowing bulbs and bottles to them in the midsummer heat, coupled with the high temperature of about a thousand degrees. There were no cooling facilities, but a Japanese supervisor with a whip at hand. One day I walked to Qingyun Road with two fellow workers. There is a Garden 63, decorated with lanterns and streamers at the door. We wanted to go in and have a look, but like the Bund, a sign reads "Chinese and Dogs, keep out." We were so furious that our teeth chattered.

Another time, my uncle and I went home after night work from the Zhonghua Book Company. It was almost 12 o'clock. We walked to the North Railway Station and saw a blazing fire at the vicinity of Qiujiang Road. We continued forward along the Songhu Railway and met groups of people along the way, sitting on the ground wailing. They told us their children died in the fire in the factory. Early the next morning before going to work, a fellow worker and I travelled to the burnt factory to see what happened. It was horrifying. It was a five-story Xiangjing Silk Weaving Factory on Qiujiang Road. The first, second, and third floors were workshops and warehouses, and the fourth and fifth were dormitories for female workers. After the

The First Blood

fire, the surrounding walls, iron windows, and doors were intact, while the workshop and dormitory inside the walls were all burnt down. The two iron doors were tightly shut, and there were charred corpses at the foot of the stairs inside the doors. According to the newspaper at the time, over 100 female workers died in the fire. Why did none of them manage to escape? It turned out that the factory assets were insured, and insurance company stipulated that if the doors and windows are opened in the accident of a fire, the assets will be deemed safely moved out, thus no compensation for the loss. The owner would rather shut the door and burn the workers to alive than to forfeit an insurance claim. Although the public was outraged about this tragedy, and capitalists received wide condemnation from the people, nothing could bring them back.

These are just a few things that a worker has seen. Data available shows that at that time, there were hundreds of various yarn mills operated in Shanghai by Japanese capitalists alone, with a total of over 100,000 employees. Behind them were 100,000 families. If there were four to five people in each family, 400,000 to 500,000 people were faring in utmost misery. And this was solely the Japanese power in Shanghai. If corporate capitalists from Britain, France, Germany, and the United States are added together, it is no exaggeration that the entire Shanghai working class was in hell.

How do people living in hell survive?

There is only one way: rebel and fight!

It is an unpeaceful world, oppressing us laborers heavily.
We sell labor all our lives, nothing of greater misery.

The October wind blows from the north, awakening us in suffering.
The proletariat have arisen, taking up the hammers to attack.
The red flag shines thousands of miles far, the hammer makes heaven and earthquake.
Unite, and together we will break through the dark clouds and glow.

(Poem by Labor Movement Leader/ Martyr Deng Zhongxia)

Revolutionaries

The only way to destroy this hell was to fight. Marx and Engels' *The Communist Manifesto* has outlined a clear program of struggle for the Chinese communists. The weapon that would smash the old world was a revolution by the united workers.

After the Second National Congress of the CPC, to make the Secretariat of the Chinese Labor Union stronger, Deng Zhongxia, a pioneer of the May Fourth Movement and outstanding labor movement leader, was specially transferred from Beijing to Shanghai to be the director of the organization (Li Qihan took up this position soon after him), the first workers' remedial class was organized at 3 North Jinxiu Lane, Binlang Road, Xiaoshadu in west Shanghai, in which revolutionary education and cultural tutoring were given to them, and a large number of outstanding workers joined in CPC organizations.

After the Third National Congress of the CPC, the leadership of the national labor movement was strengthened, and the most experienced, loyal, and outstanding labor movement leaders were appointed to organize and direct national labor movements. As Shanghai held the paramount position of these labor movements, the CPC sent Deng Zhongxia, Xiang Ying, He Mengxiong, Liu Hua, He Bingyi, and other steadfast revolutionary leaders there. All these comrades heroically sacrificed their lives.

Yet, let us set aside grief for the time being and return to the crossroad where the martyr Huang Ren shed blood, because a great and fierce revolution and struggle is often triggered by a tiny matter.

There was another death, together with Huang Ren at the age of 20. It was Gu Zhenghong, a worker, who had joined the CPC only three months before he was butchered by imperialism.

Let's take a look at what happened.

Gu Zhenghong, a worker at a cotton factory run by the Japanese, came from an indigent family.

When he was less than 10 years old, frequent droughts, floods, and plagues of insects in his hometown in northern Jiangsu cornered his father to leave his wife and children behind to go to work alone in Shanghai, living in the Zhabei slum by the Suzhou River. When Gu Zhenghong turned 16, another flood struck his hometown. The family of eight took a small boat, begging for survival all the way, and fled to Shanghai to reunite with

The First Blood

their father. However, the city was no haven for the poor. Father couldn't support the entire family on a meager salary. His second brother starved to death shortly after the arrival in Shanghai, the whole family often suffered starvation. In 1922, 17-year-old Gu Zhenghong was employed by the Japanese Number 7 Cotton Factory as a sweeper thanks to his fellow villagers.

Japanese factories in Shanghai at that time exploited the Chinese workers to the extremes, bloodsucking, truly. The working conditions were grossly harsh. Workers had to work long hours every day, often suffered cash penalties with physical and verbal abuse. Gu, honest and hardworking, could not stand the unjustified oppression of the foreman. There was a rule in the factory that every new employee had to pay the foreman their half-year wage as a thank-you gift. In extreme poverty, he naturally would not allow it. Once when the paycheck was issued, he interrogated the foreman. *On what ground is it justified that you should take my wages?* The foreman gave him an angry glare, without uttering a word, and slapped him hard.

Having a backbone, he could never meekly accept the bullying. A couple of days later, he summoned a few fellow villagers, broke into the foreman's residence, and beat the crap out of him. What audacity! The Japanese capitalist immediately expelled Gu from the factory.

With the help of fellow poor workers, Gu was employed by the Japanese Number 9 cotton factory, where he noticed no improvement in the way Chinese were treated, and even worse. *Are all capitalists heartless?*

Gu began to wonder. At this time, the remedial class organized by the underground Communist Party happened to be launched nearby, where he learned the reasons why the imperialists exploited the workers and that they had to fight the injustice, he found the savior of the poor: the CPC. After a period of trials and practice organizing strikes, he secretly joined the CPC. Thereafter, at the age of 20, he understood what was revolution, guided by Liu Hua, who was six years older and one of the leaders of the Shanghai labor.

"The poor should unite. One chopstick is easy to break, one bundle not so easy. As long as we workers unite, I don't see how we can't defeat the imperialist/capitalists and their minions." Liu Hua's speech deeply pierced him.

Revolutionaries

"Indeed, we outnumber them, don't we? As long as we unite, we are fearless." Despite the lack of education, he was able to deliver the speech properly to fellow workers, who agreed unanimously. Therefore, from the autumn of 1924 to the beginning of 1925, Gu Zhenghong, under the guidance of underground communists such as Deng Zhongxia, Xiang Ying, and Liu Hua, encouraged the workers in Number 7 and Number 9 cotton factories to actively join the West Shanghai Workers Club. The number of club members grew like a rolling snowball. In just over three months, all the nineteen Japanese yarn factories in the surrounding area had established secret Workers Clubs, with thousands of worker members.

Gu gradually became an active key member among them.

On February 2, 1925, the Japanese owner of Number 8 Cotton Factory stirred up trouble, violently beating up female workers, expelling a large number of male workers, and instructing the police station in the concession to arrest worker representatives. It was when the Fourth National Congress of the CPC had just been convened in Shanghai. Having judged the situation, the Central Committee decided to organize and lead a massive strike. Deng Zhongxia, Li Lisan, Xiang Ying, Wang Hebo, Yun Daiying, and Liu Hua quickly came among the workers. On the ninth of that month, over 34,000 Chinese workers from nine Japanese yarn mills and six Japanese Textile Societies staged a massive strike. When the striker team held high the banners that read *No Japanese abuse, No Japanese violence*, shouting slogans like *workers deserve respect*, marching toward the Bangbei in formidable array, Shanghai residents and other factory workers cheered for them, joined them side by side along the parade.

However, unexpectedly, the concession police station colluded with Shanghai Songhu Police Department and deployed a large number of armed police to arrest strikers and leaders. Fifty-six communists and union officers, including Deng Zhongxia, were apprehended. However, as the CPC continued to firmly organize larger strikes, Japanese capitalists caved in and proposed a negotiation. It was a total victory, they released the arrested and signed four agreements. (*1. Any abuse of workers must be resolved by factory owners; 2. Workers remain employed as before; 3. The deposit shall be refunded in 5 years; 4. Wages shall be paid every fortnight.*)

The First Blood

At 3 p.m. the next day, representatives of the workers union went to the police station to welcome Deng Zhongxia and other arrested workers out of prison. Tens of thousands of workers and citizens lined the streets, cheering and celebrating. What a scene!

"The February strike not only opened a page in the history of Chinese labor movement but added a new significance to the history of Chinese national liberation." Deng wrote.

Xiang Ying, who once led the February 7 Strike on the Beijing-Wuhan Railway, also wrote an article, proposing an eight-word creative and bonding purpose for the yarn mill workers union: *emotional communication, knowledge exchange, mutual help, common happiness.*

Gu joined the CPC at this very moment. There were only eight party groups in Shanghai. Because of the February strike and its victory, especially under the leadership of Deng Zhongxia and Xiang Ying, the Central Committee of the CPC proposed to recruit more workers to the party. By the end of April 1925, the number of Shanghai party branches had grown to 15, and that of party members from 109 to 220, doubling in strength.

However, the fight against the imperialist forces in China has just begun, the cruelty of the revolution only surfaced as the tip of an iceberg.

1925 was destined to be an exceptionally tragic and turbulent year in China. In April and May, industries in Shanghai, with cotton yarn as the main force, were challenged with a commercial disaster owing to the changes in the world situation. In the past, cotton used to be cheap and yarn expensive, but now it was the other way around, an even more unfavorable situation for industrial workers. In response, the workers unions and clubs under the leadership of the Communist Party changed their ways of fighting: factory workers took turns slacking work, one after another, making it difficult for Japanese capitalists to cope.

However, the imperialist powers in China were no weak enemy that crumbles meekly. On May 14, the Japanese Textile Societies in Shanghai announced a shutdown of factories to deal with the rebellion of Chinese workers. Some Japanese factories took a chance and fired workers in large numbers.

The situation had changed drastically.

Revolutionaries

Having received a report from fellow workers, Gu ran straight to the workers union station in Sanderi of Tanziwan, Bangbei in northwest Shanghai to get instructions from Liu Hua on behalf of the party organization. "We can't fall for this trick of the Japanese capitalists. Notify the workers as soon as possible. Fired as they are, show up at work as usual and never be fooled."

As expected, Gu's former employer Number 7 cotton factory owner was the first to fire workers and close the business. As soon as he found out about it, he immediately deployed several activists to break the news to the workers of this factory, who then promptly spread it to neighbor workers, informing those who worked night shifts to show up at work as usual.

But when they reached the factory entrance, the gate was locked, armed policemen and thugs holding iron rods and wooden sticks were viciously guarding it.

"We are going to work!" Hundreds of night-shift workers gathered at the gate, shouting and demanding to enter.

"We are closed."

"Not a dime." The thugs and policemen replied.

The workers, shouting slogans, attempted to break into the factory, dashing in.

Armed policemen and Japanese thugs became ferocious, beating the workers. It was chaotic, with many workers injured and bleeding. Gu Zhenghong, who had just rushed over, and witnessing the brutality, shouted furiously:

"Japanese are beating us. No violence." His roar kindled the fighting spirit and anger of the workers. Some who got inside the factory dashed to the storeroom, grabbed some picking sticks, used them for self-defense, and skirmished with police and Japanese thugs.

At this moment, Ōban Motoki, the deputy manager of the Japanese cotton factory, and Ōban Kawamura, the head of the Number 7 factory, led in a group of armed thugs to this skirmish, hitting the workers.

"No violence! No oppression!" Gu immediately stepped in front of the workers, roaring at the thugs. Unexpectedly, Ōban Kawamura went mad. He took a pistol and shot Gu in the leg.

"Japanese are killing us!"

The First Blood

"They are shooting at us!" Chinese workers at the scene became stupefied.

Wounded and bleeding, Gu gritted his teeth, straightened his body, and shouted to the workers behind: "Fear no violence. Unite and fight them to the end!"

Bang! Another deadly bullet was fired from Kawamura's barrel again, hitting Gu in the abdomen.

All the workers at the scene were horrified. Gu, who collapsed in a pool of blood, endured the devastating agony, clutching a small tree next to him with both hands, and rose trembling.

"You bandits..." Before he could finish the sentence, the gun in Kawamura's hand sounded again. This time, the bullet went straight to his head.

The 20-year-old life made a last struggling twitch. The heinous Japanese murderer saw he was still breathing, stepped forward, shot him in the chest, and slammed his head with an iron rod.

Gu Zhenghong, a young worker who had never had a nice meal in Shanghai, a young member who had only joined the party for three months, was brutally butchered by imperialist murderers.

A young life was so cruelly taken by imperialist murderers in his motherland. The death of Gu triggered a great revolutionary movement in modern Chinese history that shocked the world: The May Thirtieth Movement.

The curtain of urban revolution and armed riots was lifted from this movement.

For the revolutionaries, the days that await would be harsh and perilous, life-threatening. From this struggle, hundreds of miles of the Huangpu River and thousands of miles of the Yangtze River were dyed red with blood.

CHAPTER TWO

Flames of War on Nanjing Road

PERHAPS NO ONE EXPECTED THAT THE FALL OF ONE COMMON Chinese worker would trigger a world-shocking revolution, one that shook the power of a semi-feudal and semi-colonial nation and awakened its people.

This was the massacre on May 30 Movement that broke out in Shanghai in 1925 (the May 30 Movement was an anti-imperialist movement).

It was the death of Gu Zhenghong on May 15 that triggered the movement. The moment he was murdered, Liu Hua, an underground CPC member in charge of the labor movement in this area, got the tragic news, which he immediately reported to the leaders of the Shanghai Municipal Committee of the CPC. The Central Committee of the CPC was also promptly informed. Knowing the severity of the tragedy, it immediately assigned Li Lisan, the leader of the labor movement at the time, to Xiaoshadu to figure out what happened and guide the fight. Liu Hua and other leaders of the front-line labor union elucidated the murder of Gu at the union meeting of the cotton yarn mills that evening. Hearing this, representatives of the union were filled with outrage and determined to launch a massive strike, with eight requirements to the factory capitalists, like executing the murderers.

Revolutionaries

The next day, over 8,000 workers went on strike to protest the crimes of Japanese capitalists slaughtering Chinese workers. Their chanting of slogans echoed across both banks of the Huangpu River.

"We must take this chance to hit the imperialists hard!" Chen Duxiu, General Secretary of the CPC Central Committee, exclaimed to Qu Qiubai, Li Lisan, Cai Hesen and others.

"Our labor union is ready to hold a memorial for him. Workers proposed that we carry his body to protest against the imperialists and organize a city-wide strike at once." Said Li Lisan.

"I'll second them both, protest and strike." Chen Duxiu nodded.

Qu Qiubai suggested, "I would recommend that the central government immediately draft an emergency notice to request local party organizations to cooperate with labor unions, peasant associations, student unions, and other social groups to support Gu's memorials."

"Necessary moves. Very necessary!" Chen Duxiu waving both hands, commanded them, "Split up immediately!" and to Cai Hesen, "Write to Zhongxia and Runzhi at once. Ask them to make grand moves in Guangzhou and Changsha!"

Cai Hesen nodded: "Understood."

On the same day, Notice Number 32 of the Central Committee of the CPC signed by Chen Duxiu concerning cooperation with the Shanghai strike was issued to all party organizations nationwide. It had four key points:

1. Various groups should declare or publish an open telegram to oppose the Japanese gunning down Chinese workers;
2. Various groups should raise funds to help Shanghai yarn factory workers;
3. Propaganda teams should be built in the name of various groups to spread the fact that the constant oppression from Japanese imperialists led to the boycotts;
4. Guangzhou, Changsha and other places should call on the masses to stage demonstrations at the Japanese consulate.

Flames of War on Nanjing Road

Immediately, 35 groups in Shanghai took action, setting up the Vengeance Association against the Japanese Killing of Compatriots to support the workers' fight. The Central Committee of the CPC was fully committed; not only was General Secretary Chen Duxiu personally directing the movement, but key personnel Qu Qiubai, Cai Hesen, and Zhang Guotao came to the front. Well-known student leaders during the May Fourth Movement, Yun Daiying, Li Lisan, Li Fuchun, Li Shuoxun, and Xiang Ying, who later dedicated themselves to the labor movement, were all on the front line, organizing and directing strikes and support activities for workers, students, and social organizations.

Deng Zhongxia was sent to Guangzhou to organize and direct the massive strike of workers in the city and to Hong Kong with Chen Yannian, who happened to be there; Mao Zedong in Changsha organized workers, students, and other social organizations to actively respond to and cooperate with the actions in Shanghai; Li Hanjun and Lin Yunan in Wuhan were actively plotting a strike among railway workers to cooperate with that in Shanghai.

A great revolution was brewing.

On May 19, the Central Committee of the CPC issued Notice Number 33, which was great step forward compared with the Notice Number 32. At this time, the Central Committee of the CPC had decided to launch a nationwide anti-imperialist campaign centered on anti-Japanese. As it was preparing for a joint party caucus in Shanghai to discuss the plan of the public memorial to Gu Zhenghong, Li Lisan proposed a major demonstration plan.

However, the Shanghai Municipal Council on the opposite side fully controlled and blocked the news of Gu getting murdered and the Shanghai strike. No newspaper coverage was allowed. In response to that, on the 22nd, the Shanghai Prefectural Committee of the CPC summoned a joint meeting, where it was decided to cancel the grand parade and concentrate efforts on the memorial of Gu the martyr on the 24th.

The public memorial was held in Tanziwan on the afternoon of the 24th. Thousands of workers from the yarn factory labor unions attended. Some college students in Shanghai tried to show up with flags for support, but were intercepted by concession police, with many arrested.

Revolutionaries

The actions of the concession authorities once again enraged Shanghai citizens, especially the intellectuals. Youth leader Yun Daiying immediately convened a meeting of student representatives in the name of the Shanghai Federation of Students and criticized the concession authorities for the violence in arresting students.

On the 28th, the concession authorities made no response and kept pressuring the workers and students on strike. Challenged with the current situation, the Central Committee of the CPC and the Shanghai Prefectural Party Committee at once held a joint meeting. Chen Duxiu personally presided. He pointed out that the purpose of Shanghai students demonstrating on the streets was to motivate all walks of life to participate.

"The concession authorities are threatening to interrogate the students arrested on the 30, accusing them of disturbing law and order and going to punish them in an attempt to intimidate the people of Shanghai and suppress our anti-imperialist actions. So, I suggest that we, on this day of May 30, mobilize and gather a team of workers and students for an anti-imperialist demonstration in the concession. Let's crash the imperialist conspiracy head-on!" Qu Qiubai expressed his thoughts.

"I couldn't agree more." Li Lisan stepped forward and shook Qu Qiubai's hand, saying, "All the forces available must be mobilized to make the imperialist forces in China yield."

"Okay! May 30! Conspiracy be damned. Let's ignite the flames of the revolution on the streets." Chen Duxiu raised his right arm to asked the comrades present: "All onboard?"

"Aye!" The answer was in unison. Everyone has been waiting for this moment.

As planned, the parade would start on the morning of the 30. To ensure the success of this operation, the CPC made meticulous arrangement and set up an on-site parade headquarters in the Mengyuan Hostel on Erma Road (now Jiujiang Road) in the name of Shanghai Federation of Students. Yun Daiying served as the commander-in-chief and conducted on-site command.

In the downtown of Shanghai that day, some college students were divided into small teams, giving speeches and distributing leaflets on the streets and alleys of the concession. They were widely accepted by

Flames of War on Nanjing Road

Shanghai citizens. Angry chants of slogans echoed on the streets.

Near noon, a team of students were giving speeches in every few shops on the busiest Nanjing Road. Their words, indignant and moving, aroused strong sympathy among the citizens.

"Quickly! Post the placards and flyers." There were students running through the crowd to inform the student parade of each move. As a result, shop windows, telephone poles, and trams along the street were soon covered with various placards, flyers dancing in the sky like snowflakes. As the parade marched forward on the streets, the sound of speeches and chants of slogans like *Down with imperialism! No illegal roadblocks! Release the arrested workers and students! No Japanese goods! were loud and clear, echoing on the street.* What a spectacular anti-imperialist propaganda act!

After 1 p.m., more students and citizens gathered on the streets, the flames of anti-Japanese and anti-imperialist passions burning more fiercely. There were students giving speeches and parades on every street in downtown Shanghai.

"Shit! Shit!"

"Rebellion is fucking coming."

Waves of protests from students and citizens horrified the concession authorities. They intended to resort to force to put out the ignited revolutionary flames. As a result, concession policemen, batch after batch, armed with guns or sticks, dashed to the streets, halting students from giving speeches and dispelling audiences.

However, furious students and citizens refused to cave, leading to physical conflicts between the two sides.

"Fucking rebellion!"

"Arrest'em!"

"Do it!"

Red-eyed policemen began to arrest students who kept giving speeches and onlookers who refused to leave. The streets became chaotic.

Soon, they had arrested over 100 people by about two in the afternoon. It went slightly out of control.

Yun Daiying urgently summoned He Bingyi, his student and parade liaison officer, and ordered him to promptly notify the parade teams. "Notify the persons in charge of each school at once. On the one hand,

Revolutionaries

organize a team to rescue the arrested students and citizens at the police station. On the other, have the team that organized the parades and speeches on the streets gather on Nanjing Road. Now!"

"Yes!" He Bingyi was no tall man, but extremely agile.

But the street situation was not optimistic. The policemen went crazy. In a while, the prison was at full capacity, even the interrogation room and office were filled with arrested students and citizens.

In the meantime, some speech teams from Shanghai University, Nanyang University, Tongji University, and Fudan University assembled from all directions, chanting the slogans "Down with imperialism!" and "Release patriotic students and the masses!" Step by step, they approached the police station in the concession.

At this time, more people crowded Nanjing Road. Enraged students and citizens chanted slogans "Down with imperialism! Never buy Japanese goods!" and fought against the traitors/policemen to arrest them with their bare hands.

There was screaming, shouting, roaring, all chaotic and violent.

"Shoot'em!" At 3:45 in the afternoon, the policeman with a long-barreled gun first pulled the trigger on the Chinese students and Shanghai citizens demonstrating.

"Bam!"

"Bam! Bam! Bam!"

After the first gunshot, more intense gunfire ensued. Indian policemen lined up, criminally firing bullets at students and citizens.

Down with imperialism!

Down with foreign bandits!

Down...

The first to fall was He Bingyi, Yun Daiying's traffic man, college student at the forefront of the parade, and young CPC member.

Next was Yin Jingyi, a student of Tongji University, who was shot behind him. "Get down..." Seeing his classmate Chen Baotui who was speaking taking violent beating, he was ready to replace him and give the speech. It was at this moment, an evil bullet flew by Chen Baoquan's right side and shot Yin on his chest, instantly dyeing his student uniform red.

On the other side of Yin, a small and dashing male student let out a

Flames of War on Nanjing Road

howl and collapsed in a pool of blood. "Aqin! Aqin!"

Wailing, clueless what to do, fellow classmates held the bleeding young man.

"Vengeance!" His full name was Chen Yuqin, but among classmates he went by Aqin. He was a student at Nanyang High School, an Indonesian student of Chinese descent.

"Aqin! Hold on!" Classmates wanted to help the young man covered in blood to stop the bleeding, but failed. Seven bullets had pierced his young body.

Chen Yuqin sacrificed his young life at the gunpoint of imperialism. In the meantime, a 16-year-old worker named Wu Jinhua, an employee of *New World*, was also slaughtered by the same devious foreign bullets as Chen Yuqin.

"Heavens! What are you doing?"

"Bandits! Imperialist bandits are killing us. Wake up, China. Wake up completely!"

When he learned the tragedy of his student He Bingyi among other deaths on Nanjing Road, the parade commander Yun Daiying clenched his fists and roared like a furious lion in the Mengyuan Hostel headquarters. Yet, that was far from enough to vent the grief in his chest.

It became a major incident. The concession and British policemen panicked. In order to cover up their crimes, they ordered the blood on the road to be washed away with gallons of water, which happened to be filmed by Chen Kengran of the Union Film Company. And it became ironclad evidence of the heinous crime the imperialists had committed in China.

On the same day, the CPC mobilized various demonstration teams and civic groups, and quickly sorted out the death toll in the afternoon of the 30. They were: He Bingyi (student of Shanghai University, 23 years old, member of the CPC), Yin Jingyi (student of Tongji University, 21 Years old, member of the CPC), Chen Yuqin (student of Nanyang High School, 17 years old), Tang Liangsheng (22 years old, telephone operator of the Huayang Telephone Office), Chen Zhaochang (18 years old, kitchen worker of the East Asia Hotel), Zhu Heshang (16 years old, employee of Western Affairs), Wu Jinhua (16 years old, employee of *New World*), Shi Songsheng (20 years old, employee of an electric appliance company), Chen Xingfa

39

(22 years old, driver of a chartered car company), Yao Shunqing (28 years old, piano painter), Wang Jifu (36 years old, tailor), Tan Jinfu (27 years old, partner of Weixiangju restaurant), Xu Luofeng (26 years old, small trader), a total of 13. They died at the very gunpoint of the imperialists. Except for the 36-year-old tailor Wang Jifu, their average age was only 21, the prime of youth. However, their lives were instantly destroyed by imperialist bandits on the street Nanjing Road.

On that day, the number of casualties exceeded a hundred, and over a thousand were arrested.

This is the world-shocking Massacre on May 30 Movement in Shanghai. It triggered an unprecedented anti-imperialist movement that kicked off the Chinese urban revolution.

The flames of war were raging on the streets.

Since the opening of Shanghai as a port, it had never before happened that on Nanjing Road, foreigners publicly gunned down Chinese compatriots, and wounded and arrested hundreds of people. The appalling news quickly spread to every corner of the city.

Early the next morning, those with a doubtful mind snuck to Nanjing Road to check what happened. It was no longer as bustling as it used to be. Among the sparse crowd, there was a middle-aged man in a long gown, seemingly a teacher.

He was indeed a teacher, and rather famous. When he was informed of the massacre of students and citizens by foreigners last night, he could not believe it but he had to, because it was widely discussed among many of his friends. So, early on the 31st, he made a visit to Nanjing Road to see the blood stains left by his compatriots there. Later on that day, he wrote an article of great impact.

In the Rain of May 31st—

As I exited the car, torrential rain instantly soaked my long gown. Full of anger, I felt shackled with tight iron hoops on my head. I scurried.

There were very few pedestrians, nor many customers in the shop. Where did they go? With fear for the sound of gunshots like yesterday, for taking a bullet, did they huddle at home, as timid as a mouse, hiding under the counter? What was the point? There was nowhere to hide, to escape the sound the gunshots, to dodge the bullets. They would find you. So what was the point?

Monstrous vehicles flew by, splashing muddy water onto my clothes and my neck. I was filled with anger.

I rushed to the gate of the police station in one breath. I wanted to pay homage to the blood our fellows have shed, to lick all the blood stains with my tongue, to swallow their sacrifice. But nothing, there was nothing left, but washed off by enemy's faucet and the pouring rain, and trampled on by those heartless.

It wouldn't matter, I thought. The blood must have seeped into the soil. That would suffice, soil socked with blood of our comrades. It was a serious lesson, wasn't it? The blood would irrigate and moisturize the land, flowers would bloom and fruits be harvested.

I stared at this piece of land, fully attentive as if there was nothing else, as if my whole body had melted within.

...

It was Mr. Ye Shengtao, a well-known educator, who wrote these words. Mr. Ye found it difficult to believe the brutality of the Massacre on May Thirtieth Movement. However, witnessing the site where it happened stirred up waves of grief and anger in this kind-hearted educator, hence the immediate writing.

As one of the earliest party members of the CPC and standard-bearer of the cultural circle, Shen Yanbing could not contain the eruption of the indignation in his heart as soon as he learned this tragedy on Nanjing Road during the day. On the night of the 30, he finished a short story *The Afternoon of May 30*. The end of the story ignites the darkness like burning flame—

Tit for tat. These words kept echoing in my mind; I pushed through the crowd, furious, wanting to find a few to discuss my new faith with. Abrupt, it began to drizzle, the dusk had already descended on the city, and pedestrians on the street gradually dwindled. I turned to a narrow alley. The rain got stronger. Streetlamps shone a quiet cold light in the rain, a sultry evening, adding fuel to my flames of anger. The wind blew the drizzle to my face, a tad cool; but a special sound came with the wind and boiled my blood; it was a sound of singing, of recreational joy, of laughter, no more than a hundred steps away from the blood pools and less than an hour since the murder. How should they be having fun? My heart trembled, and I started to curse this city, shameless, filthy, and unjust. I pray for all the brutality to be washed away, for the shamelessness to be washed away, too.

The raindrops became denser, and the wind stronger: a storm is brewing in this sultry heat, isn't it?

In addition to Ye Shengtao and Shen Yanbing, Lu Xun, the standard-bearer of the New Culture Movement, was equally indignant. In *Declaration to the People of China*, he challenged and denounced in his unique style. "There are no civilized English, aren't there?" "There must be a lot more to learn about the character of English." He also advised Chinese. "Never hesitate, try it, for survival, without malice against anyone." Later, in *Miscellaneous Memories* he wrote, "I believe the Chinese have suffered enough grievances, naturally, from the ravages by the strong. However, they made no resistance against the strong. Instead, they took it out on the weak. It is most convincing evidence that the common folks, unarmed, have to suffer from both soldiers and bandits, who are not fighting against each other. Chinese have to set aside of all the insignificant traditional crafts and deign to learn from the foreigners, properly armed. Only then can the seed of hope bud."

The Massacre on May Thirtieth Movement ignited a fury throughout Shanghai. The most indignant were the Chinese communists.

They had to act, they must act, for the comrades and the people were bleeding, slaughtered by imperialist bandits in their own motherland.

There was no time to lose.

On the evening of May 30, Chen Duxiu presided over an emergency meeting of the Central Committee of the CPC. In addition to Cai Hesen, Li Lisan, Yun Daiying, Wang Yifei, Luo Yinong, and Zhang Guotao, Liu Shaoqi, a labor movement leader who was urgently transferred from somewhere else, also attended it.

"The most urgent matter now is to stop the imperialist madness. We must launch a city-wide strike in Shanghai and nationwide strike,

Flames of War on Nanjing Road

and mobilize all patriotic forces to attack them, full scale." Following his passionate speech, specific action plans were carried out for the fight against imperialism. Cai Hesen, Li Lisan, and Yun Daiying unanimously suggested that in accordance with changes in the situation of the struggle, the central government should set up an action committee at once to build an anti-imperialist and patriotic united front for all classes. In addition to workers' strikes, any anti-imperialism activities were encouraged, students' strikes, merchants' strikes, etc.

"Agree!"

"Absolutely!"

The emergency meeting achieved consensus and made a clear division of labor: under the command of Chen Duxiu, Li Lisan was in charge of external activities on behalf of the Shanghai Labor Unions, and the rest stayed in their original positions.

"Daiying, your Shanghai Federation of Students shall take the lead of all activities. You have to work harder!" Chen Duxiu patted Yun Daiying on the shoulder and exhorted:

"Understand. We act tonight!" Yun Daiying promised.

So that night, a total of 500 representatives from the schools of the Shanghai Federation of Students assembled to discuss the action plan:

1. Schools in Shanghai, big or small, would take the lead in all strikes the following day;
2. Industrial and commercial sectors in Shanghai must immediately join the strike;
3. Strike until the imperialists give in;
4. It was decided to expand the organization of the Federation of Students to deal with any changes;
5. Issue a declaration to expose the crimes of the imperialists and demand support;
6. Provincial student federations and revolutionary groups were required to lead the masses to fight.

In fact, as soon as the Shanghai Federation of Students acted, Li Lisan, Liu Shaoqi, and Ren Bishi, who had already taken an important position

Revolutionaries

in the CPC in Shanghai, dove at once into relevant business organizations and communities in the city to assemble labor unions and chambers of commerce for meetings to formulate anti-imperialist countermeasures. Under their emergency organization, chambers of commerce on Shandong Road, Henan Road, Aidoya Road (now Yan'an Road), Wuma Road (now Guangdong Road), Sima Road (now Fuzhou Road) actively responded.

On the morning of the 31st, students went on a strike, many stores also halted operations, teams of college and middle school students were seen chanting slogans and marching to the city center. Soon, teams of workers in uniforms came out of the factories. These two parade groups merged into an unstoppable torrent, making Shanghai quake. Leaders of the CPC and labor movements, such as Luo Yinong and Wang Shouhua, names that gave the enemies instant chills, were at the front, commanding and leading the protest.

However, the strike of the business community was going exceedingly slow.

The attitude of the Shanghai General Chamber of Commerce was crucial, because only when it granted permission could the city go on a full commercial strike.

Qu Qiubai complained to Chen Duxiu: "The General Chamber of Commerce is too stubborn. Send the young students to straighten it out."

Hearing the complaints, Chen Duxiu widened his eyes and suddenly ordered: "I agree. Have Dai Ying organize 10,000 students and patriotic citizens to petition the Shanghai General Chamber of Commerce!"

"I will contact her immediately!"

Soon, a petition team composed of over 10,000 students and citizens sieged the Shanghai Chamber of Commerce and demanded its chairman to issue a strike notice.

"This is too big a deal. Since our establishment, there has been no precedent." Fang Jiaobo, Vice Chairman of the General Chamber of Commerce, who was on duty, shook his head decisively.

"True. I'm well-aware of the fact of zero precedent. But it is a different time: imperialists have loaded up guns and butchered students and citizens on the streets. Can you really just sit there doing nothing" The students and citizens pressured him.

Flames of War on Nanjing Road

"This... I'm afraid..." Fang Jiaobo kept shaking his head.

"Alright, if you don't sign it, it means you are with imperialism. We have no choice but punish you the way we do the imperialists who murdered our compatriots. Students, citizens, do it--"

"Let's do it!"

"Smash the imperialist lackeys!"

In an instant, angry students and citizens picked up chairs and stools in his office, about to smashed everything.

"Stop! Don't!" Fang Jiaobo, trembling with fright, raised his hands, and caved in: "I'll sign it!"

As soon as they obtained the city-wide strike order granted by the General Chamber of Commerce, they printed and distributed them to its branches, communities, and shop owners overnight so that a full-scale strike could take place in Shanghai on June 1.

Meanwhile, Li Lisan and Liu Shaoqi presided over a joint meeting of labor unions on the 31st and decided to openly establish the Shanghai Federation of Labor Unions (formerly a secret organization) the next day.

On June 1, 1925, the first anti-imperialist fight after the Massacre on May Thirtieth Movement led by the Chinese Communist Party broke out.

In the afternoon, the Shanghai Federation of Labor Unions announced its establishment, with Li Lisan as the chairman and Liu Shaoqi as the director of the General Affairs Section (equivalent to the Secretary-General). Chen Duxiu, General Secretary of the Central Committee of the CPC, delivered a speech at the founding site. His passion and driving spirit inspired everyone present. For the first time, many worker representatives saw the true color of the May Fourth" standard bearer and the leadership of the CPC.

"Now I declare in the name of the Shanghai Federation of Labor Unions: from June 2, all workers from all walks of life in this city will strike together!" Chairman Li Lisan cried.

"Vengeance!"

"Get the murderous foreign bandits!"

"Down with imperialism!"

Immediately, workers' slogans echoed over Shanghai.

In the afternoon that day, the Shanghai Federation of Labor Unions issued the famous *June First Declaration* to all workers.

On June 1, the street situation was of great gravity. Angry students, workers, and citizens at the scene of murder of compatriots, protesting, delivering speeches, and distributing flyers, were still being dispelled and beaten by a large number of armed policemen. There was sound of gunshots, sporadic or intensive, and four more people died, with countless wounded. Also, the public concession imposed martial law from this day, banning all street gatherings and speeches, and any assembly and speakers would be punished in accordance with the public security regulations. In the afternoon, the traffic arteries along Nanjing Road and the Bund, shockingly, were filled with imperialist armies.

Obviously, Shanghai has been shrouded in the violence of imperialism.

"Fellow workers, fear nothing. Raise our hands and join the death squad." Despite tyrannical imperialist bullets, standing on the street shouting was a familiar figure to the workers. He was the only 26-year-old Liu Hua, a labor movement leader.

"But they have guns and cannons. We will die." Someone murmured timidly.

"True, we have no weapons, but we outnumber them. Unite and we shall fear no imperialists. Yes, it will be hard, but it is ten times harder for imperialists because Shanghai is our home. Ours! Not theirs! These days are coming to an end," Liu Hua replied with great confidence.

"Exactly! Their days are due! Shanghai is ours! Get up and fight, make them crawl back home. The sooner they are gone, the less death and starvation for us."

"Yes! Unite and fight—" The workers held hands and sang *The Internationale* with Liu Hua.

Under the leadership of the CPC, on June 1, the school strike in the city, small and middle, succeeded as scheduled.

On June 2, the city strike basically prevailed as scheduled.

On June 3, the commercial market in Shanghai downtown almost suspended all business for protest, raising great panic within the imperialist forces in the city.

"Toughest measures must be taken to suppress and eliminate the existence of those provocative forces!" Shouting hoarsely, the concession chose the path of absolute hostility against anti-imperialist voices and actions from all walks of life in Shanghai, against the Chinese people.

From June 4, imperialist bandits deployed forces to occupy and station in Shanghai, Daxia, Tongji, Tongde, and Donghua Universities, as well as Nanyang Affiliated High School, in an attempt to extinguish the wave of student revolution on the front line of anti-imperialist movements. It backfired, infuriating more students and teachers. CPC members such as Shen Yanbing and Hou Shaoqiu (later a martyr), together with Shanghai faculty members, established the National Salvation Comrades Association. From the student anti-imperialist movement to national salvation movement, revolutionary waves struck from all directions.

Hot Blood Daily, founded by the Central Committee of the CPC, was officially published four days after the Massacre on May 30 Movement, with Qu Qiubai as the editor-in-chief. Chen Duxiu wrote an article for the first issue. "It is hot blood and cold iron (arms) that forge world culture. Now the strong in the world have cold iron, while we weak have merely hot blood, something that promises our possession of cold iron the future. When that day comes, it will be the end of those who are strong."

In the face of imperialist violence, Chinese communists started to reckon with escalating the revolution to armed battles and urban riots.

On June 6, Cai Hesen and Qu Qiubai prepared the *Report of the CPC against the Barbaric and Cruel Massacre by Imperialism to All Chinese People* (*The Report*). Issued by Chen Duxiu, it disclosed the truth of the Massacre on May 30 Movement in Shanghai to the general public via progressive newspapers, like *Guide*, among other means.

It wrote "Shanghai, suffering heavy casualties, has become an abattoir for foreign imperialism. Is it accidental? Absolutely not. It is an inevitable pernicious result under imperialist rule. As long as capitalist-imperialism exists, the oppressed, nations and classes, are at the very risk of being slaughtered."

"The history of China from the Opium War to the Boxer Rebellion was utterly filled with bloody records of foreign forces slaughtering its people. However, the bloodshed in Shanghai opened the first page of the nation's conscious rebellion against imperialism."

"The massacre in Shanghai was a re-announcement of imperialists' barbaric ambitions — enslaving Chinese eternally and suppressing any slightest revolution, an only choice of slavery or death for them."

The Report also determinedly revealed the heinous acts of the imperialist powers, warning every Chinese, "Our life and freedom are never guaranteed by dead letters of punishment, compensation, and apology, but by abolishing unequal treaties and overthrowing all the privileges of imperialism in China. Therefore, the resistance in Shanghai and across China triggered by this massacre will be a long national fight, whose gains and losses shall not be based on whether British and Japanese imperialism punish the murderers, offer compensation, and apologize, but determined by the following two conditions: first, whether it can continue to shake imperialist privilege and rule in China for the long run and cause a permanent crisis in their economy; second, whether it can lead the people of all classes in the country to the peak of anti-imperialism and form separate mass organizations and united national organizations of each class."

The CPC bravely called on the people to take action to resist the barbaric and brutal massacre by imperialists, and persisted until the final victory. *The Report* put forward four matters worth attention, and at the end reminded all Chinese: "This major incident in Shanghai broke out because the imperialists attacked the working class. It proves that the people of all classes have already deeply realized the importance of supporting new anti-imperialism powers. Tens of thousands of students and citizens of Shanghai made no hesitation in the face of death to help the workers, one after another, amid the imperialist fire. What a respectable spirit! What a great sacrifice! It is hoped that the rising people in Shanghai and the entire country should honor the will of the bleeding martyrs and always support the interests of the workers most oppressed by the imperialists in the long-term national fight; that they should be cautious about the imperialist's traps of disuniting us, so that the working class, which is most loyal to national interests, would never be subject to peril, and the national liberation movement could dodge deadly blows."

Soon after the Report came out, the Central Committee of the Communist Youth League, as required by the Central Committee of the CPC, also published *A Report to the Young Workers of the World*. The May

Flames of War on Nanjing Road

Thirtieth Anti-imperialist Movement entered a new stage and depth.

At this time, both sides were keeping close observation on how the situation would develop. On the evening of June 6, something happened on a road in Shanghai: a middle-aged man, sniffing around alone in the street, was noticed by the workers' picket, who mistook him for a Japanese spy. Shouting "Down with the Japanese!", they flocked around him.

The middle-aged man immediately defended himself: "I am no Japanese! Never!"

"Then, what are you doing?" Just as the picket was about to rough him up, a few comrades from the Shanghai underground party arrived. They took a closer look. "Isn't this The old man'?" The Old Man was his nickname in the party, because Chen Duxiu was one of the rare few old men in their fifties in the young CPC.

"Yes, guilty," he replied in relief.

"How dangerous! Why are you wandering by yourself?"

"I just wanted to see the situation on the street."

"Too dangerous! Let's take you home."

"Thanks! Thanks!" Chen Duxiu expressed gratitude again and again.

It was a story a tad legendary, and evidence to the fact that the situation back then greatly worried the highest level of Central Committee of the CPC.

The situation was indeed urgent. First, despite the anti-imperialist mobilization taking shape in Shanghai, problems had also surfaced. For example, some factories stopped paying wages after the strike, and workers who depended on the meager wages to support their families were worried. So, students and citizens were encouraged to donate to help, but there were too many in need of financial assistance, which made it quite difficult to maintain long-term strikes and suspension of business. Second, even though the first wave of strikes and suspension of business did not fail thanks to the efforts of the CPC and the front-line workers of the labor unions, in mid-June, the warlord government of Duan Qirui and Zhang Zuolin colluded with the imperialists and launched an aggressive counterattack on the people of Shanghai in the anti-imperialist movement. Warlord Zhang Zuolin personally stationed his army in the city and led the suppression over anti-imperialist fight of students, workers and citizens.

Revolutionaries

These two matters triggered disagreement within the party.

"We must not slack! Persist to the end!"

"I have reservations about long-term strikes and market suspension."

"Imperialism has a system to frustrate the workers' revolution. We can never abandon the victory we have achieved, or the consequences will be disastrous. The revolution will suffer unbearable setbacks and more casualties!"

"Enough! Squabbling doesn't help! The iron is hot, not easy to cool down at once. What we need now is to alleviate the urgent situation of the fight in Shanghai as soon as possible, and firmly grasp the initiative. The problem is not with the students. However, whether workers and businessmen can continue the strike is the key for some time in the future. We must offer reinforcements to Shanghai on the one hand, and mobilize national power on the other, so as to put pressure on the reactionary and decadent Beiyang government while easing the pressure in Shanghai. We must crush the crazy momentum of imperialism." Having finished the speech, Chen Duxiu signaled Qu Qiubai, Cai Hesen, Zhang Guotao, and others to sit down and discuss specific strategies.

"Has Deng Zhongxia gone to Guangzhou? Send him to Guangzhou as soon as possible to organize the strike of Guangzhou and Hong Kong seamen."

"Has Changsha made any move? Hesen, have more contact with Runzhi and urge him to bring his A game."

"Transfer Xiangying from Wuhan to Shanghai. He excels at labor movement."

"There are many people in the north, experienced in labor movement and stronger. By the way, let's ask Shouchang right away to have Beard Wang transfer to Shanghai. He understands workers better than any of us, and is more experienced." At this time, Chen Duxiu, General Secretary of the Central Committee of the CPC, was playing the role of commander-in-chief for the May 30 Anti-imperialist Movement. He and several right-hand men were arranging new battlefields and fighting forces day and night. The man he referred to as Shouchang was Li Dazhao; the real name of Beard Wang was Wang Hebo, and both were revolutionary martyrs.

Martyr Wang Hebo, with outstanding revolutionary achievements,

Flames of War on Nanjing Road

had a legendary life.

He was a native of Fujian. In 1901, less than a hundred days after his mother passed away, he left his hometown to serve as a soldier with his uncle in Jiangyin, Jiangsu. His uncle, whose position in the Navy of the Qing Army was equivalent to a battalion commander, was later dismissed, and Wang Hebo had to retire and sold labor in Dalian and Vladivostok arsenals. In 1916, he worked as a fitter at the Puzhen Locomotive Factory of Jinpu Railway. When the May Fourth Movement broke out, Nanjing responded to Beijing's call for a strike. Prestigious in the factory, he led the workers to strike. In 1921, Luo Zhanglong, the head of the Northern Branch of the Secretariat of the Chinese Labor Union, was besieged by local villains on his way from Xuzhou to Puzhen and suffered atrocities. Wang Hebo, a righteous man, stood out and rescued him. Since then, Wang Hebo has built a direct relationship with the party and joined CPC. The Nanjing Underground Party established the first party group, the Pukou Party Group, where he acted as the leader. This year, he turned 40, and the workers sent him a big red plaque that wrote Man of Integrity, an accurate summary of his character.

He was a tall man, senior, thick bearded, and kind, so the workers kindly nicknamed him Beard Wang. In 1923, he left for Guangzhou to attend the Third National Congress of the CPC and was elected as an executive member of the Central Committee of the CPC. The same year, he was also elected as a member of the Central Bureau of the CPC while serving as the chairman of the Executive Committee of the CPC in Shanghai, co-managing party organization development in Shanghai, Ningbo, Songjiang, Wuxi with other comrades. In January 1924, the first cooperation between KMT and CPC officially took place. He used to be a hard laborer, and he and Mao Zedong, Yun Daiying, Deng Zhongxia, and Xiang Jingyu worked for the KMT Shanghai Executive Department. In 1925, he attended the Fourth National Congress of the CPC held in Shanghai. The same year, this labor movement leader who led the February 7 strike of the Beijing-Wuhan Railway was elected as the chairman of the Chinese Railway Labor Union. During the August 7th Conference, he was officially elected as a member of the Provisional Political Bureau of the Central Committee. In China from the 1920s to 1930s, railway workers were the strongest group

Revolutionaries

of all workers, hence his high prestige among the workers and within the Central Committee of the CPC.

Once the May 30 anti-imperialist movement began, Chen Duxiu personally ordered Wang Hebo to Shanghai from the north to lead the workers to strike on several railway lines from Shanghai to Nanjing, Zhengzhou, and Hangzhou. Having accepted the task, he instructed continuous strikes on various railway lines, effectively weakening the mad suppression of the imperialists and warlord forces over the citizens and students of Shanghai.

The May 30 anti-imperialist movement turned out victorious, owing greatly to Wang Hebo's contributions during this period. He is a martyr and shall be forever remembered.

It is worth mentioning his subsequent acquaintance with Zhou Enlai, who was transferred from Guangzhou Whampoa Military Academy to Shanghai for the daily work of the Central Committee of the CPC and the organization of armed struggles. At first sight, they hit it off, and Zhou Enlai kindly called him Brother Wang. In the third armed uprising in Shanghai, he was Zhou Enlai's right-hand man, a military commander bravely charging on the front line. When the May 30 Movement ended, he was dispatched by the Central Committee to replace Li Dazhao, who was murdered by the warlord, as the head of Beijing's underground party organization. On October 18, 1927, as he was organizing a meeting of the Beijing Municipal Committee of the underground party, he was arrested by a reactionary warlord because of a betrayal by a traitor. On November 11, he was secretly killed together with other 17 underground party leaders of the Beijing Municipal Committee of the CPC, at the age of 45.

After the founding of the PRC, Premier Zhou Enlai often thought of his "big brother." He ordered the search for the remains of Wang Hebo and other 17 martyrs. Thanks to the hard work by the police, their remains, which had been missing for over 20 years, were finally found.

On December 11, 1949, relevant central authorities organized a burial and public memorial for the remains of the 18 martyrs, including Wang Hebo, in Beijing. Premier Zhou Enlai personally presided. Li Lisan made a special report about his deeds. The person in charge of the Organization Department of the Central Committee read out the funeral oration from

Flames of War on Nanjing Road

the Central Committee to these 18 martyrs:

It has been 22 years since the heroic sacrifices of these comrades. In 1927, national scum, external imperialism, internal feudal remnants, Kuomintang reactionaries, successively betrayed Nanjing and Wuhan, served the warlords, swaggered around Beijing and Tianjin, bringing calamity to the country and people, barbaric and cruel. They murdered whoever made the slightest resistance. Countless revolutionaries were victims, including these comrades, who never yielded despite the worst torture during their imprisonment. When executed, they died shouting slogans of justice, without a tinge of fear. The spirit of sacrificing for the revolution not only deterred the reactionaries, but also encouraged later comrades, thus laying the foundation for the triumph of the national revolution.

Alas, martyrs are gone, and we revolutionaries continued the path, fearless and determined to fight people's enemies like there was no tomorrow. It has been 22 years, during which time, we fought the hardest battles, many wounded and dead, made the 25,000-li Long March. After eleven years of bitter internal and external battles, we have recently destroyed the Kuomintang's reactionary rule, established People's Government, set the capital in Beijing, and completed the great cause of the revolution. May the results comfort the martyrs underground. Greatness has no easy start. Without the first steadfast footsteps of the martyrs at the beginning of the revolution, determined and heroic, inspiring comrades of the country to fight together against the reactionaries, we would have never made it today. We owe it absolutely to them.

The remains of these comrades were buried south of arrow stall to the north of the altar of Andingmen for too long. Today, they are moved here. Rest in peace, honored by all Chinese.

Alas! What grief!
Enjoy the feast.

I allocated more words to the story of martyr Wang Hebo because rarely known are the names and deeds of many of the four to five thousand revolutionary martyrs in Shanghai Longhua Revolutionary Martyrs Memorial Hall and Nanjing Yuhuatai Revolutionary Martyrs Memorial

Revolutionaries

Hall. All of them bled for the People's Republic of China, for every one of us in a world of peace. We must always remember them.

Now let's go back to the days of early June 1925, a week or so after the Massacre on May 30 Movement.

It was another sleepless night at the Secret Office of the Central Committee of the CPC:

General Secretary Chen Duxiu sprung up from the sofa, anxiously pacing back and forth in the room. Suddenly, he stopped, waved his fist, and spoke to Qu Qiubai, Cai Hesen, Zhang Guotao, and others. "Advance, we win; retreat, we lose. But sometimes a little retreat can result in victory."

"No! Retreating at this moment is tantamount to showing our weakness to the imperialists," Qu Qiubai objected vigorously while coughing.

"There is no need to squabble. What we need most is to pay heed to how the situation develops," Cai Hesen interjected.

"I agree. It is paramount that we pay close attention to that." As soon as Zhang Guotao finished speaking, a few people were about to leave.

"Don't! There is something that we must be cautious about!" Chen Duxiu warned, with hands on his hips, "Since they have made the first killing, don't expect them to be merciful. So, everyone, be careful."

Cai Hesen exchanged glances with Qu Qiubai and Zhang Guotao, and answered, "Naturally, we will be vigilant, but you must never wander alone on the street again."

"Sure! Never again!" Chen Duxiu promised.

The situation was, as estimated by CPC leaders, developing in the direction of greater gravity every day. Strikes by workers, students, and businessmen proceeded with difficulty. Imperialist powers and the Beiyang government colluded and worsened the bloody suppression of students, workers, and citizens. They shot people dead at will on the streets and alleys of Shanghai, deployed soldiers to openly wreak havoc and make arrests in the Federation of Labor Unions and the Federation of Students. Front line protesters, including Li Lisan Liu Shaoqi, and Liu Hua were the primary targets of arrest.

Suddenly, news came from Hankou: Li Lisan, the leader of the Shanghai Federation of Labor Unions, had been assassinated.

"What? Longzhi is dead?" The news reached Chen Duxiu, stupefying

Flames of War on Nanjing Road

and distressing him and other senior leaders of the Central Committee of the CPC. Longzhi was his old first name. When he joined the labor movement, he realized that it was a name with unfamiliar characters to the workers and difficult to pronounce. So, he simply changed it to Li Lisan, easy to pronounce and remember.

The next day, all circles of the Shanghai Labor Unions held a memorial for the sacrificed Chairman of the Shanghai Federation of Labor Unions, Li Lisan.

As the Shanghai comrades and the labor union were grieving for his demise, one night, Qu Qiubai pushed in with a man while Chen Duxiu was drafting documents in his bedroom.

"Mr., look who's here!"

As soon as he heard the question, he put down the pen and raised his head. Seeing the man who followed him in, he jumped up, startled: "Longzhi? You are not dead?"

Li Lisan smiled, relaxed: "Not yet. I'm back from Hankou, alive, reporting to you."

Chen Duxiu stretched out his arms at once, hugged him tightly, and spoke with a touch of sobbing, "Alive! Great! But in revolution, we must be always ready to give our lives, especially us. Perhaps, enemy's bullets will go right through our heads. Regardless, the murderers are never to walk away unpunished."

"Longzhi, what happened?" Chen Duxiu was curious.

"The thing is that after Xing Shilian of the Shanghai Fengtian Warlord was ordered to shut down the Shanghai Federation of Labor Unions, he hired a group of thugs to assassinate six designated student and worker leaders, including Li Lisan. Faced with the urgent situation, Shanghai workers, out of love, helped him secretly escape Shanghai, all the way to Hankou. However, warlord governments in every city have listed him as the prior arrest target, so the moment he reached Hankou, information was leaked. The warlords immediately ordered his arrest, and hired Xiao Jianfei, a famous local assassin, to kill him. Unexpectedly, the assassin, of integrity and righteousness, seeing that he was with the people day and night, dedicated to fighting for their interest, judged that he was a good man, and confessed to him about the assassination arranged by Wu Peifu.

Revolutionaries

As a result, Li Lisan returned to Shanghai in disguise. Xiao Jianfei lied that he had accomplished the task. Wu Peifu bought it, and ordered newspapers to spread the news that a most wanted communist Li Lisan had died in Wuhan. It quickly spread to Shanghai, hence the workers' holding the memorial.

"Hilarious. Better stay dead. Makes it easier to fight the imperialists, and I believe you, as a "dead" man, can better mess up those warlords!" Having figured out what happened exactly, Chen Duxiu was delighted, laughing hysterically.

Let's put aside the story of Shanghai, the main battlefield, for the time being, and take a look at the entirety of China.

Beijing:

On June 2, 92 schools in the city went on strike. On the 3rd, over 50,000 students took to the streets to demonstrate; on the 5th, over 480 social organizations from all walks of life in Beijing held a vengeance rally on the massacre of compatriots by British and Japanese imperialists; on the 10th, 200,000 people held a national assembly to voice their support for Shanghai.

Tianjin:

On June 5, schools in the city went on strike and 50,000 people took to the streets; on the 10th, the Tianjin General Chamber of Commerce issued a request for the city's business community to end economic ties with the UK and Japan, and jointly defend the nation; on the 14th, over 100,000 people participated in the citizens' assembly, making five requirements to the Beiyang government and the imperialist countries in China.

In Shanghai-adjacent cities of Nanjing, Hangzhou, Suzhou, Wuxi, Jiaxing, and Ningbo, the CPC directly sent local party members such as Xuan Zhonghua (later a martyr), Zhang Qiuren (later a martyr) and Li Qiang back to their hometowns to lead students and the masses to support Shanghai.

The support activities in Wuhan and Guangzhou were more extensive, with great momentum and the longest time. Wuhan was the transportation hub connecting northern and southern China at that time. With the experience of the February 7 strike and the direct command of senior CPC leaders such as Li Hanjun, Lin Yunan, and Xiang Ying, it hit hard the

Flames of War on Nanjing Road

Beiyang government and imperialist forces in China.

Guangzhou, as the base camp of Sun Yat-sen's revolution, had a strong CPC. At that time, since seamen's strikes in Guangdong and Hong Kong were organized and commanded by Deng Zhongxia, Su Zhaozheng (former member of the Standing Committee of the Political Bureau of the Central Committee of the CPC and later a martyr), Yang Yin (former director of the Central Military Commission of the CCP and later a martyr), and Chen Yannian, it lasted for one year and four months, punching imperialism the hardest. As many as two hundred revolutionaries died in the fight.

Strong support and solidarity from all parts of the country fueled the victory of the three strikes (of workers, of students, and of business) against imperialism in Shanghai. In the two months from early June to early August, they aggressively attacked the imperialist forces and commerce in Shanghai, so many business owners, including Japanese capitalists, had to partly agree to the workers' demands. Meanwhile, police in the concession were restrained from shooting students, workers, and citizens marching and giving speeches on the street. Even so, following the shooting of 13 people during the Massacre on May Thirtieth Movement, students, workers, and citizens were still gunned down one after another. The worst thing was that when labor unions, students, and citizens halted large-scale strikes, British and Japanese imperialist forces in Shanghai colluded with Sun Chuanfang, a new direct warlord stationed in Shanghai, promising him a considerable sum of money, on one condition that Liu Hua, a worker leader in the anti-imperialist May Thirtieth Movement, be secretly assassinated.

An ordinary worker, only 26 years old, who had only worked in Shanghai for 5 years, received such hatred from the imperialist forces because Liu Hua, under the leadership of the CPC, has been charging at the front in this vigorous anti-imperialist May 30 Movement, a thorn in their eyes. They had a visceral hatred of him. In order to serve the imperialist forces, Sun Chuanfang employed a large number of spies to hunt him down.

On the afternoon of November 29th, after attending a civic meeting against the Beiyang government, Liu Hua, walking to the Jing'an Temple in the twilight to take the tram, was stopped by a few spies from the front, and blocked by several Indian policemen, fully armed, from behind.

"What do you want?" Liu Hua interrogated them.

Revolutionaries

"What else than to arrest you?" A spy pressed the gun against Liu Hua's waist, "Tie him up!"

Having handcuffed him, they took him the police station. It happened to be seen by Zhang Zhaodi, a textile worker who knew him, and the news of his arrest was immediately spread to the party organization.

At once, secret rescue and public condemnation and demonstrations took place simultaneously. However, the police station transferred him to the Songhu Martial Law Command as soon as the following day.

"Mr. Liu, we are well-aware of your position as a worker leader in Shanghai, young and promising. Commander Sun also think highly of you, and hopes to make friends and make greatness in Shanghai together." In the interrogation room, the judge sent by the warlords, expressionless, attempted to cotton up with him.

Liu Hua snorted, without further response.

"In fact, our commander asks only a little." The judge gabbed on and on. Receiving nothing but silence, he continued: "As long as you persuade workers to halt the strike, we promise immediate release. How about that?"

"No way!" Liu Hua answered indignantly.

"Name your price?"

Liu Hua tilted his head back, "Sorry, nothing can bribe me. Tell your commander. The strike will stop only when the imperialist forces crawl the hell out of Shanghai, out of China, when all unequal treaties are abolished, when feudal warlords abandon their traitorous rule, when the Chinese nation and the working class are liberated. Can you make that happen?"

"Bullshit." The judge was speechless, and snarled, "Do you really fear no death?"

"Fear is no solution. One day inevitably, we will be killed by the imperialist-capitalists, by reactionary governments. So, we must rise up and fight. To fight, there is no space to fear death."

"Make him suffer!"

The torture never destroyed the iron will of the young communist and working-class leader. In the meantime, workers and students in the entirety of Shanghai launched strikes to rescue and support Liu Hua; meetings with over 10,000 attendants to condemn the reactionary government's arrest of Liu Hua were held. The Shanghai Federation of Labor Unions, which ceased activities in August, also announced that they would once again publicly lead the new labor movement.

The warlord government was afraid that it might not be able to eliminate Liu Hua as required by the imperialist forces should the strike continue to expand. Therefore, in the middle of the night on December 17, a group of military police stuffed him into a police car, drove to a wasteland, and executed him in secret.

His demise once again shocked and enraged the people of Shanghai. Hundreds of thousands of fellow workers of his desperately took to the streets, holding the picture of the deceased, and condemned the violence. The Shanghai Federation of Labor Unions immediately published an open telegram to the whole country, mourning that "our dearest and bravest leader" had been murdered. "Workers, unite, on the blood of our leader, and keep fighting."

On December 21st, Liu Hua's friend and famous poet Jiang Guangci wrote, tears in his eyes, a revolutionary poem *In the Dark Night – In Honor of Comrade Liu Hua*, passionately and affectionately:

...
You tried to tell me your wandering days;
That you were a proletarian — top to bottom.
That you were a soldier, fought battles
That bullets were raining around;
That you sold hard labor, suffered cold,
That you knew the misery of the unfortunate.

You said, "Studying as I am,
Never have I had a day of happiness!
Bread today, clothes tomorrow, books the day after.
Studying hard brings me no ease, does it?
Oh, my friend, I want to avenge, to fight back,
At daggers I am with this dark society."

Revolutionaries

Alas! If there is justice in the world,
Why do the evil sing while the kind weep?
Why do those who slack have it all while those who work have nothing?
Could it be destined to be?
Liu Hua! You represented the unfortunate,
A traitor of God, enemy of darkness!

You had the genius of a leader, the ability to command,
Resolutely dedicated to the mass of workers;
Tens of thousands of the abused and oppressed, by foreign capitalists,
Fortunately, had their beacon.

The tragic death of Gu Zhenghong enraged the public,
Gunshots, shouts, blood splashes, and noise, chaotic on Nanjing Road;
Even the Huangpu River turned red,
Even the great Shanghai was shrouded in murderous aura.

You led tens of thousands of oppressed people to seek for liberation,
Strove for freedom, human rights, and justice;
I pictured your hardworking look,
Alas! I have only one word, "Greatness!"
But friends and enemies never go hand in hand,
Darkness fell
So they, enemies of the oppressed,
Were determined to, alas! kill you...

The stars in the sky wept with shimmering tears;
The waves of the Huangpu River sobbing;
Where was humanity, justice, and light — absent,
But every fiber of this world was lamenting.
Alas, my friend, my comrade, my warrior,
Not openly beaten to death by lackeys in Tianfei Temple,
Not gunned down in front of the masses at the intersection of Nanjing,
But in the dark, you were secretly executed —
Dead as you were, I believe your heart lives.

Flames of War on Nanjing Road

I shall buy some flowers for you,
For the camaraderie of ours — and wail;
But where have they discarded your dead body,
Amidst the wild mounds, or on the seashore where no one can find?
Or thrown to wild beasts in remote barren hill?
Alas! My friend! You are gone,
Miserably

Tens of thousands of workers lost a brave leader,
They are crying with me, all tears;
In their pure heart, their simple imagination,
This enormous grief has no end.
Alas, my friend, my comrade, my warrior,
Dead as you are, tragically as it was,
Your name will be engraved on the monument of human liberation,
Eternally, gloriously, radiantly.

A hero was murdered, a poet enraged, and the revolutionary anthem sounded. A tragic murder during imperialist forces' suppression of the Chinese people developed into an anti-imperialist movement, in which the country was awakened and rose up. Heroes did not die for nothing, but a greater spiritual value than one's physical life.

Jiang Guangci, the author who sang the poem *In the Dark Night* against darkness, was later regarded a revolutionary martyr himself. I saw his portrait and deeds in the Longhua Revolutionary Martyrs Memorial Hall. This pioneer of proletarian revolutionary literature and art had been intelligent since childhood. At the age of 12, he wrote:

How about the torrential flood? Scaring off traveling merchants.
Waves raging and roaring, keeping away fishing boats.

Locals called him a prodigy. During the May Fourth Movement, he was already leader of a student movement and of literary youth in Wuhu area. In 1920, referred to Shanghai, he made acquaintance with revolutionaries such as Chen Duxiu and Chen Wangdao, and later joined the Socialist

Revolutionaries

Youth League. In May 1921, Jiang Guangci, Liu Shaoqi, Ren Bishi, and Xiao Jinguang were sent to study at the Communist University of Eastern Laborers in Moscow, where they met Lenin, a long-admired revolutionary icon. When Lenin passed away in January 1924, Jiang Guangci wrote the famous poem *Mourning Lenin* and became one of the pioneers of Chinese revolutionary literature. After joining the CPC in Moscow, he returned to Shanghai, officially began his career in revolutionary literature and joined the literary society Creation Club. After the May 30 Movement, he created a series of works reflecting the revolutionary truth of the labor movement, such as the novels *Young Wanderers* and *The Shorts*, one of the first achievements of Chinese proletarian revolutionary literature.

Next, he co-founded the revolutionary literary group Sun Society with Qian Xingcun and Meng Chao, and edited literary publications such as *Sun Monthly* and *Literature and Art of the Times*. Since most of his works unveiled real social mass struggles, directly condemning imperialism and reactionary warlord governments, they were banned by the authorities repeatedly, and he himself was wanted, too. However, he never gave in but kept successively creating excellent works, and later grew into one of the founders of the Chinese Left-wing Writers Alliance. And his novel *The Roaring Land*, written in 1931, further consolidated his lofty status as a warrior of words of the early proletarian revolution. In April 1931, his pulmonary disease deteriorated and he passed away in Shanghai on August 31, at the age of 30. Like Deng Zhongxia, Yun Daiying, Xiao Chunü, Qu Qiubai, and others, he was the backbone of the early propaganda of Marxist-Leninist literature as well as an early communist fighter, who had made outstanding contributions in the bloody revolution. People shall remember him for eternity.

The May Thirtieth Movement, directly led by the CPC, shocked both China and foreign countries, hitting imperialism hard like never before. Chen Duxiu, then General Secretary of the Central Committee of the CPC, once published an article on behalf of the CPC in the later period of the movement, commenting that the Chinese working class "Has exhibited great strength in this anti-imperialist movement. This period has thrown light upon the path for future development, which is to take fighting for the people as beacon; has warned us to prepare detailed strategies to better

Flames of War on Nanjing Road

resist imperialist aggression, the political and economic destruction and oppression of domestic warlords, and strive to liberate China."

He summed up two experiences of this movement:

"(1) effective mobilization of the proletariat, together with urban laborers and small businessmen, to fight in the past two months;

(2) correct identification and harnessing of the internal conflicts between imperialism and warlords."

This initial hard-earned victory at the price of martyrs' blood, led to a rapid development of the CPC organization. When the Fourth National Congress of the CCP took place in early 1925, there were 994 party members nationwide, and by the end of the year, the number exceeded 10,000. Before the May 30 Movement, Shanghai had 220 party members. After that, the number surged to 1,652, of which workers accounted for 78%. The increase in the party's class forces has laid a significant foundation for the CPC to lead the people to overthrow the "three mountains" (feudalism, imperialism, and warlords) and found a new China. Meanwhile, this brutal and bloody fight made Chinese communists fully aware of the importance and urgency of armed struggles.

Therefore, at the end of 1926, the Central Committee of the CPC made an important decision: to urgently transfer Zhou Enlai, who had served as the Director of the Political Department of the Whampoa Military Academy, member of the Standing Committee of the Guangdong District Committee and Minister of Military Affairs of the CPC, and Director of the General Political Department of the National Revolutionary Army, to Shanghai as Military Leader of the Central Committee of the CPC to organize an armed riot among Shanghai workers.

Thereafter, the city welcomed more cruel and fierce revolutionary fights.

CHAPTER THREE

———

Shanghai University: A Crucible for Revolution

I BELIEVE THAT WHAT DESERVES TO BE CALLED A CRUCIBLE FOR revolution should be a place that forges backbone, ambition, and talent of the revolutionaries.

Is there such a place? Yes, there is. In Shanghai, there was a university a hundred years ago. Although it only survived five years, it wrote an immortal chapter in the history of the Chinese revolution.

I prostrate myself in worship of it...

One year when I visited the Whampoa Military Academy in Guangzhou, the antithetical couplets and the top scroll at the gate left an enduring impression on me:

The couplets–Seek Fortune and Power Elsewhere, Prepare to Fight and Bleed Here;

The top scroll–Come the Revolutionaries.

This was one of the school regulations Sun Yat-sen set for Whampoa Military Academy. Unfortunately, when Chiang Kai-shek took control of it, it deviated from what Sun Yat-sen had intended but cultivated his henchmen for the upcoming counter-revolutionary cause. Of course, it also nurtured a great number of outstanding military talents to the revolutionary cause of founding the PRC, including marshals, senior generals, and generals, as well as communists such as Zhou Enlai and Yun Daiying, who once taught

Revolutionaries

there and inspired many communists.

To write this book, that day, accompanied by an expert on party history in Shanghai, I visited Huaihai Road and Shaanxi Road to pay homage to several early revolutionary sites of the Central Committee of the CPC in Shanghai. When I reached North Shaanxi Road, the expert urged me to look at the former site of Old Shanghai University. I mistook that he found out that I was a part-time doctoral supervisor at Shanghai University, but he explained, "This is not the Shanghai University of today."

"No?" I was puzzled.

"No. We Shanghai locals call it the Old Shanghai University."

It was established in 1922 in the early stage of cooperation between the KMT and the CPC. It had been a private Southeastern Higher Vocational Normal School, located in Qingyunli, Qingyun Road (now Lane 167, Qingyun Road), Zhabei District, and was rather small, with only 160 students, including those from its affiliated middle school, most of who were boarding students from Anhui.

In the wave of the May Fourth Movement, students at this school walked out of the gate and saw the outside world, especially the scale and education level of other schools. Discontent with the quality of their alma mater, they protested. Under this circumstance, principal Wang Litang absconded to Japan with the tuition they paid. They were outraged when they found out. Student Chen Yinnan united a couple of key students and they decided to recommend a new principal they deemed fit and overthrow the old one.

"Which celebrity do you think is qualified?" Passionate youth, fearless, were imagining the perfect candidate for the position. Eventually, three made the cut. First, it was Chen Duxiu, the standard-bearer of the May Fourth Movement, one of the key founders of the CPC, and editor-in-chief of *New Youth*. He was their first choice; the second was Zhang Taiyan, a prestigious educator, and with him, it would become a famous university; the third was Yu Youren, who had attracted much attention for his advocacy of education to save the nation.

"Wake up!" Some teachers and students burst into laughter the moment they heard their intention to invite one of these major figures to be the principal.

Shanghai University: A Crucible for Revolution

"Why not? It is revolution everywhere, isn't it? But we have no revolutionary university yet. Why can't we have an expert run one?" The young had fearless imaginations and words, and took actions—With dreams, these key students began to scour their traces everywhere. They discovered that Chen Duxiu was elusive, untraceable. They didn't know that Professor Chen was also the General Secretary of the CPC. It was no wonder his whereabouts were difficult to track. Zhang Taiyan rarely moved around, but he resided in Suzhou and had little interest in running a school. The students inquired about Yu Youren's residence in Shanghai, a destination easier to find. However, afraid of another rejection, they turned to Shao Lizi, a close friend of Yu Youren. It took relatively less effort to find him.

"It is an amazing idea to build a revolutionary university. Mr. Sun Yat-sen has always wanted that." Shao Lizi took the idea serious, nothing of a joke. However, it was difficult to convince his friend to take up this great task.

"I'll give it a shot." He told Yu the invitation to be a principal when he arrived at his residence. Yu became emotional, saying: "Zhonghui, you and I both are followers of Mr. Sun Yat-sen. It is a great idea to establish a school that enlightens Chinese with revolutionary thinking. But I am afraid I am not good enough for the job."

Shao Lizi was styled Zhonghui. They built a friendship when they were studying at Fudan Academy, the predecessor of Fudan University. Next, the two co-founded *Shenzhou Daily*. When the revolution was on fire, they went to Tokyo to meet Sun Yat-sen and joined the Tongmenghui (Chinese United League) together, the beginning of their participation in the revolution. Following the success of the Revolution of 1911, Shao Lizi and Ye Chucang co-founded the *Republic of China Daily* in Shanghai, which became the front of leftist progressives of the KMT at that time. The newspaper, persecuted by the warlord authorities for criticizing the Beiyang warlords and propagating democratic ideas, suffered difficulties in operating. Shao Lizi tried his best to keep it afloat and experienced countless hardships. At times, he had pay for printing paper himself, so that it could be published. *The Supplement of Awakening*, which he developed by himself, played an important role in promoting the New

Revolutionaries

Culture Movement. In 1920, Chen Duxiu came to Shanghai to organize the Marxism Research Association, of which Shao Lizi was one of the important members, and prepare for the establishment of the CPC. In August, Shao Lizi became a member of the CPC and joined the Shanghai Communist Group (as a KMT member).

He persuaded Yu Youren to take the job as the principal by saying that it was a great responsibility because the CPC also looked forward to creating a school to train revolutionary talents. Knowing that he and Li Dazhao were classmates in Japan, during the persuasion, he consulted Chen Duxiu and Li Dazhao within the Communist Party. The two leaders of the CPC agreed that Yu Youren was a perfect candidate for the principal of a revolutionary university jointly run by the KMT and the CPC.

"Zhonghui, you serve as the vice principal." Chen Duxiu entrusted an important task to Shao Lizi.

"Everyone believes you are perfect for the job." Shao Lizi delivered the result to Yu Youren.

"Really?" Yu Youren asked in surprise.

"Indeed." Shao Lizi repeated the words of Li Dazhao and Chen Duxiu.

Yu Youren answered cheerfully: "Then, shall we go to the school for a look?"

"Let's go."

In fact, at that time the school could not wait for a new principal, because the fights within the school had become fierce. The school plaque had been smashed multiple times. Hearing the news that Yu Youren would probably take the job, the students looking forward to improvement posted welcome slogans and colorful flags on the walls inside and outside the campus. Informed of that, Yu Youren decided he had to take a look.

One day in October 1922, Yu Youren, accompanied by Shao Lizi, arrived at the school in a hired car. It was raining, but as soon as he showed up at the school gate, the students waved the welcome flags, lined up to greet him, and there was loud music and firecrackers. Many even jumped with excitement, despite rain covering their bodies and faces. It was a moment that moved him greatly. He exclaimed said: "What promising and respectful students!"

At the welcome meeting, Yu Youren was invited to give a speech.

Shanghai University: A Crucible for Revolution

He took the stage, and said emotionally: "I was touched by your spirit in the rain just now. I used to make small firecrackers when I was a child. I wanted to make bombs and landmines to blow up old China and the old world to pieces! Today, I am deeply glad to see you, aspiring. So, right here I promise you that I am going to, with all of you, build China's first real revolutionary university!"

As soon as he finished the speech, the students shouted "Hurrah" three times.

He proceeded: "I am confident! Because I have help from the talented and famous personal friend of mine, Mr. Shao Lizi, to build and manage it together! I will also invite all progressive revolutionaries and educators in China to be your professors, your lecturers. I would like to invite Mr. Sun Yat-sen to give lectures, too—"

"Long live China!"

"Long live the revolution!"

The words of Yu Youren, who they regarded as "a great revolutionary, founding father, pioneer of speeches, and advanced educator," like a blaze, ignited this decayed school, fiercely burning red...

Shanghai University-that day, he wrote these characters with great enthusiasm, and a school that had a major influence in modern Chinese history and nurtured a considerable number of outstanding revolutionaries was born.

"Shouchang, you must help me with this!" The news that Yu Youren and Shao Lizi were appointed as the principal and vice principal of Shanghai University quickly spread in the public. It was during the "honeymoon" period of Li Dazhao and Sun Yat-sen discussing cooperation between the KMT and the CPC. One day, Yu Youren learned that Li Dazhao had come to Shanghai and invited him for a meal at the Beijing-Tianjin Tea House in the Tongxing Building on Sima Road. As they talked about the founding of Shanghai University during the dinner, he made a request to Li Dazhao.

"Naturally! We are lucky to have you as the principal. We will help as much as we can," Li Dazhao promised. He added that from the needs of the Chinese revolution, the school, in addition to the courses available in ordinary universities, should focus on opening the Department of Social Sciences, and make it a key task in the school to train the cores for national

Revolutionaries

revolution.

"Indeed! The paramount factor to run a school is the teaching faculty. You know a wide network of teachers in Beijing, must recommend a few best to me," Yu Youren urged.

Li Dazhao nodded with a smile, stroked his beard, dipped his finger in water, and wrote down several names on the table. "How about them?"

"Fantastic! This is beyond my imagination!" He stood up immediately and bowed to Li Dazhao, who was a few years younger. "Thank you! I cannot thank you enough!"

"We are a team now. We help each other. Cultivating a group of useful revolutionary talents is the most important and fundamental task. I and the Communist Party of China shall contribute our best."

Soon, the *Republic of China Daily* published the Shanghai University Notice:

> *The school, originally named Southeast Higher Vocational Normal School, was renamed Shanghai University, for Southeast overlaps that of National Southeast University, and the school system was changed as decided in the reorganization, with Mr. Yu Youren appointed as the principal.*

An advertisement of merely a few words, perhaps due to the celebrity effect, attracted an endless stream of applicants. At this time, the CPC admitted progressive students expelled or suspended for their revolutionary ideas from other schools to Shanghai University. Therefore, in less than half a year, the old campus could no longer accommodate that many students. It was relocated to new school buildings at 132 Ximo Road in the public concession (now Shaanxi North Road), and endured five brilliant years (until in 1927 it was shut down for being a Red School by the Chiang Kai-shek group who betrayed the revolution).

"Cultivate talents able to found a nation, Promote cultural undertakings," words Yu Youren wrote as the aim of Shanghai University.

When school started, students were thrilled the moment they found out about the composition of the teaching faculty:

Deng Zhongxia (he had the pseudonym Deng Anshi at the time), a student leader of the May Fourth Movement, well-known labor movement

Shanghai University: A Crucible for Revolution

activist, and Editor-in-chief of *Chinese Youth*, served as the school's General Secretary, taught ethics courses, and presided over its daily operation;

Qu Qiubai, a famous scholar proficient in Russian and one of the main leaders of the early CPC, served as the Dean of the Department of Sociology, concurrently teaching the history of social movements and of Chinese philosophy;

Chen Wangdao, a well-known scholar proficient in Japanese and English and with outstanding Chinese literacy, the first Chinese full-text translator of *The Communist Manifesto*, served as the head of the Chinese Department and also taught grammar and rhetoric;

He Shizhen, a prestigious educator served as the Dean of the English Department and taught an Outline of Political Science;

Artist Hong Ye (the teacher of outstanding painters such as Pan Yuliang) was appointed Dean of the Department of Art.

The faculty of Shanghai University perfectly demonstrates why there was the saying Beijing University best in the North and Shanghai University the best in the South.

There were other teachers, such as Cai Hesen (who taught the History of Social development), Zhang Tailei (who lectured the History of the Labor Movement), Yun Daiying (who taught the History of Imperialist Aggression in China), Ren Bishi (who taught Russian and gave lectures on the youth movement), Shi Cuntong (who, the first secretary of the Chinese Socialist Youth League, taught the History of Social Movements and Social Thought), Shen Yanbing (who became better known as the writer Mao Dun, taught the History of Chinese Literature), Gao Yuhan (who, as an early member of the CPC, lectured on Hegelian philosophy), Jiang Guangci (who taught Soviet Literature)...

There were also part-time lecturers such as Peng Shuzhi, Tian Han, Yu Pingbo, Zhu Ziqing, Xiao Chunü, Feng Zikai, Zhou Jianren, Li Ji, Shen Zemin, Yang Xianjiang, Hu Puan, Li Chunfan, Zhou Yueran, Hou Shaoqiu, and others.

Sun Yat-sen, Chen Duxiu, Li Dazhao, Wu Yuzhang, Li Lisan, and others also gave lectures there; so did famous KMT "revolutionaries," Wang Jingwei, Dai Jitao, and more.

This revolutionary crucible rose on the banks of the Huangpu River in the 1920s like the rising sun, illuminating the city and affecting the entire country.

It earned the title of crucible of the revolution because at its early founding, there was no school dedicated to cultivating revolutionary talents in the country, and it was mainly leaders of the CPC who took up the teaching tasks and daily operation of the school. Many of the students who enrolled were not unfamiliar figures later on, such as important figures in the history of the CPC, Wang Jiaxiang, Yang Shangkun, Qin Bangxian, and so on; such as cultural celebrities, Ding Ling, Yang Hansheng, Dai Wangshu, Yuan Muzhi, Shi Zhecun and so on.

From establishment in 1922 to 1927, it merely survived five years. However, no other Chinese institutions of higher education can ever match the brilliance of this short life. This school cultivated not only a great many political figures and cultural figures who changed and influenced China, but revolutionaries who sacrificed their lives for the nation. Their heroic deeds and immortal spirit are still inspiring us for generations to come.

May 4, 2019, was the centennial of the May Fourth Movement, a great revolutionary movement in modern Chinese history we are most familiar with. As we solemnly commemorated it, we definitely thought of the person who had marched in the forefront of the Peking University student parade, which set off from the Red Mansion in Beijing a hundred years ago, who took the lead in front of Tiananmen Square chanting slogans "Down with imperialism!" and "Abolish all unequal treaties!"

We know him well. He was one of the early leaders of the CPC and a famous leader of the labor movement, Deng Zhongxia.

He is a well-known figure among Chinese. However, there are two things about him that are little known: one is his contribution to the convening of the First National Congress of the CPC; the other is his engagement in the great cause of cultivating revolutionary talents in Shanghai University.

As Li Dazhao was preparing the early organization of the Beijing Communist Party, Deng Zhongxia was an activist. It was he and Li Dazhao, Luo Zhanglong, Zhang Guotao, and Liu Renjing who received Grigori Naumovich Voitinsky, who was appointed by the Communist International to assist with the preparation for the establishment of the CPC. At the end of June 1921, the Beijing Party Organization received a notice from the

Shanghai University: A Crucible for Revolution

Shanghai Party Organization regarding the convening of the First National Congress of the CPC. Beijing recommended two representatives, the first choice being Deng Zhongxia and the second Zhang Guotao, considering that they had contact. However, Deng Zhongxia had already scheduled a trip to Nanjing in July to attend the annual meeting of the Youth China Association, and would go to Chongqing to give lectures in mid-July. "This is fixed. Better not change it!" In this case, Liu Renjing and Zhang Guotao, the youngest ones, were selected as representatives of the Beijing Party Organization to attend it in Shanghai.

As a result, Deng Zhongxia was not on the list of 13 representatives of the First National Congress of the CPC. However, quite influential and well-known among the young CPC members at the time, he was still an essential preparatory member commissioned by Li Dazhao for the event, drafting the report of the Beijing Party Organization. On June 28, he attended the annual meeting of the Youth China Association in Nanjing; on July 4, he arrived in Shanghai from Nanjing and stayed in the Bowen Girls' School in the French Concession. In the following three or four days, not only did he submit the report of the Beijing Party group to the Shanghai preparatory group for the First National Congress of the CPC, but discussed major party building matters with representatives in attendance.

Representative Bao Huiseng wrote in a reminiscence article: "Before the congress, representatives from all over the country arrived in Shanghai and lived in the Bowen Girls' School in the French Concession, including Comrade Mao Zedong. Comrade Deng, invited to attend a summer seminar in Chongqing, went there as scheduled to give a lecture, thus unable to participate in the congress, but he lived with representatives in the Bowen Girls' School for three or four days. And he exchanged ideas with all of them." This greatly helped with the convening of the congress. During his short stay, he discussed the arrangements with Li Hanjun and others in Shanghai. Because at that time there were two leaders of the CPC, North Li and South Chen (Li Dazhao in the north and Chen Duxiu in the south), Zhang Guotao, who represented North Li, presided over the Congress while Chen Gongbo, under the command of South Chen, took minutes of the meeting. And representatives from Shanghai covered meeting services. After all these were confirmed, Deng Zhongxia and Wang Huiwu, the wife

Revolutionaries

of Shanghai representative Li Da, who was in charge of congress affairs, inspected the venue of the event.

"Alright. I can leave assured." After the inspection, he walked out of Li Da's apartment and took a deep breath, with a hint of glow on his face.

He must have been elated in that very moment, because founding a proletarian party in China was something he had been working hard for and looking forward to with Li Dazhao and other revolutionary comrades since the May Fourth Movement. Now, in order to mobilize and awaken more youth, workers, and intellectuals, he handed over an important historical opportunity to shine to other comrades. Instead, in a long gown and with an umbrella, he walked towards the next revolutionary task.

The appointment to the Shanghai University as Chief of General Affairs was not only a decision of the CPC, but also what he himself was more than willing to do. As the standard-bearer of the May Fourth Movement and the February 7th Beijing-Wuhan Railway Strike, and participant in the great cause of the founding of the CPC, he attached great importance to the nurturing of revolutionary talents. In Shanghai University, he actually executed the work of Principal, as Yu Youren rarely worked on campus. Deng Zhongxia, the Chief of General Affairs, became the de facto executor.

Deng Zhongxia, who studied at Peking University, was deeply influenced by Principal Cai Yuanpei's idea of education to save the nation. Having absorbed Marxism, he realized that in order to save China, people's thinking must first be enlightened. Upon his arrival at Shanghai University, he personally formulated the school constitution, clarifying that the purpose of was to train talents able to build a nation and promote cultural undertakings, that social science and revolutionary literature were the focus, and employed celebrities from all walks of life to teach or give lectures there. Under his leadership, social science courses of this university differed from ordinary universities by focusing on arming students with Marxism. He particularly emphasized reading to practice.

"What is reading to practice? To understand Chinese society and find a way to save it and the Chinese people, a task students in this university must dedicate themselves to!" he said.

Therefore, as guided by educational ideas of revolution, Chinese communists such as Chen Duxiu, Li Dazhao, Cai Hesen, and Li Lisan

Shanghai University: A Crucible for Revolution

became teachers at the university. Lectures about the flames of the October Revolution, the protest against the Paris Commune, the legend of the February 7 strike fascinated the students. For a time, in the school, classrooms were full of deliberate discussions, streets full of passionate speeches, stages full of performances about blood shed for the nation, and printing machines full of stacks of publications and leaflets.

On campus, the Social Science Research Association, Social Issues Research Association, Art Research Association, and Spring Breeze Literature Association came into being one after another.

Within a year, the reputation of the university spread. Applicants in 1923 were not only young people from Sichuan, Yunnan, Guangxi, Guizhou, Hunan, and Anhui, but also young overseas Chinese who had returned from foreign lands such as Southeast Asia and Japan.

Old school building failed to accommodate waves of new students. On February 22, 1924, the campus was relocated to new buildings on Ximo Road. At this time, Deng Zhongxia immediately started to create the organizational system of the school, making major adjustments to the original departments. The university section had three departments: Department of Social Sciences, Department of Natural Sciences, and Department of Arts. And a secondary school section was added (with high school and junior high school classes). As a result, it had truly become a well-known national university with a complete number of departments.

As a professional revolutionary, Deng Zhongxia believed that revolutionary fire should go beyond the campus to a wider world. Therefore, based on his experience in running a cram school in the Changxindian Subdistrict of Beijing, as well as the characteristics of Shanghai's industrial and commercial advancement, he decided to make use of the university to open night schools for civilians and workers. It was a decision that turned out a great move that ignited the fire of revolution among people in Shanghai.

The number of applicants for the first term of the night school for civilians of Shanghai University reached 450. But as many as 560 attended the classes. There were more students in the following terms. For a time, studying at Shanghai University was a hot topic among Shanghai residents. With the opening of night school for workers, it became a sacred place for revolutionaries and Shanghai masses. It was at this time that Liu Hua, who grew into a leader of the Shanghai labor movement, received education in Marxism and joined the CPC.

Dissemination of advanced ideas and improvement of cultural knowledge enabled workers and students to see the hope and prospects of self-liberation and proletarian revolution. Many took the initiative to join the CPC and the Communist Youth League. Consequently, the Shanghai underground organization of the CPC continued to expand, from one small group during the First National Congress of the CPC to four, with Shanghai University as the first, consisting of a total of 11 party members. This branch had Deng Zhongxia, Qu Qiubai, Yun Daiying, Zhang Tailei, etc. who were all leaders of the Central Committee of the CPC and the Central Committee of Communist Youth League, and died revolutionary martyrs.

It was their great personality and the qualities of Communist Party members that deeply influenced and inspired the students Shanghai University to embark on a firm revolutionary path.

Yang Zhihua (wife of Qu Qiubai), a female revolutionary, recalled Deng Zhongxia, a model for others:

He was our Chief of General Affairs, with dark hair, thick and long eyebrows that separate a tad far from one another. When he raised his head to look at us, his eyes sparkled. He was energetic, witty and decisive, keeping school life tense and orderly. He used to enjoy telling us stories about Karl Liebknecht and Rosa Luxemburg. He was a courageous and persevering revolutionary we respect and love.

For the proletarian revolutionaries, Liebknecht and Luxemburg were worshipped by guerrillas all over the world no less than the Cuban revolutionary Che Guevara.

Yes, true revolutionaries are,
Committed to their dream career,
Often they choose the most exposed and dangerous spots for themselves.
When dawn has not yet come,

Shanghai University: A Crucible for Revolution

They have fallen in the darkness,
Among all the fallen,
Please remember one:
Rosa Luxemburg.

Yes, the day when victory comes in the future,
We may be alive,
May be dead,
But our program will last forever.
And liberate all mankind!
(By Karl Liebknecht)

On the stage, Deng Zhongxia delivered a passionate and eloquent speech that touched the heartstrings of many students at Shanghai University. The heroic images of the female revolutionary Rosa Luxemburg and Marx's comrade Karl Liebknecht, whom Lenin called the Eagle of Revolution, was deeply imprinted in their hearts.

Later on, many of them followed their path, becoming heroic Chinese warriors.

Because it was co-run by the KMT and the CPC, there were intense conflicts between the revolutionary leftists represented by the communists and the KMT right forces during the course of operations. Although communists outnumbered KMT members, KMT right-wing forces led by He Shizhen, head of the English department, and Chen Dezheng, director of the secondary school, relied on the remaining nepotism of the old school and tried to suppress and obliterate the dissemination of revolutionary ideas in the school and Marxist education. Deng Zhongxia united the CPC forces at school to fight back and uphold the truth of the revolution, and eventually defeated the rightist forces. This added more fuel to the flames burning in the revolutionary crucible of Shanghai University, thus deepening the hatred of KMT reactionary forces for Deng Zhongxia.

From April 1923 to April 1925, during the two years he managed the university, he and other early leaders of the CPC molded it into a revolutionary base camp. Prior to the May Thirtieth Movement, he was ordered by the Central Committee of the CPC to leave. However, the

Revolutionaries

biggest casualty and charging at the forefront of the world-shocking anti-imperialist May Thirtieth Movement were those from the university, because of the night schools he founded for civilians and workers and the revolutionary education during his management. The sacrificed CPC member Huang Ren was a student at the university, worker/party member Gu Zhenghong, gunned down by the imperialists, studied at the night school for workers, and the sacrificed labor movement leader Liu Hua was an excellent cadre trained there. Statistics show over a hundred people arrested by the reactionary warlord government and imperialist police during the May Thirtieth Movement were from the university.

In the revolutionary history of the school, Deng Zhongxia deserves a front seat.

His tenacity and persistence in faith and truth have influenced and inspired students for generations to come.

After the departure from the university, he led and commanded the famous Guangdong-Hong Kong strike in Guangzhou, and subsequently served as secretary of the Guangdong Provincial Party Committee of the CPC. However, a few years later, it was a pity that due to the influence of left-leaning Wang Ming, he was removed from all his positions in the party. In 1931, when he returned to Shanghai again, he could hardly scrape a living. The only employment he could get was as a porter on the dock, about which he never complained.

On the evening of May 15, 1933, on his way to handle some affairs at the Red Mutual Help Association at 37 Jundeli, Huanlong Road, French Concession, Shanghai, he was arrested by a group of French Concession policemen. After having been taken to the police station, his identity was at first not exposed. No matter how he was tortured, he insisted that his name was Shiyi and he was only visiting friends. However, for his frequent appearance in the Shanghai University and the May Fourth Movement, the February Seventh Strike, among other activities, and because traitors testified, he was imprisoned on September 5. Aware that he was compromised, he never lost the backbone of a communist when fighting the enemy face to face.

"Yes, I am Deng Zhongxia, a member of the Central Committee of the CPC, and once the Political Commissar of the Second Red Army. What

Shanghai University: A Crucible for Revolution

else do you want to know? Is that enough to have me executed? What else?" He turned their enemies' torturing interrogation into revolutionary questioning for the anti-revolutionaries.

Chiang Kai-shek was excited when he learned that Deng Zhongxia, a senior leader of the CPC, had been captured, and ordered him to be taken to Nanjing. In the middle of the night on September 6, he was secretly escorted to Nanjing by train. To avoid any unexpected accident, over a dozen armed military policemen were deployed to guard the carriage in which he was detained, and a young communist from eastern Shanghai was handcuffed to him, and the entire train was meticulously guarded, leaving no weak spots for any attack. When the military police dozed off, Deng Zhongxia, not drowsy at all, was lecturing revolutionary principles to the youth party member stuck on the same pair of handcuffs—

"For some, death is terrifying. But a revolutionary, in the cause of a revolution, should fear no death but be prepared for die in the right path at the right time."

"Revolution has a price, always. We must be ready to dedicate everything to the cause of communism at any time."

"I am a big target. My enemies will never let me live. It is glorious to die for the party. One is killed, thousands will rise. Remember, the revolution will triumph eventually. You're still young. Get stronger. In the future, when you get out, work hard and make the party proud."

The young party member handcuffed with him was Ma Naisong. He realized that Deng was seizing every second of his time to consciously educate him. Deeply moved, he was more determined to fight their enemies to the end.

Having arrived in Nanjing, Deng Zhongxia was imprisoned in the Detention Center of the Nanjing Military Police Headquarters, located on the Qinhuai River. It was divided into three blocks: A, B, C. Political prisoners were basically detained in A. The prison cell was like a well, poorly ventilated. There was only a small hole at the door for guards to monitor prisoners. Deng Zhongxia was imprisoned in cell 11 of A block. When he entered, there were already a dozen political prisoners inside. One saw a small tag hanging on the chest of the newly arrived that read Deng Shiyi/Deng Zhongxia. Shocked, he questioned: "Are you really Deng

Revolutionaries

Zhongxia?"

"Yes, I am."

"Alas! I knew you when you were leading the revolution in the Honghu." The prisoner was Zheng Shaowen, also a member of the CPC. He asked vigilantly: "Identity exposed?"

Deng Zhongxia nodded.

"What a pity!"

On the contrary, Deng Zhongxia calmly comforted him. "It's ok. We revolutionaries are well prepared for it."

"Come, everyone, meet Comrade Deng Zhongxia!" Zheng Shaowen immediately summoned all cellmates.

"You are really him?" Most of them were communists. They knew the name Deng Zhongxia rather well. Finding it hard to believe that an important figure of the party was present with them in such a place, they huddled around for a look, quite curious.

"Yes, I am him." He shook hands with them one by one.

"I would never expect to see you here!" Someone held his hand with great excitement.

He smiled. "Isn't it a glorious moment for us communists to meet in prison?" His words soothed everyone.

"Hey, listen, everyone," Zheng Shaowen suggested. "Comrade Deng Zhongxia is an important leader of our party. He has served as the Provincial Party Secretary of multiple provinces and Political Commissar of the Red Second Army. He has made great contributions to the revolution. A pioneer. What do you say we give him the upper bunk to sleep?"

There was an unspoken rule in prison that newcomers had to sleep by the urinal at the door first, and then move inside step by step when a newcomer arrived or someone left.

"Definitely!"

"Come, take my spot!"

"I've made space." Before Zheng Shaowen's voice died away, they were eager to offer him their spots. It moved him greatly.

That night, Zheng Shaowen brought a bowl of rice and a plate of a stir-fried dish to him. Deng Zhongxia, rather surprised, asked, "What's going on?"

Shanghai University: A Crucible for Revolution

"We ordered this. We comrades pooled our money and had it delivered from an outside restaurant."

"You..." he choked with sobs as soon as he heard those words. He took an affectionate glance at his fellow sufferer, wiped his tears, and categorically ordered. "Only this time, no more!" Next, he insisted to a weak cellmate, "Let's share it."

During his imprisonment at the Detention Center of the Nanjing Military Police Headquarters of the KMT, revolutionary Tao Zhu was a fellow detainee, and also the secretary of a secret party branch there. One day, when they were let out for exercise, Tao Zhu asked Zheng Shaowen: "How is our big brother doing?"

"Very good! What's up?"

"When you are back, tell him that comrades in the branch care for him and ask about his plans."

Zheng Shaowen delivered the message to Deng Zhongxia. As soon as he heard it, he jumped off the bunk, excited, and solemnly spoke: "Good question! When a revolutionary leader falls into these situations, comrades should care about his political stand. Please tell them, dead or alive, I am a member of the CPC, always have, always will be!"

Therefore, cellmates trusted and respected him even more. His image as a pioneer left an unforgettable impression on many revolutionaries. Those who interrogated him somehow respected him, because no torture could break him. Therefore, his enemies sent traitors who had betrayed the party one after another to coax and persuade him, but nothing worked.

One day, the Investigation Department of the KMT Central Party Headquarters sent several government dignitaries to cajole him, promising him fortune and power as a senior official. Deng Zhongxia sneered at it. Sternly, he said: "I am a revolutionary. I have dedicated my life to the cause. You dignitaries are nothing but bloodsucking shit. Save it. It's insulting me!"

"Mr. Deng, you are a revolutionary forerunner in the CPC. But the fact is the top CPC leaders are young people who have just returned from Moscow. They steal the thunder from communist veterans like you. We feel sorry for you! The CPC is on a path, soon to die. A great politician like you, why make more sacrifices for them?" Some resorted to such a vicious trick

81

Revolutionaries

in an attempt to "sprinkle salt on his wound."

Deng Zhongxia was infuriated. Solemnly and clearly, he confronted the dignitaries Chiang Kai-shek sent. "Let me ask you a question. How come is that one with incurable cancer is laughing at one with a simple fever? The CPC never hides our shortcomings and mistakes. We are confident. We dare to expose all of them, we can overcome all of them. We understand that mistakes are limited when compared with our correct position. And you, betraying the revolution, slaughtering the people, committing unforgivable crimes. How shameless of you to speak of the shortcomings and mistakes of others! What absurdity!"

Their enemies, at the end of their wits, accepted that a CPC member like him would never surrender. Deng Zhongxia, imprisoned as he was never forgot his responsibility as a leader of the CPC.

During his imprisonment, due to the influence of Wang Ming's left-leaning dogmatism, party organizations in different places suffered several damages. On the other hand, the betrayal of the vicious traitor Gu Shunzhang within the party led to the brutal murder of many communists by their enemies, devastating some CPC members in prison. Deng Zhongxia had a first-hand experience, so he started a party class in prison, encouraging cellmates to fight by the integrity of revolutionary martyrs.

"Arrested as we are, we communists must have backbone. Be strong. Under no circumstances shall we surrender."

"A person who lives for personal wealth and power drags out an ignoble existence. It is not living at all. A person who sacrifices himself for the benefit of most Chinese, of the industrious public, lives forever even if he dies. We only live once. Make it meaningful. Have a worthy death."

"I know him. There is no way he will give in." Chiang Kai-shek, who was on the forefront of the suppression of the CPC in Jiangxi, concluded after hearing out the report from his minions. Having worked with Deng Zhongxia in the early years, he knew his character well. Immediately, he sent a secret telegram to Gu Zhenglun, commander of the military police headquarters in Nanjing: "Execute Deng Zhongxia at once."

On September 19, 1933, Deng Zhongxia was transferred to the prison priority cell. Aware that his life was about to end, he wrote through the underground party organization in the cell. "Comrades, I am off to

Shanghai University: A Crucible for Revolution

Yuhuatai. Keep fighting! We shall triumph in the end!"

In the early morning of September 21, before dawn, there were sudden hurried footsteps outside the cell. Then, the prison guard shouted loudly: "Number eleven, Deng Zhongxia!"

Death called. He dressed calmly, walked out of the cell, head held high, and chanted: "Long live the CPC!"

"Long live the proletarian revolution!"

"Down with the KMT reactionary government!"

Those solemn slogans awakened the whole prison at once. Cellmates rushed to the bars, in tears, and bid him farewell.

"For a dying man, you are surely a pain in the ass!" Some ferocious prison guards forcefully choked him by the neck, trying to make him bow his head and shut him up. He stubbornly struggled, held his head high again, and kept chanting slogans until the prison van drove away.

Under Yuhuatai, criminal bullets pierced through his head and body, blood of the martyr spilling on the slopes of the green hills.

Deng Zhongxia, a well-known leader of the labor movement and great proletarian revolutionary fighter, died at the age of only 39.

Arise, ye prisoners of starvation!
Arise, ye wretched of the earth!
For justice thunders condemnation:
A better world's in birth!
No more tradition's chains shall bind us;
Arise, ye slaves, no more in thrall!
The earth shall rise on new foundations:
We have been nought, we shall be all!
...

On the campus of Shanghai University, loud and tragic, the Internationale resounded. It was Qu Qiubai, dean and head of the Department of Sociology, giving a politics lesson to the students.

He was highly proficiently in Russian because when at the age 18, he traveled to Beijing alone and got himself admitted to the Russian Language Institute of the Ministry of Foreign Affairs of the Beiyang Government. It

Revolutionaries

charged no tuition, precisely favorable for Qu Qiubai, who came from a poor family. During his studies, he learned about the October Revolution in Russia, and made acquaintance with Chen Duxiu and Li Dazhao early, due to his frequent visits to Peking University for some courses. Especially after participating in the May Fourth Movement, he joined in the Beijing Marxism Research Association organized by Li Dazhao. In 1920, with a keen interest in the Russian revolution, he accepted the invitation from the *Beijing Morning Post* and *Shanghai Current Affairs Newspaper* and went to Moscow as their special correspondent.

The trip to Moscow changed his outlook on life and encouraged him to be a proletarian revolutionary fighter. During the two years in the Russian capital, he not only went deep into the factories and mines, rural areas, military, schools, and families of the world's first socialist country, conducting investigations and interviews, but also had face-to-face exchanges with the revolutionary pioneer Lenin many times. Lenin introduced Bolshevik history and how the October Revolution happened to this young Chinese and recommended to him several books on Oriental issues. Face-to-face instruction and teachings of the great mentor were valuable revolutionary experiences to him that was never easily available to common Chinese progressive intellectuals. In addition, he later worked at the Communist University of the Toilers of the East in Moscow as a translator and Chinese teacher. He was given a more direct learning opportunity of the original Marxist-Leninist classics and read a large number of Russian literary masterpieces, which he particularly enjoyed.

"The great Soviet socialism, like the rising sun, spurting out, illuminates the world, illuminates all the oppressed nations. And I–among hundreds of comrades who have been to the Soviet Union–deeply believe that we from now on, are no longer children of the old age, but of the new, that we are active revolutionaries! Socialism and communism will replace the old world, head to toe!" In Shanghai University, sometimes he taught his students to sing *The Internationale* in Russian, sometimes he read classic quotations of Marxism-Leninism with his characteristic soft and sonorous voice in his Changzhou dialect. Based on what he saw and heard, he depicted those students who yearned for socialism and communism the beauty of the Soviet socialist system and the free life of their people, greatly

Shanghai University: A Crucible for Revolution

exciting them.

"At present, our revolution has reached a critical turning point!" It was another of his political lessons on the Chinese revolution. As always, the large classroom was crowded. What surprised the students was that he uttered those words passionately, without any opening remarks.

The huge classroom went suddenly silent. Only his sonorous voice echoed there. "Yes, a critical turning point! KMT rightists recently held a meeting in the Xishan area of Beijing, publicly raising the anti-revolutionary banner against the CPC. In Guangzhou, there were similar voices, with Dai Jitao taking the lead, that they want pure Three People's Principles (Nationalism, Democracy, the People's Livelihood). They are after only one thing, that is: to completely undermine the cooperation between the KMT and the CPC by launching a frenzied attack on the Chinese revolution!"

In the audience, students widened their eyes. On the podium, Qu Qiubai took off a cashmere scarf around his neck, waved his right arm, and shouted, "Conspiracies, exposed conspiracies!"

"We must expose these conspiracies! And their leader is–" he paused, turned around and wrote on the blackboard: Dai Jitao!

"This man! He talks about the golden mean of the Confucian school, reconciliation, and the so-called unification. Ultimately, he strives to draw the united front of the CPC and the Chinese Revolution to their KMT rightist reactionary forces. As a result, the Chinese revolution will never win!" He cried, "Revolutionaries need to wake up! Act! Now!"

This is Qu Qiubai, a revolutionary professor at Shanghai University. His abilities and personal charm had a lifelong impact on many progressive students.

Famous writer Ding Ling, who transferred from the night school for civilians, was also a student at Shanghai University. She and her best friend Wang Jianhong (who was Qu Qiubai's first wife and died of illness after half a year of marriage) came to Shanghai from their hometown of Hunan together and began their lives in Shanghai University, which had a lifelong impact on their revolution and love. Ding Ling wrote a special memoir article titled *The Qu Qiubai That I Know* a few decades later, in which she described her first impression of him and his impact on her at the school:

That day, they brought a new friend, who was lanky, wearing a pair of glasses for his astigmatism, and spoke Mandarin in a southern accent. When we first met, he spoke it, vigilantly. At the right moment, he would quip and cheer up the room. We had a few exchanges of polite and calm glances. Jianhong and I both believe he is an excellent communist. This pal is Comrade Qu Qiubai, who later led the Communist Party to convene the August 7 Meeting. He replaced the opportunist Chen Duxiu, who made the mistake of putschism. Qu worked in the literary and artistic field, making outstanding contributions, shared a close friendship with Lu Xun, and calmly died in a KMT prison.

Ding Ling recollected: "Qu Qiubai told us stories about the Soviet Union, which intrigued us enormously. Back when we were in the civilian girls' school, another comrade who had returned from the Soviet Union was invited to talk about the situation there. The two lecturers differed greatly, one with a numb tongue while the other was eloquent. When he found out that we had read some books by Tolstoy, Pushkin, and Gorky, he talked more. Like listening to adults telling stories when we were children, we were fascinated. He listened with great interest and praised our wandering life this year and our unrealistic fantasies. He encouraged us to follow them to Shanghai, to Shanghai University for lectures in the Department of Literature."

Having spent some time in Shanghai University, she compared Qu Qiubai with many highly experienced teachers, and concluded:

Qu Qiubai was the best teacher. He was with us after class almost every day. As a result, our little garret became lively. He talked broadly about Greece, Rome, about the Renaissance, about the Tang, Song, Yuan and Ming Dynasties. He told stories of not only the dead, but the living. He never treated us as children, or as students when lectured, but as fellow travelers, exploring ancient and modern times, east to west, south to north. I often wonder why he taught philosophy in the Department of Social Sciences instead of Department of Literature. What is philosophy? Something profound, right? He must be proficient in philosophy. But he never talked about philosophy with us, only literature, social life, and all the stories. Later, in order to help us quickly grasp the beauty of Pushkin's language, he guided us to read his poems in Russian, in a special way. After a brief introduction to the alphabet and phonetics, we read the original poems directly, and he explained the grammar, the inflections, the characteristics of the Russian language, and the beauty of Pushkin's words in the poems. For one poem, we had to read over two hundred new words and learn much grammar. But as if we have absorbed everything ounce of knowledge in the reading of the poem, when we covered three or four poems, we felt we had mastered Russian.

Deeply impressed to the point of life-changing, Ding Ling gained unprecedented strength and direction from the professional revolutionary and literary artist Qu Qiubai during her years in Shanghai University:

During the winter vacation, Qiubai hardly went out; even when school started, he often stayed home. He wore a comfortable, old black silk cotton robe every day, allegedly the belonging of his deceased grandfather, who used to be an official. He wrote poems every day, one after another, all love poems for Jianhong. I received one poem as well, which called me an angel with an honest heart, probably to thank me for my help in their romance. Jianhong wrote as well, one poem after another every day. They also read poems together, fascinated by all the works of the poets of ancient China, Li Bai, Du Fu, Han Yu, Su Shi, Li Shangyin, Li Houzhu, Lu You, Wang Yuyang, Zheng Banqiao, and others. He also carved seals, engraving his favorite verses in all sorts of delicate small stones. Jianhong had always been good at Chinese classical literature, but her passion for it was fully ignited thanks to his cultivation and influence.

Jianhong is two years older than me, and better educated. Since we knew each other, I have been greatly influenced by her in terms of thinking patterns and personal interest, which were all about the pursuit of socialism, the fantasies of life, and the contempt for the secular. Although we appeared somewhat arrogant, we were sociable and sometimes accommodating. Now, I couldn't help playing flute or singing a few Kun opera verses (he taught both), and my heart felt lonely without them. I yearned for the vast world, I missed other old friends. I often had some new plans, but only hidden in my heart. I looked at the passing time and got lost in melancholy.

Revolutionaries

Qiubai took up a lot of work at school, and later added translation. It was perhaps at that time he started to translate for Borodin. I saw that he was handling it well, always in a neat suit, clean and energetic, going in and out. He never led guests upstairs, nor did he talk about his work, his friends, his comrades with us (at least not me). He was vigorous those days. Often after a whole busy day, he was still in good spirits when he came back. He talked and wrote poetry with Jianhong. Sometimes to meet a deadline, he would work at his desk all night, with a cup of tea and some cigarettes, and Jianhong would keep him company. He could translate 10,000 characters in one night. I have read his manuscript, each line in perfect order with delicate handwriting. There was hardly even a word revised.

I never knew how he managed his time, as if there was still free time. The two of them came to my little garret across the street many times for a discussion, because only my room had a stove fueled by kerosene, thus warmer. Yunbai bought it for them. They insisted to put it in my room. There was a circle of small holes in the lid, and firelight shot out from them, glimmering on the ceiling in the shape the of a flower. When they came, we always turned off the light, leaving only the flickering, and the atmosphere in the room was amazing. He was chatty and often talked humorously about some anecdotes from the literary world at that time. He has made the acquaintance of Shen Yanbing and Zheng Zhenduo. He liked Xu Zhimo's poems. He showed interest only in Yu Dafu of the geniuses of the Creation Society. At that time, I had no say in these people, events, articles, and the disputes between the Literary Research Association and the Creation Society. I was just a primary school student, listening with interest. It was my first lesson on romanticism, naturalism, realism in literature, life, art, etc. Back then, Comrade Qiubai talked extensively, and I often failed to grasp the main points of his speeches. But I was sure that he was extraordinary and superb. He seemed to stand above all kinds of opinions.

Once, I asked him what I should learn and do in the future and now. He raised his head without thinking and replied: "Learn as you like. Just do it, spread your wings and fly. The higher, the farther, the better. You are a bird born to soar. Yes, you are." His words gave me infinite confidence and a lot of strength. I believed what he said and made my decision.

Ding Ling later became an important writer in the history of modern

Shanghai University: A Crucible for Revolution

Chinese literature and created a great many excellent revolutionary literary works. In Yan'an, Mao Zedong once commented that she could wield both pen and gun.

There were more people like her who were inspired by Qu Qiubai and firmly embarked on the road of revolution.

"Flowers are blooming this year, best in white jade basins. For a mild autumn, frost marks are seen nowhere." This is a poem Qu Qiubai wrote in middle school. This revolutionary young man in love with literature and art, who had been good at poetry since the age of seven, had pride deep in his bones. Having joined the revolution, he gradually became humble, treating comrades with kindness and patience.

Yang Muzhi was a revolutionary, who came from the same hometown as Qu Qiubai. He was also one of the students in Shanghai University. He recalled the work performance of Qu Qiubai, who served as a temporary member of the Standing Committee of the Political Bureau and presided over the work at that time, and his humility and self-knowledge: extremely busy as he was, he was never on his high-horse, but always humble for his lack of grass-root work experience. Many times, he reflected on himself: I'm not as good as Peng Pai and Mao Zedong in the peasant movement; not as good as Su Zhaozheng and Deng Zhongxia in the labor movement; not as good as He Long and Ye Ting in military affairs. I once consoled him, smiling: "You excel at promoting Marxism-Leninism."

He shook his head decisively. "In this respect, I am far behind Chen Duxiu and Li Dazhao."

Revolutionary ambition and quality are actually a kind of spiritual and personality force that is drenched in ideals and beliefs. As a professor in Shanghai University, his firmness, self-confidence, clarity, and decisiveness exhibited in his tortuous revolutionary experience left a deep impression on the students. This is extremely valuable and important for common workers and intellectuals to embark on the revolutionary road. Also, it reflects his great personality as a revolutionary leader.

When Shanghai University ceased operations, it was at the time of the harshest failure of the Great Revolution. It was at the lowest ebb. Communists were murdered at a great scale by the powerful KMT reactionaries. At that very hour, Qu Qiubai climbed to the position of the

Revolutionaries

party's supreme leader. Next, due to the influence of Wang Ming's left-leaning, his political status fell from the peak to the bottom. He was only employed as editor-in-chief of a newspaper in the Soviet area. When the main Red Army evacuated from the Soviet area for the Long March, he was stuck in Jiangxi, surrounded by danger. At that time, he was already very ill, often breathless after a simple walk. Chen Yi and Xiang Ying. leaders of the Central Committee of the CPC who remained in Jiangxi, decided to send him and the equally frail elder He Shuheng to Shanghai to recuperate. However, the escort squad was attacked by a local armed security group on the way. He Shuheng fell off a cliff and died while Qu Qiubai was arrested.

It is painful to see that during the difficult years of the revolution, the two early leaders of the CPC suffered such a fate.

Imprisoned, Qu Qiubai was betrayed by a traitor. Chiang Kai-shek, who was on the forefront of the suppression of the CPC, believed that it would help him build more prestige and slander the CPC if Qu Qiubai, an important figure of the CPC, could be turned. So officials, a total of nine, one by one, came to Changting, Fujian Province where he was held custody, trying to turn him against the CPC. However, they all got the same answer from him. "I love my history more than birds loves their wings. Save it. Never taint my history!"

In the end, they played the card of Gu Shunzhang (the most dangerous and highest-ranking traitor of the CPC), who was said to receive all sorts of preferential treatment of the KMT, to coax him. "Never swim against the tide."

Qu Qiubai sneered: "I am Qu Qiubai, not Gu Shunzhang. I will rather swim against the tide than sell my soul."

Soon, Chiang Kai-shek, who was commanding the suppression of the CPC in Nanchang, received the report from bureau of investigation and statistics of the military council, saying that Qu Qiubai was "stubborn, resolute and unturnable."

"So, he prefers the fucking hard way, does he?" Chiang Kai-shek swore fiercely, and issued a secret order for his execution at once. "Shoot him the spot!"

On the morning of June 18, 1935, Qu Qiubai had his last meal in Zhongshan Park in Changting. With head high and smoking a cigarette in

Shanghai University: A Crucible for Revolution

his hand, he walked to the execution ground. Along the way, he chanted *The Internationale*, sometimes in Chinese and sometimes in Russian.

"Mr. Qu, do you really not fear death?" The executioners who escorted him found it unbelievable, questioning, in whispers, the man about to die.

Qu Qiubai chuckled, rather relaxed. "True communists have long prepared themselves for this since the day we joined the revolution. Death is nothing, for that we believe that communism will prevail in China and in the world!"

"Hopeless!" Executioners shook their heads.

Reaching the middle of a lawn in front of Luohanling outside Changting West Gate, Qu Qiubai stopped, sat cross-legged and smiled at the executioners: "This is it! Do it..."

They hesitated for a moment and raised their guns together.

"Long live the CPC!"

"Long live the Chinese revolution!"

"Long live communism!"

With a burst of criminal gunshots, Comrade Qu Qiubai, one of the key leaders of the early CPC, great Marxist, outstanding proletarian revolutionist, theorist, and propagandist, and one of the important founders of China's revolutionary literature, fell in a pool of blood at the age of 36.

For young revolutionaries, there is nothing luckier than having an outstanding revolutionary leader to be their mentor and professor, isn't there?

The revolutionary enlightenment and ambition that teachers like Qu Qiubai brought to the young students at Shanghai University are undoubtedly great and irreplaceable.

The aforementioned He Bingyi, who bravely stood in front of the guns of imperialists on Nanjing Road, was such a student at Shanghai University.

Born in landowning family, at the beginning he was just a rebellious young man with a personality. With the financial support of his wealthy family, plus his intelligence and talent, he was admitted to college. From his contact with the revolutionary Li Yimeng, he began to absorb progressive thoughts. Subsequently, having heard that the Department of Sociology at Shanghai University was promising, he gave up science and engineering and enrolled in the Department of Sociology at Shanghai University with

Revolutionaries

Qu Qiubai as the director.

"You are insane! It is not a good school at all. How can you go there?" His father found out about the change, so furious that he sent letters one after another demanding his son to go back to the right path.

He Bingyi, who had only attended a few classes of Qu Qiubai, replied in a long letter to his father, introducing Shanghai University and elucidating why he wanted to study at the Sociology Department there. He said: "Why do I study sociology? Because I am one of the new youth of the 20th century, not an old pedant of the 19th, who lived on articles and studied for imperial examinations. Born in this bizarre 20th century, I am to make it better, to seek happiness for the people, that is, to study the truth of the life of human society and the various phenomena to identify whether they work. This is why I intend to study sociology. It matches my personality and ambition." He Bingyi expressed his zero interest and contempt for studying to be an official. He also told his family his experience at Qu Qiubai's lectures.

"Although Shanghai University is a private school in Shanghai, I believe it is the best, its sociology perfect. I respect and worship its system, its organization, its spirit." He went on passionately: "If I go, I can hear the god of the future calling me, as if saying: 'You are on the road to light, all the comfort ahead; a boundless future; your life begins here; the flower of your life blooms here.'"

"May my life bloom with the flower of a revolutionary dream," a wish He Bingyi made after he understood the truth of a life of revolution in Shanghai University. Next, when he dedicated himself to the anti-imperialist fight, the young flower of his life withered for good in the May Thirtieth Movement.

In addition to that, he applied his experience of the severe test of his ideals and beliefs in the revolutionary storms in Shanghai University and Shanghai to educate and guide his younger brother to embark on the road of revolution together. Later, the younger brother He Bingjun died heroically in Shanghai in 1928, at the age of 20.

What beautiful flower of life! Like a snowflake in winter, it danced in visible midair, in a determined direction, radiating charm and light to the world. Insignificant as it appeared throughout the revolutionary history, it is valuable and shines—this is the spirit and belief that students at Shanghai

92

Shanghai University: A Crucible for Revolution

University learned from revolutionary leaders and mentors.

Among the martyrs of Shanghai University, there was a young man named Li Shuoxun, a Sichuanese revolutionary, who was admitted to the university at the end of 1923 and joined the CPC at school. He was a student in the Department of Sociology. In Qu Qiubai's class, he experienced the raging waves of the great socialist revolution and the light of Marxism-Leninism. In 1924, this outstanding man became director of the Executive Committee of the All-China Students Federation. Having witnessed his classmate Huang Ren die on the street, he vowed to fight anti-revolutionary atrocities with revolution. Following the May Thirtieth Movement, in order to meet the needs of urban armed fights, the All-China Students Federation took up a secret task from the CPC: to set up a military committee and train young military cadres. Li Shuoxun, appointed chairman of this committee, began his revolutionary years in the underground military armed combat, and made outstanding contributions to the following armed uprising in Shanghai. Having worked as Chairman of the All-China Students Federation for years and concurrently as Secretary of the Shanghai Nanshi Ministry of the underground party, he threw himself into the Nanchang Uprising. When he returned to Shanghai, he served as Secretary of the Military Commission of Jiangsu Provincial Party Committee and Secretary of Jiangnan Provincial Military Commission. Together with Li Weihan, Chen Yun, and Liu Xiao, he successfully formed the Fourteenth Red Army and the Fifteenth Red Army in southern Jiangsu to support the Jiangnan area in armed revolutionary fight. In August 1931, the man was ordered by the Central Committee of the CPC to lead armed fights in Hainan. But as soon as he landed in Haikou, he was betrayed by a traitor and imprisoned. In prison, KMT reactionaries were well aware of his importance in the CPC and tortured him brutally, hoping he would give in. However, he would rather die than surrender. They broke the bones in his foot. Before his execution, the 28-year-old CPC member and outstanding military strategist could no longer stand, but he raised his arms, shouting "Down with KMT reactionaries!" "Long live the CPC!" Before he died, the martyr Li Shuoxun left a last note to his wife Zhao Juntao:

Tao: In Hainan, I have already decided never to surrender. Afraid execution is not far. I bid you farewell. Before and after, people die for the cause, of whom I am one. Never grieve for me too much, but raise our children well. Try to send them back home, and stay alive and independent yourself. My body will be buried properly, thus no need to come for it. Yours, Xun

His wife was also a student in the Department of Sociology at Shanghai University. They met there, married in 1926 and joined the CPC. She was one of the leaders and educators of early women's movement.

It was a hot summer in 1923. It was in this summer that an important figure in the history of the Chinese revolution came to Shanghai. His name was Yun Daiying, one of the Outstanding Three of Changzhou, his hometown. The other two of the Outstanding Three were also important teachers at Shanghai University and early leaders of the CPC: Qu Qiubai, who has been mentioned before, and Zhang Tailei. Their achievements in Shanghai and Shanghai University will always stand erect like a monument on the banks of Huangpu River.

Yun Daiying worked in Shanghai University as a Professor while maintaining the positions of a young student leader and one of the leaders of the Chinese Socialist Youth League. He was also the creator of the newly founded *Chinese Youth* magazine. He studied in Wuhan before and became a revolutionary leader, leading student demonstrations during the May Fourth Movement and founding progressive newspapers with Lin Yunan and others, which built his reputation among young students.

"Shanghai University is our first school to train a new generation of revolutionaries. You are the perfect candidate to teach. Together with Zhongxia and Qiubai, you can ignite the flames of revolution there!" Chen Duxiu placed great hopes on him and encouraged him to take the job.

This young revolutionary had glorious moments in Shanghai and Shanghai University and later left the city for Guangzhou, where he served as a Political Instructor in the Whampoa Military Academy. He worked with Zhou Enlai to train revolutionary military talents, and then organized the Nanchang Uprising and the Guangzhou Uprising.

On April 5, 1929, Mao Zedong in Ruijin once telephoned the Central Committee of the CPC, suggesting that Yun Daiying be Secretary of the Front of the Fourth Red Army. However, the Chiang-Gui War broke out and the suggestion was not followed.

However, when he returned to Shanghai in the Spring of 1930, he suffered persecution for opposing Li Lisan's left-leaning adventurism, and was demoted to Secretary of the Hudong District Party Committee.

On May 6, 1930, Yun Daiying, dressed in a long shirts, worker-style, took a pack of flyers to Yangshupu Taopeng Road (now Tongbei Road) to rendezvous with underground party members at the gate of Old Yihe Yarn Factory. Unexpectedly, there was an abrupt police investigation. Because of deep short-sightedness, the young youth leader, who did not wear glasses to avoid being identified that day, failed to notice it was police approaching, and was thus unable to escape. He reacted quickly: as the police were searching for him, he disfigured his face with both hands—he knew that in Shanghai and for his enemies, his face was too familiar. He was chief writer of *Chinese Youth* magazine, a teacher in Shanghai University, commander-in-chief of the student demonstration in the May Thirtieth Movement, let alone the great number of people who have seen him as he gave speeches on the streets, in factories and night schools.

Disfigured Yun Daiying was not identified at the beginning. Detained in the Longhua KMT Songhu Garrison Headquarters prison, his identity was not exposed either despite severe torture. As a result, he was merely sentenced to five years of imprisonment for spreading flyers in an attempt to instigate a rally. During imprisonment, he encouraged cellmates to fight as a revolutionary propagandist and orator. He used to chant *Prisoners of the Age*, which greatly encouraged the revolutionaries in prison—

Prisoners, of the age
We do not sin;
We all, are captured from the battle front,
From that of class fights...

Prisoner, are not prisoners, but captives!
Regardless of torture,
Our blood stays boiling

...

We are never afraid of death,

Revolutionaries

Victory is up ahead!
Impregnable fortress,
Handcuffs and fetters, shackling our bodies,
Never our hearts

...

In September of that year, the Third Plenary Session of the Sixth Central Committee of the CPC was held in Shanghai, and Yun Daiying, despite imprisonment, was still elected as an alternate member of the Central Committee.

After he was escorted to Nanjing Military Prison, many cellmates learned his identity, and no one sold him out. Even the prison guards were under the spell of his personality, and did not report him to their superiors. The Central Committee of the CPC and Zhou Enlai, extremely concerned about his safety, tried their best to rescue him or have him released early. Just when the underground party branch had notified him to prepare for an early release, something irreversible happened. Gu Shunzhang, an alternate member of the Political Bureau of the Central Committee of the CPC, was captured in Wuhan. In order to survive, he offered a grand gift to Chiang Kai-shek: exposing Yun Daiying in Nanjing prison.

Chiang Kai-shek was overjoyed. He knew Yun Daiying well since Yun was in Whampoa Military Academy and admired his talent. Chiang Kai-shek always offered money and power to coax captives for information. "Yun Daiying is an exception. He is asked to leak no information. As long as he promises to work for me, he can walk free." This time, Chiang Kai-shek was rather "less-demanding." He sent people to deliver the message to Yun Daiying in prison.

Yun Daiying, who had already been exposed, laughed the moment he heard the offer. "I will never collude with the traitors of revolution!"

"Shoot him on the spot!" Chiang Kai-shek, irritated, ordered the kill immediately.

Before dawn on April 29, 1931, a group of armed KMT military policemen pulled him out of the cell. After a few steps, they loaded their guns. However, they were actually intimidated by his aura of righteousness. Their hands trembled, and for a long while none pulled the trigger. Wang

Shanghai University: A Crucible for Revolution

Zhennan, director of the KMT Military Law Department, was so furious at what was happening that he had other executioners fire bullets at the prisoner.

Travelled the world, reminiscent of the past steps
Old pals, faring well, or gone for good
No more scruple for the common things
Imprisoned, yet stand head held high

Yun Daiying's demise devastated comrade Zhou Enlai. In the summer of 1937, taking the opportunity of travelling to Nanjing for the cooperation negotiation between the KMT and the CPC, Zhou Enlai chanted Yun's last poem at Yuhuatai, paying tribute to his dead friend. In the first summer after the founding of the PRC, Zhou Enlai once again wrote words of commemoration for him. "It has been 19 years since the leader of Chinese youth, Comrade Yun Daiying, sacrificed himself. His proletarian consciousness, work enthusiasm, strong will, frugality, readiness to sacrifice himself, approachability, and persuasiveness will always be a model for Chinese youth."

Indeed, young leaders like Yun Daiying influenced and educated countless young revolutionaries in the early Chinese revolution, among whom there was the following pair of martyrs, teacher and student, in the martyrs list in Shanghai Longhua Martyrs Memorial Hall and Nanjing Yuhuatai Martyrs Memorial Hall—the teacher was Hou Shaoqiu, and the student Zhang Yingchun.

Both of them came to Shanghai University under the influence of Yun Daiying. Later, they served as Executive Committee Members of the KMT Jiangsu Provincial Party Headquarters in Shanghai as representatives of the CPC. They had a solid friendship with famous scholar Liu Yazi, who was also an Executive Committee Member.

In March 1927, having just attended the inauguration of the members of the Provisional Municipal Government of Shanghai Special City, Hou Shaoqiu was ordered by the Central Committee of the CPC to go to Nanjing, which was under the control of reactionary forces, for face-to-face fighting. In those darkest days, the CPC members who openly fought

Revolutionaries

against Chiang Kai-shek's reactionary forces included Hou Shaoqiu's student Zhang Yingchun and others. On the night of March 29, when the team of Party Headquarters of Jiangsu Province led by Hou Shaoqiu left Shanghai for Nanjing, passing through Suzhou, Wuxi, and Changzhou railway stations, thousands of people welcomed them, waving colorful flags. When they arrived at Nanjing Railway Station, as many as 40,000 to 50,000 people from all walks of life greeted them.

In Nanjing at that time, revolutionary and anti-revolutionary forces had entered a stage of fierce fighting. Leaders of the CPC like Hou Shaoqiu and progressive people of KMT Jiangsu Provincial Committee, who have been fed up with Chiang Kai-shek's anti-revolutionary behavior, decided to respond to the KMT's decision to remove him from being chairman of the KMT's Military Committee, among other positions, which was made during KMT's Third Plenary Session of the Second Central Committee held in Wuhan, and proposed to establish a new Jiangsu Provincial Government in Nanjing. Hou Shaoqiu, as the representative of the CPC and executive member of the KMT Provincial Party Committee, led the arduous fight against the aggressive Chiang Kai-shek reactionary groups.

Every minute of the week after Hou Shaoqiu and the others arrived in Nanjing counted: revolutionary forces and reactionary forces respectively launched battles to get ahead.

On April 9, when reactionary forces were at the gate, Nanjing immediately became the center of a raging storm.

That night, Hou Shaoqiu presided over an emergency meeting of leaders of revolutionary groups in Nanjing, and decided to convene a mass meeting the next day and present a petition to Chiang Kai-shek.

On the morning of April 10, the next day, the Nanjing Citizens Purging Anti-revolutionaries Meeting organized by the Jiangsu Provincial Party Headquarter was held. Tens of thousands of people participated in the event, a spectacular sight. On behalf of the Provincial Party Headquarters, he condemned Chiang Kai-shek's reactionary actions. In the afternoon, representatives from all walks of life rallied at the gate of Chiang Kai-shek's General Headquarters to petition. Eventually, Chiang Kai-shek pretended to agree to the petition. Unexpectedly, around 5 pm, a group of armed gangsters broke into the petitioning masses, frantically firing at the innocent petitioners, who were totally unarmed. It was a horrifying and bloody moment.

In the face of the sudden and severe situation, at 11:00 that night, main CPC leaders in revolutionary groups such as the Nanjing Federation of Labor Unions urgently gathered at 10 Dashamao Lane to hold an intra-party meeting to deal with what just brutally happened. Unexpectedly, around 2 a.m., the venue was besieged by secret agents in plain clothes of the KMT Nanjing Police Station. Except Liu Shaoyou, then-Member of the Standing Committee of the Nanjing Municipal Committee of the CPC (real name Liu Pingkai, later Secretary of the Nanjing Prefectural Party Committee of the CPC, Secretary of the Shanghai Hudong Party Committee, Secretary of the CPC Hubei Provincial Party Committee, and Acting Secretary of Yunnan Provincial Party Committee. On July 26, 1931, he died after being arrested by his enemies in Kunming), escaped, nine people, including Hou Shaoqiu, were arrested.

Chiang Kai-shek was delighted the entire time, hearing that leaders of Nanjing Prefectural Party Committee of the CPC were caught in one action. Next, he sent people to persuade Hou Shaoqiu to surrender, promising him the position of Chairman of the Jiangsu Provincial Government on the condition that he publicly withdrew from the CPC.

Hou Shaoqiu replied one word: "Never!"

A few days later, on a dark night, Chiang Kai-shek ordered Wen Jiangang, Director of the Nanjing KMT Police Station, and Chen Baoyuan, Chief of Secret Service, to personally direct a detective team to conduct a most cruel massacre of the nine underground party leaders of Nanjing Prefectural Party Committee of the CPC, including Hou Shaoqiu. Secret agents put them into sacks, stabbed them to death, secretly transported their bodies to Jiulong Bridge outside Nanjing's Tongji Gate at night, and dumped them into the Qinhuai River.

The corpses of the nine communists, including Hou Shaoqiu, were never found. By accident, pedestrians passing by saw sacks thrown off the bridge into the river. It was not until 1949, after the government persisted with investigations, that this heinous murder of Chinese communists committed by Chiang Kai-shek's KMT reactionary groups was eventually exposed.

Revolutionaries

Their names are in the Nanjing Yuhuatai Martyrs Memorial Hall and Shanghai Longhua Martyrs Memorial Hall. Let's get to know them.

Hou Shaoqiu, born in Songjiang, Shanghai, then-Secretary of the Communist Youth League of KMT Jiangsu Provincial Party Headquarters, was 31 when he was murdered;

Xie Wenjin, then-Secretary of the Nanjing Prefectural Party Committee of the CPC, was 33 when they stabbed him to death;

Chen Junqi, female, then-Committee Member of the Nanjing Prefectural Party Committee of the CPC, was 42 when she was slaughtered;

Liang Yong, then-Member of the Nanjing Federation of Labor Unions, was 23 when they murdered him;

Liu Chongmin, then-Member of the Nanjing Prefectural Party Committee of the CPC, was 25 when his life ended;

Wen Huazhen, then-Secretary of the Nanjing Prefectural Committee of the Communist Youth League, was killed at the age of 25;

Xu Jinyuan, then-Member of the KMT Jiangsu Provincial Party Committee, was 21 when he sacrificed his life;

Zhang Yingchun, then-Executive Committee Member and Director of the Women's Ministry of the KMT Jiangsu Provincial Party Committee, died at the age of 26;

Zhong Tianyue, then-Member of the Nanjing Federation of Labor Unions, was 22 when he died.

At the Yuhuatai Martyrs Memorial Hall, I did some research on their files and discovered that, except for martyr Liang Yong, who came from Shandong, the other eight were either Shanghai natives or had inextricable connections with the city. It can be said that as revolutionaries, they either had most of their revolutionary experience in Shanghai, or they started it from this city. For example, although Liu Chongmin, Wenhua Zhen, Zhong Tianyue, and Xu Jinyuan were not Shanghai natives, they came to this city, or enrolled in Shanghai University, or joined in the Shanghai Federation of Labor Unions as soon as they understood revolutionary principles and sought for truth. They accepted revolutionary education of Marxism, embarked on the road of revolution, joined the CPC, and almost all became the backbone of the May Thirtieth Movement. In 1927, before Chiang Kai-shek's April Tenth Massacre, the organization dispatched

Shanghai University: A Crucible for Revolution

these revolutionaries to bloody Nanjing at the most critical revolutionary juncture as duty called. Some of them were brutally stabbed to death in a sack and dumped into the Qinhuai river by their enemies merely ten days after their arrival.

Next, let's focus on two revolutionary martyrs Xie Wenjin and Chen Junqi, who died in Nanjing.

Few know who Xie Wenjin was. In fact, this Wenzhou-born revolutionary and the first batch of CPC members in Shanghai, including Chen Wangdao, Yu Xiusong, Shi Cuntong, and others were all alumni of Zhejiang Provincial No. 1 Normal School. As early as 1920, Xie Wenjin came to Shanghai and studied with Liu Shaoqi and other early revolutionaries in the Foreign Languages Society, the cradle of young revolutionaries set up by communists such as Chen Duxiu, Chen Wangdao, etc. in Yuyangli No. 6. In 1921, he joined the CPC in Shanghai, which sent him to study at the Communist University of the Toilers of the East in Moscow. There, those who studied with him and those who gave him lectures later became important figures of the CPC, such as teacher Qu Qiubai, classmates Ren Bishi, Luo Yinong, Wang Yifei, Peng Shuzhi, Xiao Jinguang, Jiang Guangci, and others. Having returned to China, he went to his hometown of Wenzhou to sow the seeds of revolution, encouraging groups of enthusiastic Wenzhou progressive youths to go to Shanghai. He either introduced them to study at Shanghai University, or led them to directly participate in labor movements, including Cai Xiong, Lin Pinghai, Dai Guopeng, Lin Qubing, Wang Guozhen, Jin Shisheng, Chen Zhuoru, Dai Shutang, and more. Later, these youths died in several armed uprisings in Shanghai. After the liberation, a Wenzhou scholar named Su Yuanlei recalled: "One of the major reasons they dedicated their lives to the revolution is the political inspiration by Xie Wenjin and his personality."

Among the nine martyrs, Chen Jun was the oldest, 42 years old.

Chen Junqi came from Nanxiang Town, Jiading District, Shanghai. It is difficult to fathom that a middle-aged woman, born rich, whose father was a member of the Imperial Academy of the Qing Dynasty could go through severe ordeals and perils for the revolution, and sacrifice her life somewhere away from home. Her embarking on the revolutionary road was related to her personal pursuit of a progressive career and to rid herself of her miserable marriage. Back then, the women's liberation movement was one of the important components of early revolution. Her special family situation was extremely beneficial to the women's liberation movement and the underground party liaison. Therefore, the middle-aged woman of Nanxiang secretly shuttled back and forth between Shanghai and Nanjing, and became a woman Committee Member of the KMT Jiangsu Provincial Party Headquarters during the KMT-CPC cooperation period. On April 2, 1927, under the leadership of Xie Wenjin, the KMT Jiangsu Provincial Party Headquarters was urgently relocated from Shanghai to Nanjing, and she followed him. For over a week, she and her comrades rushed around day and night, organizing women from all walks of life to fight against the anti-revolutionary forces of Chiang Kai-shek, and unfortunately she was killed after being captured by their enemies, along with eight other comrades.

At that time, *Republic of China Daily* in Hankou published a poem called *The Grief of Zhongshan*, which described the bloody massacre Chen Junqi and other martyrs suffered—

Dark terrifying clouds shrouded Zhongshan;
thready drizzle was threadier, soaking the gloomy flowers and plants.
Whose grief, whose lament?
Dark terrifying clouds shrouded Zhongshan;
howling wind in the sky, raging waves on the river, a more heartbreaking ensemble.
Whose grief, whose lament?
Whose grief, lament, curse, echoed across the sky.

Next, let's go back to the unfinished legendary stories of martyrs Hou Shaoqiu and Zhang Yingchun, teacher and student, among the nine CPC martyrs. Their stories were related to Yun Daiying, who was teaching at Shanghai University, and inspired more legendary revolutionary careers and magnificent historical stories—

Hou Shaoqiu, born in Songjiang, and Zhang Yingchun, born in Wujiang, were fellow villagers of the Wu area. In the history of Wujiang, the unique geographical advantages of Yangtze river delta and a great

Shanghai University: A Crucible for Revolution

number of refined scholars, together have created long-lasting elegance and refinement in the history of Chinese civilization for thousands of years.

Whitebait and bass fill the sparkling spring river, travelers from afar are attracted for a visit.

The river is too beautiful to be drawn, the chirp of the birds is heard deep in the reeds.

The market is closed before dusk falls, the blue sky clear and the mountains lonely.

A rainbow rises over the southern bridge, moonlight shines upon Taihu Lake on a clear night.

Wujiang by Zhang Xian, a poet in the Northern Song Dynasty, beautifully portrayed this water town south of the Yangtze River, where people were wealthy and materials were abundant.

It was unexpected that this idyllic water town should nurture two core revolutionary heroes.

There was only one explanation: the forging of ideas and beliefs.

Indeed, that must be it. It was how the life and destiny of a group of Chinese intellectuals in the early twentieth century was reshaped, and how a revolutionary road was extended, dyed red with life and blood.

Hou Shaoqiu was a gifted scholar in Songjiang. In August 1918, he was admitted to Nan Yang Public School in Shanghai (the predecessor of Shanghai Jiaotong University), the second-highest of all students, to study civil engineering. However, on the train back to Shanghai from his hometown on May 6, 1919, some news in a newspaper made the engineering student interested in national affairs, thus altering the track of his life. The news was the May Fourth Movement.

On May 7, he and his schoolmates participated in the anti-imperialist demonstration of tens of thousands protesters. The enthusiasm of the citizens and students and how they were fighting deeply touched this man. "The power of the masses inspired me. The first thing I did after I returned to school was draft an article that advocated domestic products and to boycott Japanese ones, and published it in the corridor (a key point on campus)!" Hou Shaoqiu recalled.

Revolutionaries

On May 11, the Shanghai Student Union was established. Hou Shaoqiu, representing Nan Yang Public School, was recommended to be the Secretary of the Education Department of the Student Union, thus embarking on student movement-themed Revolution to Save the Nation. *New Youth*, the magazine, and *Gray Horse*, an article, turned him into a revolutionary who believed in Marxism. He was expelled from the school under the accusation of aggressive behavior and had zero interest in studying because he edited and published the *Question Weekly*, which was nicked name *Ear News* by Songjiang people. That a progressive college student in the May Fourth Movement was expelled caused a sensation in Shanghai, where the flames of revolution were already burning hot. *Awakening*, the supplement of the *Republic of China Daily* published a signed article, pointing out that: "Imagine that an expulsion terrifies those engaged in the new cultural movement. Ridiculous, isn't it?"

But Hou Shaoqiu calmly confronted the abrupt misfortune: "That shall never change my will to fight."

At this time, a private girls' school in Songjiang was closed due to feudal forces and financial distress. He was sorry that one of the earliest girls' schools south of the Yangtze river had shut down. However, it happened that a country gentleman named Zhu Jixun intended to revitalize it. He heard that Hou Shaoqiu, who was teaching in Yixing, was a native talent, so he invited him for the revitalization. Zhu Jixun was a good friend of Liu Yazi, a celebrity from Wujiang and member of the Tongmenghui, who also studied at Nan Yang Public School. Therefore, Hou Shaoqiu was more than willing to work with this fellow villager and senior alumnus on the task.

They teamed up and the Songjiang Girls' School soon came back to life. Hou Shaoqiu, who mainly focused on teaching, introduced a large number of prestigious experts and advanced ideas to the school, thus earning it a good reputation in Shanghai. Shen Yanbing (whose pen name was Mao Dun), who was then-member of the Shanghai Prefectural Party Committee and District Committee of the CPC, praised their achievement. "I admire their courage to reject all coldness, refusing all weakness of suppression, and keep minding their own business regardless."

Hou Shaoqiu's successful operation of the school attracted the attention of the CPC in Shanghai. Not only was he recruited as one of

Shanghai University: A Crucible for Revolution

the earliest CPC members in Songjiang, but in the winter of 1923, Luo Zhanglong from the Central bureau of the CPC, who was responsible for party building in the surrounding areas of Shanghai, and Yun Daiying, head of the Central Committee of the Communist Youth League of China, were sent to Songjiang to found a party organization. That day, Hou Shaoqiu, extremely excited, personally travelled to Shanghai to greet them. The three of them took a little steamer on the Suzhou River in Shanghai and sailed up the Huangpu River to Songjiang, passing the Waibaidu Bridge.

In the following days, they lived and worked together, giving lectures to the people, convening secret meetings from time to time to promote Marxism and the October Revolution, answering urgent questions raised by the progressives, and initially establishing party, youth league, and student organizations in Songjiang, thus the presence of revolutionary tinder was there from then on. Luo Zhanglong was particularly impressed with the days of working with Hou Shaoqiu in Songjiang, together with Yun Daiying. He once recalled: "Comrade Hou Shaoqiu is handsome, capable, talented, eloquent, and a good writer." He also composed the poem titled *Three in Songjiang*:

> *There were busy days, full of meetings, and brain-racking were the decisions regarding south Jiangsu.*
> *To ensure every plan is perfect, debates went on until dawn broke.*
> *For high taxes and heavy burdens on the tenants South of Yangtze, fights were seen everywhere in the countryside.*
> *Dedicated to reforming and benefiting generations to come was Mr. Hou Shaoqiu.*

Side-by-side in the days of revolution, Yun Daiying and Hou Shaoqiu forged a profound revolutionary friendship. Hou took Yun as a role model, learning everything from him.

In February 1924, the KMT Shanghai Executive Department of was established. It was a historic event. And it greatly affected the subsequent cooperation between the KMT and the CPC. Thereafter, many outstanding Chinese communists had officially entered the political arena. In this organization, in addition to Wang Jingwei, Hu Hanmin, and Yu Youren,

Revolutionaries

important figures of the KMT at that time, Deng Zhongxia, Mao Zedong, Yun Daiying, Xiang Jingyu, Luo Zhanglong, and Liu Yazi, a friend of the CPC, were among them. Of the 20 executive committee members, 12 were CPC members, and they were the ones who presided over the daily work, such as Deng Zhongxia and Yun Daiying. At this stage, the CPC used the legal organization of the KMT-CPC cooperation to actively develop relevant revolutionary forces and party organizations around Shanghai, recruiting the progressives to join the revolutionary ranks. After Sun Chuanfang was stationed in Shanghai, he offered a bounty of 2,000 silver dollars for whoever captured Hou Shaoqiu. Students and friends who heard the news hurried to warn him. He replied calmly. "Don't be afraid. I'll try to avoid it. If unfortunately I am captured, I'll bravely die for the revolution!"

At the end of 1924, there was tangled fighting between warlords of Jiangsu and Zhejiang. Songjiang Jingxian Girls' School, which Hou Shaoqiu worked hard to revive, was forced to shut down. He led the students to relocate the school in Shanghai. "Come study at the Affiliated School of Shanghai University, we need you!" As soon as Yun Daiying's recommendation of Hou Shaoqiu as the Director of the reorganized Affiliated School was approved, Yun immediately informed him the good news. From that day on, they truly fought side by side as professional revolutionaries, the busiest and shiniest days of Hou's life.

In the bloody storm of the May Thirtieth Movement, Hou Shaoqiu was Yun Daiying's right-hand man. He directly instructed the demonstration of the member units of the Students Federation and led the anti-imperialist protests on Nanjing Road. Meanwhile, he was also the organizer/leader of the all-Shanghai teacher protest team. On the following day after the imperialists' bloodbath on Nanjing Road, he, together with CPC members Yang Xianjiang, Mao Dun, Dong Yixiang, and others in Shanghai co-founded a National Salvation Association of faculty to support the strikes of students, of workers, and of markets in the May Thirtieth Movement. Back then, there were a group of so-called celebrities in the education circle, who in fact disapproved of students of taking to the streets and fighting against the imperialists. They kept advocating the cliché of education to save the nation. With the foresight of a proletarian revolutionary, Hou

Shaoqiu sternly pointed out that at a turning point in history, national salvation precedes education, saving the country from crisis comes first so that the foundation can be laid for education.

Influenced by Yun Daiying, plus his own talent, he exceled at speeches and debates, thus attracting and motivating students and colleagues, and became an outstanding figure in the May Thirtieth Movement. More importantly, his talent and courage in developing and organizing party building in the surrounding areas of Shanghai and in openly fighting against the right-wing forces of the KMT inspired a group of steadfast revolutionaries just like himself.

His student, an important young female revolutionary, joined him in the fight. This Qiu-Jin-styled (female revolutionary) female communist, who then earned a reputation in Shanghai and Jiangsu, was Zhang Yingchun, one of the nine martyrs murdered by KMT executioners along with Hou Shaoqiu and others.

Martyr Zhang Yingchun's stories are told in both the Shanghai Longhua Martyrs Memorial Hall and the Nanjing Yuhuatai Martyrs Memorial Hall.

Her hometown, Lili in Wujiang, is a neighboring town that I have been familiar with since childhood. It is located at the border of Jiangsu and Zhejiang, approximately 30 kilometers away from Suzhou. Together with Tongli, Zhili, and Guli, it is called the Four Li's of South of the Yangtze. It was a famous historical market. There is still the special atmosphere of a peaceful old town south of the Yangtze.

Zhang Yingchun, born in Lili, was courageous when she was a teenager. Her father Zhang Nong had four daughters. In the years when women were advised to remain uneducated, she had been demanding education since childhood. Her father, who ran a private school, gave her this opportunity and she became the only girl there. She was clever and studied hard, which made her the favorite student of her father and other teachers. Gradually, her female gender was no longer an issue. She was treated equally as a boy. At that time, Liu Yazi's South Association in Lili kept promoting the heroine Qiu Jin. From novels, plays to poems, the little girl was deeply fascinated. She therefore aspired to be as outstanding a woman as Qiu Jin. However, she was born physically weak. Her father, who basically raised her as a son, was an enlightened man and wanted the best possible for her–thus sending her to study at the girls' school founded by educator Ni Shouzhi.

Their predecessors travelled across the sea to Japan. They absorbed the best knowledge there and returned to the motherland. Day and night, they worked hard to teach, to run the school... Stay frugal, work hard, everyone, we girls are just as good as boys!

These were the lyrics of the school anthem, a reflection of the great ambition and anti-feudal spirit of the founders.

At this school, she met someone important in her life, classmate Liu Junquan, Liu Yazi's fourth sister. In current terms, they were besties. They sat together in class, went home together after school, inseparable.

Due to the influence of Liu Yazi and others, the turmoil outside and the wave of revolution kept disturbing the peace of the quiet town of Lili. In 1915, Yuan Shih-kai restored the dethroned monarch and announced himself emperor, causing an uproar and opposition from the Chinese people. And that young Zhang Yingchun aggressively criticized Yuan Shikai in public, causing a sensation at the time.

She drew the attention of Liu Yazi. Her father Zhang Nong joined Liu Yazi's Southern Society, which gave her the opportunity to inhale the fresh air of revolution. Meanwhile, with her father as a role model, her talent for poetry stood out and her works were often published.

"Yingchun of Lili, a rarely talented woman!" Liu Yazi sang her praise frequently.

The revolutionary wave of the May Fourth Movement, together with the motivating and thunderous slogans of "Make the Country Strong" and "Save the Country" in Beijing and Shanghai, reached the heart of this young woman from Lili. In the summer of 1920, with the support of his father, she came to Shanghai alone with the belief that a strong country comes from strong people and strong people must build up their body, thus her application to study at the first women's sports school in the Shanghai College of Fine Arts, located in Linyin Road, Old West Gate.

"Thunder roars, waking the sleeping lion; revolution sweeps across China...May the young waste no time and promote sports as if a personal duty." By that time, there has already been such an advanced theory of school management and ambitious goals.

In Shanghai, after the ordeal of the May Fourth Movement, the wave of

Shanghai University: A Crucible for Revolution

revolution was raging, progressive newspapers and organizations springing up like mushrooms, advanced thoughts becoming popular among the young. Therefore, schools were shrouded with an atmosphere of patriotism, democracy, and progress. Among them, Zhang Yingchun, like a stranded fish back in the water, often practiced swordsmanship with the sports skills she had acquired, and passionately expressed personal ideas, resembling Qiu Jin, thus she simply nicknamed herself Qiu Shi.

Unfortunately, she caught erysipelas (a common bacterial infection in the skin) in her calf and had to go home for treatment. It happened that Liu Yazi was also in Lili.

"Mr. Liu, there are too many students coming to Jingxian School. Our biggest problem is that there are not enough teachers. You are wise and well-connected. Please introduce some progressive female teachers for the school!" One day, Hou Shaoqiu asked Liu Yazi for a favor.

"Sure! You have asked the right man." Liu Yazi knew about the Songjiang Jingxian Girls' School Hou Shaoqiu was running. Without giving it much thought, he blurted out the name of Zhang Yingchun to Hou Shaoqiu.

Hou Shaoqiu was overjoyed when he met her, as she had already joined the CPC. From then on, the revolutionary teacher and student/colleagues began their wonderful lives.

At that time, Jingxian Middle School had actually become a crucial base of the CPC for training female revolutionaries in Shanghai and Songjiang. Zhang Yingchun was fully dedicated to helping Hou Shaoqiu expand the school, running endless errands. In the face of the temporary difficulty of fundraising during the construction of new school buildings, she even donated all her salary from the school, and organized nine fundraising teams to collect donations in Songjiang and Shanghai. At that time, a woman making frequent public appearances would suffer finger pointing behind her back.

"How about I cut my hair short?" One day, she picked up a pair of big scissors, looked into the mirror, and cut her beautiful hair herself. Since then, a woman who called herself Qiu Shi was often seen on the streets of Wujiang, Songjiang, and Shanghai, giving speeches.

She gradually earned herself the popular title "Qiu Jin of Wujiang."

After the May Fourth Movement, China's revolutionary ideological

Revolutionaries

trend, in addition to science to save the country, education to save the country, the student movement, and the labor movement, included another important component: the women's liberation movement, equally magnificent and profound. The liberation movement to mobilize and encourage Chinese women to consciously save themselves was an important part of the CPC's awakening the people. In this movement, Soong Ching-Ling, He Xiangning, Cai Chang, and Xiang Jingyu were the leaders and standard-bearers of women. In Shanghai, Jiangsu, and Zhejiang, knowledgeable, courageous, capable, and energetic revolutionary women like Zhang Yingchun were naturally uplifting. She earnestly practiced what was advocated in the women's liberation movement, for example, by being the first to apply for a women's sports school in her hometown, to cut her hair short, to get rid of a corset, all because she was a member of the CPC.

"When we join the party, we accept the command of the party, mind and body, and personal interests come second!" she confided firmly, having joined the CPC.

As the Northern Expedition went on, the fight between the revolutionary and anti-revolutionary forces entered a fierce stage. Hou Shaoqiu, as head of the Communist Youth League organization within the KMT in Shanghai, was always at the center of the confrontation between the two forces. The danger he was exposed to was beyond imagination. Zhang Yingchun was tasked with sharing and substituting his work and paying attention to his safety. She resolved countless dangers for him with her unique female sensitivity and carefulness.

"Yingchun, the organization has decided that we should move the party headquarters to Nanjing tomorrow. Inform the committee members at once to prepare to leave, the sooner the better!" On the afternoon of March 29, 1927, Hou Shaoqiu called her to his residence and assigned this important task decisively.

"Understood!" She was about to dash off immediately after receiving the order, but he stopped her: "Wait, one more thing."

"What is it?" She stopped to ask.

Rather worried, he prepared his student mentally. "This trip to Nanjing is dangerous. We have to plan for the worst. Figure out a way to deliver a message to your family."

Shanghai University: A Crucible for Revolution

She nodded. "I understand. It can wait until we are in Nanjing!"

But as soon as they arrived in the city, the situation worsened, leaving no time for her to send any information to her family in Lili. When they learned that she had died in Nanjing, the whole family were skeptical. For confirmation, his father, Zhang Nong, travelled to Nanjing twice, but there was no way to confirm it. He fell ill from anxiety and died vomiting blood. Father and daughter, both dead. What sorrow!

In early 1949, Chairman Mao invited Liu Yazi to Beijing to prepare for the founding of the nation. When he first set foot on the road in Beijing, Liu Yazi recalled the revolutionary martyrs Hou Shaoqiu and Zhang Yingchun, involuntarily reciting the commemorative poem *Dead together, Hou and Zhang, heroically. Heart aches, for their tongues cut off.* When their enemies murdered Zhang Yingchun and Hou Shaoqiu, they were extremely cruel. Not only did they stab and mortally wound them, but they first cut off their tongues. Liu Yazi found it difficult to fall asleep when he thought of how tragically the comrades had died. So, when he attended the founding ceremony, facing the cheering crowd in the square, he recited to the martyrs with respect the verse *Rest in peace, for that people have finally earned peace...*

Yun Daiying, Hou Shaoqiu, Zhang Yingchun, three revolutionary martyrs, one was a teacher at Shanghai University, one the director of the affiliated school to the university, and one had studied at the university. To a certain extent, it was the university that brought their lives together. The time of their demise was 1931, 1927, and 1927 respectively, and their ages were 36, 31, and 26.

How young! What dazzling young talents! But for the revolution, for China of today, they died young. How tragic!

They are representatives of many revolutionaries of Shanghai University who heroically sacrificed their lives.

CHAPTER FOUR

——

1927, the Year Dyed Red by the Blood of Communists...

THE NOBILITY OF REVOLUTIONARIES LIES IN CONFRONTING DEATH selflessly and fearlessly.

It was perhaps destined or coincidental but legendary that following the failure of the Great Revolution in 1927, Wang Shouhua, Zhao Shiyan, and Luo Yinong, three important figures of the CPC died heroically almost at the same time at the same age of 26.

There were three armed uprisings of workers in Shanghai, of which they led the first two.

Wang Shouhua was the first who sacrificed his life among the trio. He was from the city of Zhuji, in Zhejiang Province. His real family name was not Wang, but He. He used to be called He Jiyuan. His father was a *xiucai* (a scholar in the Ming and Qing dynasties who passed the imperial examination at county level) in the late Qing Dynasty, taught in his hometown all his life, and died of illness. His eldest brother also died of the same cause. And the family declined. Seventeen-year-old Wang Shouhua was admitted with flying colors to the Zhejiang Provincial No. 1 Normal School in Hangzhou. This was a school known as the Zhejiang Revolutionary Crucible. The May Fourth Movement allowed him, who was pursuing progress, to understand the principles and ambitions of transforming the old world. In his diary, he wrote: "I vow to live with no regrets."

Revolutionaries

The October Revolution broke out, and Wang Shouhua, like many Chinese youths, yearned to go to Soviet Union to learn and experience the new world of socialism. In 1920, when he returned home during the summer vacation, he spread Marx's theory of communism everywhere, but the villagers were skeptical. He promised: "When I come back, we will build socialism and establish a new China!" No one in his family or the village understood nor supported him. Only his farmer mother unexpectedly financed him 100 silver dollars to study in Russia.

In June of that year, Wang Shouhua came to Shanghai. Introduced by his classmate Xuan Zhonghua (a martyr, one of the leaders of the Shanghai labor movement, and former secretary of Zhabei Ministry of the CPC; on the evening of April 17, 1927, his enemies tortured him cruelly for three days and he never gave in, so he was beheaded by a group of executioners. He died extremely heroically, at the age of 29), he came to the progressive work-study mutual aid group and Shanghai Foreign Languages Society started by China's first batch of Marxists to learn Russian. In April 1921, before the founding of the CPC, far-sighted leaders such as Chen Duxiu and Li Dazhao began to send outstanding youth to receive a Marxist education and learn revolutionary experiences. Therefore Wang Shouhua, Liu Shaoqi, Ren Bishi, Luo Yinong, Xiao Jinguang, and others went to Moscow, the holy place of the October Revolution they yearned for.

Luo Yinong was a Hunan native, one year younger than Wang Shouhua. His father was a well-known local gentleman. Similarly inspired by the May Fourth Movement, when he turned 17 (the second half of 1919), this young man from Xiang River, in a long gown holding an umbrella, came to Shanghai. He first worked as a proofreader in a newspaper agency. It was this job that exposed him to more progressive magazines such as *New Youth*. One day, a middle-aged man stepped into the proofreading room and started a chat with him, asking about his origin, hobbies, and ambitions. The final question was whether he feared trouble. Luo Yinong replied, "I am all alone surviving in Shanghai. Pretty fearless, I would say."

The middle-aged man was delighted, praising, "Typical Hunan fierceness."

Soon, he found out that the middle-aged man was Chen Duxiu, a well-known standard-bearer of the May Fourth Movement and one of the

1927, the Year Dyed Red by the Blood of Communists...

founders of the CPC. Since then, this smart, open-minded, strong, and aspiring man was often invited to Chen Duxiu's apartment in Shanghai, where he read the earliest Chinese version of *The Communist Manifesto*. One day, Chen Duxiu suggested to Luo Yinong, who had been studying Russian in the Foreign Languages Society for some time, "Go to Russia!"

It was exciting news for him. Naturally, he had to consult with his family. And he encountered the same outcome as Wang Shouhua, in that family members and villagers believed he was crazy, but his father was supportive and believed it would bring glory to the family. Soon, the father decisively financed the son 100 silver dollars for travel expenses.

Clever and studious, Luo Yinong found favor with Chen Duxiu, general secretary of the CPC. After he enrolled in the Communist University of the Toilers of the East in Moscow, he made rapid progress, joined the Communist Youth League and the CPC successively, and became Secretary of the Moscow branch of the CPC. He also served as a Professor of Materialism and translator for the Chinese class, equally competent as Qu Qiubai, who came to Russia through other channels and was also teaching in the university.

However, Wang Shouhua's trip to Moscow was much more tortuous and difficult than Luo Yinong's. Back then, reactionary warlords were wary of Chinese youth going to the socialist Soviet Union. To dodge the eyes of warlords, Wang Shouhua and others acted separately when they arrived in Harbin, no longer travelling together with Liu Shaoqi, Luo Yinong, Ren Bishi, and others. And he was captured, together with Liang Baitai (a martyr, the first Minister of Justice during the Soviet Regime, killed by the Communist Purge Group in 1935, at the age of 36.) by the minions of the warlord Zhang Zuolin. After being released, they arrived in Vladivostok by sea. At that time, the roads to Moscow were perilous, as white bandits were rampant. Later, it was discovered that the group of Liu Shaoqi, Ren Bishi, Xiao Jinguang, Cao Jinghua, and others also encountered a lot of trouble, except they were luckier. It somehow took them several months to reach Moscow.

In Vladivostok, an unfamiliar land, Wang Shouhua and others could only work while doing revolutionary work. Meanwhile, he joined the CPC and became Director of the Far East Ministry of Workers of China.

Revolutionaries

Li Dazhao personally designed a study abroad plan for Zhao Shiyan, who was selected to be sent abroad. He left Shanghai at the same time as Wang Shouhua and Luo Yinong. He accepted Marxism earlier than both of them. The Sichuan teenager came to Beijing at the age of 14 and soon made the acquaintance of Li Dazhao. On May 9, 1920, he boarded the French ocean liner Amonique to Paris, another sacred place of revolution—where the Paris Commune took place. There were many Chinese youths travelling together with Zhao Shiyan, a total of 130, among whom most were familiar faces. In the second half of this year, Zhou Enlai, Deng Xiaoping, Cai Hesen, Chen Yi, and Xiang Jingyu visited important cities in the center of the European revolution, such as Paris and Berlin. Most of these youths later became significant leaders of the CPC, yet few survived the cruel revolutionary fights to see the founding day of the PRC.

1925 was an important year. As required by the Central Committee of the CPC, many young outstanding party members who studied in France and the Soviet Union were transferred back to the motherland. They raced to the forefront of the revolution. And Shanghai, as the main battlefield, was the common destination of their return.

The world-shocking May Thirtieth Movement was an important background for the Central Committee of the CPC to recall young core members studying abroad to China to participate in and lead the revolution. At the time, there was insufficient experience in the labor movement and the student movement, and a group of organizers and leaders were killed. The main party leaders Chen Duxiu, Li Dazhao, and others realized the urgency to take special measures for the revolution.

Wang Shouhua, Luo Yinong, and Zhao Shiyan were first assigned to Shanghai, Guangzhou, and Northeast China. Wang Shouhua returned to China earlier than the other classmates, because there was a woman in his hometown of Zhuji waiting to marry him. Next, he went to Shanghai to attend Fourth National Congress of the CPC. Throughout the May Thirtieth Movement, he and his classmates Li Lisan, Liu Shaoqi, and others worked in the Shanghai Federation of Labor Unions. He served as Chief of the Propaganda Department, witnessing scenes of workers led to strike and fight imperialism on the streets.

At this time, Luo Yinong formed the Guangdong District Committee of the CPC with Chen Yannian and Zhou Enlai in Guangzhou, leading workers to strike in Guangdong and Hong Kong to support the May Thirtieth Movement in Shanghai.

Zhao Shiyan was serving as the Secretary of the Beijing Prefectural Committee of the CPC and the Local Executive Committee in the north, assisting Li Dazhao in the anti-imperialist and anti-warlord fights in several northern provinces, including establishing the Inner Mongolia Alliance of Workers, Peasants, and Soldiers and armed forces. He was also a well-known talent in the party who could wield both pen and gun. *National Salvation Times*, an influential progressive newspaper in the northern region praised him: "Mr. Zhao, as the famous editor-in-chief of the northern political review, is widely admired by common revolutionary youth for his speaking style, thus the spread of his fame throughout the country."

In China after the May Thirtieth Movement, southern revolutionary camps represented by the Guangzhou National Government, the example of cooperation between KMT and the CPC, were antagonistic with northern reactionary warlord regime of the Beiyang government in Beijing. Thanks to progressive forces of the CPC and the KMT, the Northern Expedition aimed at overthrowing the Beiyang government of the reactionary warlords commenced in July 1926 and advanced rapidly from south to north. Chiang Kai-shek was commander-in-chief of the Northern Expedition while He Yingqin, Li Jishen, Bai Chongxi, Li Zongren, Zhu Peide, and Tan Yankai were all front-line military generals in that operation. However, leaders of the political departments of the Northern Expedition and party representatives of various military forces were almost all CPC members who joined the KMT in their personal capacity. For example, Director and Deputy Director of the General Political Department of the Northern Expedition were Deng Yanda and Guo Moruo respectively; Li Fuchun, Lin Boqu, Zhu Kejing, and Liao Ganwu served as party representatives or directors of political departments in various military forces. The masses in Guangdong, among other provinces, offered tremendous support to the expedition. For example, the CPC organized thousands of workers who participated in the strike in Guangzhou and Hong Kong to form a transport team to travel up north with the army.

At the beginning, the Northern Expedition was a just battle to overthrow

Revolutionaries

the reactionary warlord government and oppose the rampant suppression by imperialist forces in China. Therefore, it was invincible from the start, thus encouraging revolutionaries and the oppressed people everywhere. At this time, the CPC decided to take the advantage to strive for greater success in the revolution. As Shanghai was the key center connecting north and south China, and the largest city, and the army of the Beiyang warlord government stationed there had only one to two thousand soldiers plus about two thousand policemen, meaning only three to four thousand versus over 200,000 worker pickets and hundreds of thousands of students, the CPC was preparing an armed uprising in the city to cooperate with the Northern Expedition so that the Shanghai regime could be taken over.

All preparations were rapidly unfolding. It was also at this time that Zhao Shiyan and Luo Yinong, who had already accumulated experience in military armed struggles, were successively transferred from the north and Guangzhou to Shanghai by the Central Committee of the CPC. On May 7, 1926, the CPC's armed uprising to cooperate with the Northern Expedition was quietly yet nervously proceeding: the Shanghai District Committee of the CPC decided to establish a special military committee. Thereafter, Wang Shouhua, Zhao Shiyan, and Luo Yinong began their years of armed uprising side by side —

In a small building in Hengfengli on Sigaota Road (now Shanyin Road), there were suddenly people bustling in and out. People assumed it was a business gathering. Some participants appeared rather stylish, men in silk gowns, women fully made up—seeming to be no gathering of the poor. In fact, this was the organ where the Shanghai District Committee of the CPC was located at that time. Those who bustled in and out during that period were all trainees in the secret class of Zhao Shiyan, Luo Yinong, and Wang Shouhua. They chose that house because it was located in Chinese territory adjacent to the Japanese concession, just in case.

The revolutionary situation has been pressing on at every stage. There were six sessions of the secret training courses, which lasted over a month. At each session, trainees would study for a week, intensively two to three times during the week, usually in the evening or afternoon. They were all heads of the Shanghai party organization and labor union. The secret courses mainly disseminated basic military knowledge, while the core

1927, the Year Dyed Red by the Blood of Communists...

training of explosives and firearms use was directly taught by the central government in another secret location, where there were only a dozen students, in absolute secrecy. In contrast, the stronghold of the Shanghai District Party Committee on Shanyin Road assembled the fundamental backbone of workers' armed uprising, who educated and mobilized the people, and taught the simplest military defenses and military techniques.

Instructor Luo Yinong lectured about Marxism-Leninism and the current situation, Zhao Shiyan taught party organization building, and Wang Shouhua focused on the labor movement. Despite the secret training courses being short, the effect was delightful. A considerable number of outstanding students joined the party organization. Statistics shows that at the end of 1925 after the May Thirtieth Movement, there were over 1,350 CPC members in Shanghai. By the end of the classes Zhao Shiyan, Luo Yinong, and Wang Shouhua held in 1926, the total number of CPC members in Shanghai had exceeded 2,500.

The Northern Expedition was steadily victorious, approaching Zhejiang and Shanghai. At this moment, Xia Chao, governor of Zhejiang Province declared "independence." Who would get Shanghai became the focus of attention of the hour.

On October 19, Shanghai District Committee of CPC, as ordered by the Central Committee of the CPC, formally decided to launch the first armed workers' uprising. Luo Yinong was recommended as Commander-in-chief while Zhao Shiyan and Wang Shouhua were both Commanders, responsible for mobilizing the people and related labor union organizations.

The time for the uprising was set for October 24.

Everyone was waiting for news from Zhejiang—Luo Yinong, Zhao Shiyan, and Wang Shouhua in Shanghai were ready all the time for any news from Hangzhou. However, eventually bad news came that Xia Chao, Governor of Zhejiang suffered a heavy blow, as he led troops marching towards Jiaxing, from Sun Chuanfang, who marched from north to south to Hangzhou. On October 22, Xia Chao had to retreat to Yuhang with the surviving soldiers. On October 23, Sun's army entered Hangzhou and he sent troops to pursue and attack Xia Chao, beating him to death on the Yuhang Highway.

"We are losing! Abort the uprising immediately!" On the evening of

October 23, the planned armed uprising could no longer proceed. Luo Yinong, Zhao Shiyan, and Wang Shouhua analyzed the situation, promptly reported it to the central government, and immediately made a new decision upon approval. However, it was late at night. Worker pickets in some areas failed to receive the notice to abort the mission in time, and they began to clash with the police. The outcome turned out different from what was planned. Over 10 worker leaders, such as Tao Jingxuan, Xi Zuoyao died in the conflict, and more than a hundred were arrested.

In the early morning of the next day, the first uprising was announced to be at an end and a failure.

The Central Committee of the CPC was deeply concerned with the failure of the armed uprising. Wang Shouhua was summoned to Wuhan to report what happened to Zhang Guotao, the person in charge of the work of the Central Committee. It emphasized again the importance and possibility of armed struggles in Shanghai, and called for another armed uprising by taking advantage of the strong momentum of the Northern Expedition, so that it would be likely the CPC could take control of Shanghai.

Hearing comrades in Shanghai speaking confidently about the sure success of the armed uprising, the young Central Committee of the CPC was also full of anticipation and hope. Certainly, Zhang Guotao and others would fully support Shanghai for a decent armed uprising. "Knock the imperialists and reactionary warlords down to the ground!" This was the common wish of most Chinese communists those years.

With such aspirations and victorious Northern Expedition, the second workers armed uprising in Shanghai was under vigorous preparation.

However, the Sun Chuanfang warlord group entrenched in Shanghai launched a large-scale raid against the armed uprising leaders Luo Yinong, Zhao Shiyan, and Wang Shouhua. One night, Wang Shouhua convened a meeting with labor union cadres. As he was about to speak, he cautiously noticed two policemen walking towards the venue from the window. While instructing everyone to be calm, he messed up his hair. The policemen did not find him after entering the room, but they knew something was happening with so many people gathering. So, one policeman guarded and monitored the scene with a gun while the other returned to report it. When a large group of policemen arrived, Wang Shouhua had already

1927, the Year Dyed Red by the Blood of Communists...

escaped over the wall under the cover of fellow workers.

"What? Commander Luo is nowhere to be found?" At about the same time, late at night abruptly, Zhao Shiyan was surprised when he received the report from the workers' picket line.

"Damn! Please don't be arrested!" Zhao Shiyan stomped his feet in anxiety, and personally led a team to look for him in the secret military training spot near Lafeide Road (now Fuxing Road).

"Here!" When everyone was desperately anxious, a worker picket saw him lying asleep by the stairs of the training spot.

"Ha-ha. I fell asleep, didn't I?" Luo Yinong was embarrassed when he saw his comrade-in-arms Zhao Shiyan and workers laughing around him. He was exhausted.

However, judging from the current situation, the Northern Expeditionary Army was one step away from taking over the city of Hangzhou. It was now or never for Shanghai to launch another armed uprising.

On February 15, 1927, the Central Committee of the CPC held an emergency meeting and decided to launch an armed uprising of workers within the city when the Northern Expeditionary Army turned to Songjiang on the way to Shanghai after attacking Hangzhou.

"We must succeed this time! Comrades, let's get fully committed to it." Commander-in-chief Luo Yinong waved his fist at the military meeting of the Shanghai District Committee of the CPC held on the 16th, vowing to win.

Wang Shouhua became more nervous, because the armed uprising was an armed riot organized with workers on the picket line as the principal force by the main body of the Federation of Labor Unions. On the other hand, Zhao Shiyan, experienced with armed struggles, while inspecting all aspects of uprising preparations, reminded everyone at a special meeting held by the Shanghai District Committee of CPC on February 18. "In this riot, everything is still unpredictable. Stay highly vigilant!"

It was also on this day that the Northern Expeditionary Army conquered Hangzhou. The Shanghai District Committee immediately announced that on the 19th, the All-Shanghai Labor Alliance strike would take place under the call of the Federation of Labor Unions. The slogan was

Revolutionaries

Support the Northern Expedition Army, defeat Sun Chuanfang. Obviously, it was unanimously believed the best time for an armed riot has come.

On February 19, 20, 21, and 22, the workers' strikes were formidable, with 360,000 participants. Against only two thousand warlord soldiers and two thousand policemen, it was believed to be a piece of cake, a sure victory.

Therefore, during the day of the 22nd, representatives of various circles of Shanghai industry and commerce, the CPC and the KMT announced the establishment of the Shanghai Municipal Civil Provisional Revolutionary Committee.

Victory seemed around the corner!

At 4 p.m. that day, the Shanghai District Committee of the CPC issued a special emergency notice to mobilize Shanghai residents to riot at 6 p.m. When the artillery of the uprising sounded, worker pickets in each district immediately attacked the military police, engaging in close combat with their enemies on the streets. However, when the second armed uprising of Shanghai workers reached a climax and was in urgent need of support from the Northern Expedition army, Chiang Kai-shek unexpectedly ordered Bai Chongxi's troops marching in Jiaxing to stop attacking Shanghai, and Niu Yongjian's troops, which agreed to cooperate with the CPC organization in Shanghai, stood by indifferently.

Without peripheral assistance, the workers' armed uprising, which lacked weapons, ammunition, and military experience, fell in the dilemma of fighting alone. Seeing another bloody tragedy coming, the Shanghai Municipal Civil Provisional Revolutionary Committee decided to call it off right away.

The workers, who fought hard and shed blood, were grossly disappointed.

The leaders of the armed uprising, Luo Yinong, Zhao Shiyan, and Wang Shouhua, reproached Chiang Kai-shek: an untrustworthy traitor, the true enemy of the revolution.

However, the harshest reproach could not change the failure of the armed uprising. Many revolutionaries in Shanghai sulked.

On the evening of February 23, the Central Committee of the CPC and the Shanghai District Committee of the CPC convened a joint

1927, the Year Dyed Red by the Blood of Communists...

meeting and announced two important decisions: to immediately abort the second armed uprising of Shanghai workers, but expand the armed organization, and prepare for the third; and to establish a Special Action Committee (SAC) for the armed uprising as the highest leading body of the mission, where General Secretary Chen Duxiu personally served as its Secretary, with committee members including Zhou Enlai, Luo Yinong, Zhao Shiyan, Wang Shouhua, Peng Shuzhi, and others. Under it, a special military committee was set up, with Zhou Enlai serving as the secretary.

Next, before the formal uprising, he was appointed as commander-in-chief of the action.

Although the first two armed uprisings ended up in failure, they toughened the workers and communists. Meanwhile, the dying reactionary warlords were more rampant. They organized the Broad Swords Squad, who were ordered to arrest and kill whoever they saw holding a slogan. Yet, it never deterred workers and progressive students. Ren Qixiang, an old worker of the former Commercial Press, said: "Their brutality can't frighten us. We still perform smart propaganda activities. To outwit our enemies, our propaganda team was divided into two groups. The first went on the streets shouting slogans to deliberately lure the Broad Swords Squad to hunt them while the second posted slogans and distributed leaflets on the streets, and quickly escaped, exhausting the killers.

As a result, warlords resorted to brutal actions, beheading workers and students killed in the uprising, hanging their heads on telegraph poles, and discarding corpses on the streets. Simultaneously, they conducted random searches on the streets and alleys to plant fear in the citizens.

"Tit for tat!" At the SAC meeting on the evening of the 24th, Luo Yinong, indignant, was ready to fight back.

Zhou Enlai signaled them to calm down, analyze why the previous two uprisings had failed, and compare the strength of both sides.

"The main problem lies in our insufficiently strong principal force in the uprising." Wang Shouhua suggested.

"Plus, the surrounding cooperation and support forces have not been coordinated well, thus the fiasco." Zhao Shiyan pointed out.

Luo Yinong, waving his fist, added, "The workers pickets are not armed at all. At critical moments, they basically cannot be of much help."

Revolutionaries

"You all make sense. Therefore, an armed uprising is not only a problem of a few of us, of Shanghai workers and students, but of the entire picture. If one piece loosens, the whole fails," Zhou Enlai concluded, and stressed the establishment of the three principal forces of the next armed uprising: workers picket lines, a self-defense group, and a special team. Undoubtedly, workers picket line was the strongest of three principal forces, at least 3,000 to 5,000 people; to command and motivate this enormous team, formation, training, and weaponry were required. To ensure the fighting capacity of the three principal forces and their rapid and effective action, transportation and information dissemination must be guaranteed.

"Shanghai is a coastal city with rivers flowing through. In addition to effective land preparations, we must also get support from the navy." Zhou Enlai proved himself the most important military strategist in the early days of the CPC. He had practiced armed struggles in Guangzhou and accumulated experience in leading the Whampoa Military Academy, thus he was more than familiar with military command.

The preparations for the third armed uprising since that day were made in an orderly manner under the direct command of Zhou Enlai.

Since the workers picketers were the principal force, their training became a top priority. The experienced Zhou Enlai, utilizing his own influence and personal connections, secretly transferred Hou Jingru and Peng Ganchen (martyr, important mainstay of the August First Nanchang Uprising, died on the battlefield in 1935 at the age of 36) to Shanghai. They were communist members of the Northern Expeditionary Army/ first graduates of the Whampoa Military Academy. They had come to Zhejiang to train the core members of the worker picketers and impart to them military skills such as the use of firearms and street fighting tactics. They were both members of the CPC. He asked them to bring some military leaders from the Northern Expedition Army along with them to secretly join the workers picket formation as the uprising commander and the military tactical commander. This was actual combat training. What distinguished itself from the previous two armed uprisings was that the third was no longer a simple strike, demonstration, and parade, but a true armed struggle.

Luo Yinong was assisting Zhou Enlai in the overall preparation for the uprising; Zhao Shiyan was in charge of the tasks pertaining to the backbone of the three principal forces; Wang Shouhua was organizing workers picketers in the name of the Shanghai Federation of Labor Unions and mobilizing peripheral workers to go on strike and demonstration and more.

One day, Commercial Press welcomed a special guest, who got out from a car in a formal hat, a long gown, businessman-styled, and unloaded many things from the car.

"Alas, it's you! It's too dangerous. Commander Zhou, you shouldn't have come deliver weapons in person?" It turned out that Zhou Enlai was the guest. He came with guns for the worker picketers of Commercial Press.

Having entered the house, Zhou Enlai teased. "The most important theory in the art of war is to keep doing the unexpected. The streets outside are all nervous. Nobody would expect us to deliver munitions by car in broad daylight, would they?"

On the street, it was a white horror. In secrecy, flames of the uprising were raging. By the end of February, 5,000 workers pickets under the charge of Wang Shouhua had been formed, and the number of strikers from peripheral forces reached nearly 300,000.

Simultaneously, in order to impede the northern warlords from supporting the reactionary forces in Shanghai, Zhou Enlai ordered Luo Yinong to personally organize workers of Shanghai-Hangzhou and Shanghai-Nanjing railways to set up strike committees to flexibly respond to possible complex situations.

The situation after early March was favorable for the armed uprising as the preparations under the leadership of Zhou Enlai, Luo Yinong, Zhao Shiyan, and Wang Shouhua were about to be finished. However, the Northern Expedition Army under Chiang Kai-shek's command was slow and even showing no progress on the occupation and attack of Shanghai. What next?

"Never act rashly again!" Chen Duxiu, General Secretary of the Central Committee of the CPC and highest leader of the armed uprising, advised, "We can't act too early! At least two basic conditions must be met: one—there are no troops stationed in Shanghai; two—the Northern

Revolutionaries

Expedition Army arrives in Songjiang and keeps marching forward, or we act when they arrive in Longhua." But at the critical moment, Zhou Enlai, Luo Yinong, Zhao Shiyan, Wang Shouhua, among other military special commissioners of the uprising, did not fully follow his advice. They believed that as long as one of the following three conditions was met, i.e., the Northern Expedition Army arrived in Longhua or attacked Suzhou, or the warlord troops stationed in Shanghai started to retreat, an uprising could be launched.

On March 20, the Northern Expedition Army conquered Songjiang. In the evening, advanced guards had arrived at Longhua.

The third armed uprising of Shanghai workers was ready.

At 12 p.m. on March 21, Commander-in-chiefs of the uprising Zhou Enlai, Luo Yinong, and Zhao Shiyan, in gray cotton jackets, peaked caps, and gray scarves, issued orders to the uprising branch headquarters from the front-line headquarters: start the armed uprising!

Immediately, millions of workers, students, and citizens in the city, under the command of Wang Shouhua, went on strike. Sirens that marked the beginning of the uprising resounded across the sky. The entire city witnessed the storm of a great revolution coming.

The battle was tense but often good news came in: first, Nanshi workers picketers occupied the Nanshi Police Station, Nanshi Arsenal, and Nanshi Railway Station; the outcome in Pudong was more exciting, as the battle ended in two hours; and workers fully occupied Wusong.

Except for Zhabei, all districts triumphed as expected that night. However, the adversaries entrenched in the North Railway Station and the Commercial Press Club (the former Oriental Library) did not surrender. With heavy weapons such as tanks, mortars, and machine guns, they neutralized the worker picketers' attack, leaving them with massive casualties. The moment Zhou Enlai, Zhao Shiyan, and Luo Yinong learned of the urgent situation at the forefront, they raced to the battle, immediately ordered a temporary ceasefire, and pretended to retreat.

That night, the three stayed on several fronts, separately plotting to attack the last two critical strongholds.

Since the reinforcements were cut off by the workers pickets, defenders entrenched in the Commercial Press Club were quickly besieged, an easy

1927, the Year Dyed Red by the Blood of Communists...

prey.

A white flag was raised. It was pure jubilation in Shanghai!

Now there was only the last stronghold to be taken: the North Railway Station. As planned, they would wait for the support of the Northern Expedition Army to deal with the heavily armed foes there. However, for an entire day on March 21, the Northern Expedition Army never moved an inch forward to the city. What happened?

"Chiang Kai-shek finally shows his fangs." Luo Yinong slammed his fist on the table. Zhao Shiyan also denounced him as a traitor to the revolution in front of Zhou Enlai.

"I have known what he is like since Whampoa Military Academy," Zhou Enlai calmed the SAC comrades. "We shall never need the Northern Expedition Army to conquer the North Railway Station. We are determined and confident. On our own, we shall eventually eliminate the warlord remnants."

"Yes! We will make it happen ourselves!"

"On our own! Expel the reactionary warlords out of Shanghai!"

"Down with the reactionary warlords!"

"Establish a revolutionary regime!"

On the 22nd, when the first rays of sunlight shone upon the North Railway Station, tens of thousands of strike teams, worker picketers, armed special forces, and citizens besieged the stubborn enemies in the station.

Subsequently, after a daytime of psychological warfare, at 5 p.m. when the sky had just darkened, the order to attack the North Railway Station came: at once, a blast of gunfire, shouts of slogans, and fighting echoed around the North Railway Station. The foes' commander, Bi Shucheng, understood that they were losing and secretly fled to the concession. Thus, their forces fell into the predicament of an absence of leadership. The workers' uprising army took advantage of the momentum, broke through the defense, took over the last stronghold, and seized nearly 4,000 rifles and handguns, and dozens of both light and heavy machine guns.

The first armed contingent of Chinese workers rose from the struggle from that very moment. For the first time, the Shanghai working class held their heads high in Shanghai.

It was a day of victory, a day to be remembered, a day to celebrate

Revolutionaries

the revolutionary success, a day when the CPC understood the power of armed struggle.

That day, Luo Yinong, Zhao Shiyan, and Wang Shouhua hugged each other in tears. Next, they gathered around Zhou Enlai and praised him from the bottom of their hearts: "Enlai, you came and we won. We and the people of Shanghai cannot thank you enough!"

Zhou Enlai smiled: "Without your previous two uprisings, the third would never have succeeded. Thank you."

The hearts of the four revolutionaries were tied tightly together.

The news of the triumph of the armed uprising spread fast. It took less than half a day to fully cover the entire city of Shanghai.

According to the planning and preparations of the revolutionaries, at 9 a.m. on March 22, the second meeting of citizens' representatives took place on the new stage in the city center. Over 4,000 representatives attended it and 19 members were elected for the Shanghai Municipal Government, including CPC members Luo Yinong, Wang Shouhua, Hou Shaoqiu, and Li Zhenying, as well as Gu Shunzhang, who became a traitor later.

Simultaneously, the Shanghai Provisional Municipal Government was formally established, and members of the municipal government elected Bai Chongxi, Niu Yongjian, Yang Xingfo, Wang Xiaolai, and Wang Shouhua as its executive members, and Lin Jun (a native of Chuansha, Shanghai University student, also known as Lin Shaobai, one of the student leaders in the May Thirtieth Movement, who later participated in the Nanchang Uprising, was a member of the CPC, and murdered by the KMT in 1944) as Secretary-general. However, Niu Yongjian, who was elected as the Chairman of the Provisional Municipal Government, and Bai Chongxi, who was elected as the highest military commander of the Northern Expedition in Shanghai, refused to take the jobs. It was actually a conspiracy of the Chiang Kai-shek group. However, the news of the revolutionary victory of the Shanghai armed uprising kept inspiring the country and the world. Eight newspapers, including *Pravda,* covered the Shanghai Victory in detail. The Central Council of All-Soviet Labor Unions, on behalf of all their workers, kindly congratulated the Shanghai Federation of Labor Unions. "We are always ready to assist you like brothers. Whether a difficult moment of failure or a happy moment of victory, we are always there for

1927, the Year Dyed Red by the Blood of Communists...

you!"

The young CPC and everyone in Shanghai were immersed in the joy of victory. Although Zhou Enlai, Zhao Shiyan, among others expected a total victory of the Northern Expedition, a cooperation between the CPC and the KMT, at the price of sincerity and kindness, Chiang Kai-shek, an epitome of landlord class and bourgeoisie power, thought otherwise. His anti-revolutionary face was constantly changing, trying to deceive the Chinese communists and the general public. Under his instructions, trouble was stirred up on the day of uprising victory: 19 groups representing the interests of Shanghai capitalists, including the Shanghai County Chamber of Commerce, Zhabei Chamber of Commerce, Banking Association, Money Industry Association, and so on announced the establishment of Shanghai Commercial Federation, whose standing committee was composed of 17 bourgeois leaders including Yu Qiaqing, Wang Xiaolai, and others. It was an obvious move to engage in a stand-off with Shanghai Federation of Labor Unions.

On March 26, Chiang Kai-shek arrived in Shanghai. In the evening, Yu Qiaqing, Chairman of the newly established Shanghai Commercial Federation, paid him a visit. On the third day, Chiang Kai-shek met with its nine representatives and appeased his "class brothers" with promises. Representatives of Shanghai bourgeoisie took the hint, thus the Money Industry Association organized 84 private banks to generously raise one million silver dollars at once, plus two million silver dollars from the banking industry, as a gift to Chiang Kai-shek.

Chiang Kai-shek, who gave favors once money was paid properly, was never as simple as the bourgeoisie representatives expected. His ambition was not limited to Shanghai, a lucrative city, but the entirety of China. He wanted to take advantage of the power of the Northern Expedition to swallow the entire country, but the biggest problem was that the CPC already had an armed force of thousands in Shanghai, the largest city. To him, it was rather troubling.

"I never fear men like Chen Duxiu, who only wields a pen. What is intimidating is Zhou Enlai and the workers and students, who are armed," Chiang Kai-shek once admitted to his henchmen.

Chiang Kai-shek had a system in dealing with revolutionary forces and

Revolutionaries

rivals. To suppress and disarm the workers in Shanghai, his series of actions were carried out secretly and vigorously.

First, 500,000 silver dollars was allocated to Yang Hu, Director of the Secret Service of the National Revolutionary Army Headquarters, to hire thugs and organize teams to prepare for the destruction of the Shanghai Federation of Labor Unions and the suppression of the labor movement. According to Chiang Kai-shek's instructions, Yang Hu, in addition to forming the Shanghai Commercial Federation against the Shanghai Federation of Trade Unions under the leadership of the CPC, resorted to a more toxic trick: founding the China Association for the Advancement of the People. Gang leaders Huang Jinrong, Du Yuesheng, and Zhang Xiaolin personally organized it, with Green Gang leader Pu Jinrong as the chairman and Red Gang leader Zhang Boqi as the military commander. The Green Gang and the Red Gang in Shanghai were rather powerful. By early April, the China Association for the Advancement of the People had grown to tens of thousands of members. In order to conceal their tracks, all members wore blue T-shirts and white armbands with the black Chinese character "Work." Workers and citizens mistook them as members of the Shanghai Federation of Labor Unions. These thugs, who pretended to be Labor Union members, also copied many of Shanghai Federation of Labor Union's logos with the help of their spies inside it. They were waiting for the opportunity to disarm the workers pickets at one fell swoop.

On the surface, Chiang Kai-shek threw an olive branch to the CPC, and specially sent someone to deliver a golden banner that wrote the words "Struggle Together" to the worker picketers, exhibiting his "respect" for the working class in Shanghai.

Perhaps it was precisely this window dressing that fooled Chen Duxiu, who, at the CPC Shanghai District Committee meeting on March 26, once accused him to be a new warlord and murderer of communists, published a Joint Declaration of Wang Jingwei and Chen Duxiu, with Wang Jingwei, a KMT leader in Wuhan, a week later on April 5. It said that: "The majority of CPC comrades, who understand CPC revolutionary theories and trust the KMT will never doubt Premier Sun's policy to cooperate with the CPC." Since Chiang Kai-shek's anti-revolutionary tricks had been exposed in places like Nanchang and Guangzhou, CPC members in Shanghai

1927, the Year Dyed Red by the Blood of Communists...

and other regions were worried about the situation, and various rumors were spreading. However, the joint declaration assured and guided the CPC comrades. "The resolution of the Plenary Meeting of the KMT's Supreme Party Headquarters has clarified to the world that there will never be any expulsion of CPC members nor persecution towards labor unions. The Shanghai military authorities expressed their obedience to the central government. Despite disagreements and misunderstandings, there are reasonable explanations." It called on the KMT and the CPC to halt mutual suspicions, accept no rumors, respect each other, and negotiate everything, and more.

Chiang Kai-shek, who rose to power by conspiracy, exceled at making the most of this opportunity. He believed that the time had come to suppress the revolution, eliminate the CPC, and disarm the workers of Shanghai. Having colluded with imperialist powers in China, like Japan, the UK, and the US, his first move was to, in the name of KMT Central Supervisory Committee, submit a fake report of the CPC's betrayal, informing police stations or military police nearby to keep watch on over 200 dangerous CPC members, including Chen Duxiu, Tan Pingshan, Lin Zuhan, Bao Luoting, and others in various locations and restrain their actions. He also suggested, "Should there be any resistance or riot, execution must be performed, just in case."

Chiang Kai-shek, holding a butcher knife, kept pretending to be kind. Once a series of secret orders were delivered, he gave great publicity to his departure from Shanghai to Nanjing on April 9, creating an alibi for his "irrelevance" with everything that would happen in Shanghai.

On the way from Shanghai to Nanjing, proud of his plan, he couldn't hide his smug face.

Shanghai, without Chiang Kai-shek, was shrouded in a murderous aura. The two forces led by Bai Chongxi and Huang Jinrong quickly made the second move in accordance with his anti-revolutionary plan: arresting armed uprising leaders Zhou Enlai, Wang Shouhua, Luo Yinong, and Zhao Shiyan, among other important figures in the CPC.

His victory was built on disguise and a scam.

To lure Zhou Enlai, Si Lie, Commander of the Second Division of the Twenty-Sixth Army, was ordered to "invite" him to the division

Revolutionaries

headquarters to discuss certain affairs regarding weapon management of the Shanghai worker picketers. "Si Lie wrote to me, asking for a talk together, and I fell right into their trap," Zhou Enlai told the story some days later.

In this way, Zhou Enlai, who had been working in the Oriental Library since the uprising succeeded, hurried to the headquarters of the Second Division on Baoshan Road with several deputy commanders. However, Si Lie was merely giving idle chitchat without discussing anything. It was an obvious trap to lure Zhou Enlai for a house arrest. Zhou Enlai, who had always been gentle, became furious. He pushed over tables, vases, and cups to the ground, pointed at Si Lie, and reprimanded: "You are a traitor of Three People's Principles and Three Major Policies of Premier Sun. You suppressed and deceived workers, confiscating weapons they seized from the warlords. There is no good end for you."

Si Lie lowered his head, murmuring, "I was just following an order."

It was a secret order from Chiang Kai-shek. Si Lai played both good cop and bad cop to prevent Zhou Enlai from leaving. That night, the Central Committee of the CPC and the workers picketers were extremely worried.

In the next early morning, Zhou Enlai was rescued by underground CPC officers of the Second Division, escaping danger.

"Imbecile! What stupidity!" When Chiang Kai-shek heard the news, he abusively cursed Si Lie.

On April 11, 1927, 29-year-old Zhou Enlai escaped possible execution from his adversaries.

But that night, another 26-year-old leader of the armed uprising in Shanghai was not so lucky. He was Wang Shouhua, Chairman of the Shanghai Federation of Labor Unions and member of the Standing Committee of the Shanghai District Committee of the CPC.

In that armed uprising, in addition to the organization and selection of people for the Federation of Labor Unions and worker picketers, he was also in charge of the liaison and coordination with KMT members, bourgeoisie representatives, and gang leaders. Since Wang Shouhua was one of the CPC members in charge with extensive influence among Shanghai workers, Chiang Kai-shek met him on March 27, requiring him to have the labor union follow the command of the military authorities,

1927, the Year Dyed Red by the Blood of Communists...

which Wang categorically declined.

"I want him gone." Before leaving Nanjing, Chiang Kai-shek gave a secret order to Huang Jinrong and other accomplices. It happened to be what the gang leaders wanted. They believed it would be a disaster for the gangs when the worker picketers took over Shanghai. Some of them who had long wanted to kill him together came up with a wicked scheme.

The office of Shanghai Federation of Labor Unions was located in the Huzhou Hall. There was proposal in the gang to smash it, but Yang Hu and Du Yuesheng rebuffed it. "Rather than make a fuss at Huzhou Hall, we might as well pretend to invite Chairman Wang to come discuss some matters. Lure this pain-in-the-ass into our trap."

Great plan!

So, on the afternoon of April 9, Wan Molin, the henchman of the Green Gang leader Du Yuesheng, came to Huzhou Hall with a sincere invitation to Wang Shouhua for a banquet. To go or not to go? There was disagreement among the heads of the Federation of Labor Unions and the Shanghai District Committee of the CPC.

"You can't go. Du Yuesheng has always been seemingly in agreement but actually at odds with us, an insidious snake." Li Zhenying, one year older than Wang Shouhua, strongly disapproved of going to this banquet where treachery clearly awaited. However, Wang Shouhua, who was in charge of the work related to gangs, shook his head after some consideration, and decided: "I used to deal with thugs of the Green Gang and the Red Gang. They abide by the code of brotherhood. If I go, we may come to some agreement. If I don't, they will see me as a coward."

Under that circumstances, the Shanghai District Committee of the CPC finally decided to have Li Zhenying, who had more military experience, accompany him. However, well aware that Du Yuesheng would never let Li Zhenying follow him into the Du Mansion, Wang requested Li before entering the tiger's den. "Two hours later I am not out, things must have gone south. Report it at once."

Wang blocked Li outside the spooky Du Mansion. At 8 p.m. in the evening, he swaggered inside.

"Chairman Wang is here!" Wang Shouhua walked through the spacious courtyard of Du Mansion. In the brilliantly illuminated lobby, Du Yuesheng

Revolutionaries

announced politely. But immediately he changed his tone. "We have a suggestion. Chairman Wang, please have the worker picketers join our side." The "our side" was the newly established China Association for the Advancement of the People, as instructed by Chiang Kai-shek.

"Your side? The China Association for the Advancement of the People?" He sharpened his vigilance.

"Yes." Du Yuesheng confessed, concealing nothing in the answer or his facial expression.

"Want to steal the fruit of our victory?" Wang Shouhua solemnly interrogated him.

"Don't make it sound bad! After all, I know you are not from Shanghai. It is better that we natives manage this city," Du Yuesheng responded to the interrogation in the local dialect.

Wang Shouhua shot him a cold glimpse. "Mr. Du, never forget, the worker picketers are not a force with any gang in Shanghai, but a revolutionary team led by the CPC."

"Fuck the revolutionary team! I am going to eliminate all communists." Suddenly, behind Wang Shouhua, another leader of the gang, Zhang Xiaolin, could no longer bear it. Before Wang finished speaking, he shouted "Kill him!" At once, several thugs, who were ready to ambush him, jumped in, punching and kicking him to the ground unconscious. Next, Du Yuesheng and others stuffed the unconscious man into a car as planned and drove towards Fenglin Bridge.

It was a criminal night.

When the car arrived at the predetermined location, the thugs pushed Wang out of the car, stuffed him into a sack, and started digging a hole on the spot. At that moment, there was a sudden moan in the sack. He had regained consciousness.

"Shut up!" The thugs picked up their shovels and hit the sack repeatedly.

There were no more sounds from the sack. Then, they threw it into a deep pit and filled it with mud.

Wang Shouhua, a 26-year-old young communist and important leader of the three armed uprisings in Shanghai, was dead. This early CPC revolutionary, who was a classmate of Liu Shaoqi, Ren Bishi, and Xiao Jinguang, left his dear comrades-in-arms and Shanghai workers too soon.

1927, the Year Dyed Red by the Blood of Communists...

Before his death, he once declared. "Revolution is the pursuit of truth. We should try our best to follow the path we should take now. If we die along the path, there will be someone else to carry on."

As expected, on the second day after the workers could not find Wang Shouhua, Chiang Kai-shek sent the gangsters from the China Association for the Advancement of the People to attack the workers' picket line. Armed with knives and guns, they launched a surprise attack—and activated the Zhou Fengqi-led division of 26th Northern Expeditionary Army, on the excuse of internal dissension among workers, to perform the shocking April Twelfth Counter-revolutionary coup.

By far, the Chiang Kai-shek reactionary group completely showed their fangs, raising butcher knives to the communists and revolutionaries across the country. Hundreds of thousands of martyrs fell in a pool of blood.

Let's first take a look at Shanghai on April 12, 1927.

In the early morning, Zhou Enlai was escaping from the tiger's den to the "general headquarters"—the Oriental Library, where he used to direct the fight and work of the uprising team—on the way, accompanied by Huang Yifeng (a CPC member and Director of the Shanghai Railway Bureau after liberation), he passed by Luo Yinong's office near Dongsi Kazi Bridge on North Sichuan Road, only to discover that the library had been occupied by KMT troops and the workers picketers there disarmed.

"Where is Luo Yinong? Is he safe?" Zhou Enlai was deeply concerned about the safety of his comrades-in-arms. The next day, he learned that Luo had escaped with the help of workers.

With Luo Yinong, the "culprit" of the CPC's armed uprising, still walking as a free man, Chiang Kai-shek soon offered a bounty of 50,000 silver dollars in Shanghai for his capture. Luo Yinong, who had a foreign accent, had to leave the city as instructed by the Central Committee of the CPC.

Early in the morning, Zhao Shiyan personally saw him off at the dock. Two young communists who had fought side by side for years shook hands affectionately, saying goodbye and encouraging each other.

Luo Yinong next attended the Fifth National Congress of the CPC in Hankou, and was later transferred to serve as Secretary of the Hubei Provincial Party Committee of the CPC. In early November, he secretly returned to Shanghai, attended the Provisional Politburo meeting of the Central Committee of the CPC, where he was elected as a Member of the Politburo Standing Committee. On New Year's Day in 1928, this man, who had just turned 26, held his wedding ceremony with Ms. Li Zheshi at the seat of the Central Organization Bureau. Qu Qiubai, Yang Zhihua, Zhou Enlai, Deng Yingchao, Li Fuchun, and Cai Chang attended the event.

However, the newlywed, who set off immediately to prepare for the Sixth National Congress of the CPC in Moscow, was sold out by He Jiaxing and his wife, who had already betrayed the revolution, and was arrested when he came to the British concession to meet with the comrades of the Shandong Provincial Committee of the CPC on the morning of April 15, 1928, merely four months after his wedding.

The next day, various newspapers in Shanghai covered the news of his arrest, as a "communist criminal." The report summary said that with the prime criminal captured, the CPC would soon be extinguished, showing how smug the enemies were about the capture. The Central Committee of the CPC was deeply worried and ordered Zhou Enlai to rescue him. However, the reactionary authorities paid special heed to the arrest. Chiang Kai-shek, to avoid any accidents, ordered the Songhu Garrison Command to execute him at once.

On the evening of April 21, a group of reactionary military police murdered Luo Yinong, member of the Standing Committee of the Provisional Politburo of the Central Committee of the CPC and one of the leaders of the Shanghai armed uprising, at the Longhua Execution Ground.

"Zheshi, farewell. My spirit will be with you forever. I hope you learn what I have learned. I shall rest in peace... Victory will be ours at last!" This was his last note from prison to his wife.

His newlywed wife was anxiously waiting for her man to return home, but he never came. Instead, the news of his arrest quickly spread in the newspapers. Li Zheshi was worried about her husband all the time, but meanwhile she had to change her residence every day, because the enemies were also hunting down the families of communists like her everywhere.

On the morning of April 22, Gu Shunzhang appeared in front of her and whispered: "Go to Longhua, there is a wire hanging over a road at

1927, the Year Dyed Red by the Blood of Communists...

the intersection. There are four square iron sheets on it that read "Wenzhi University." Check the notice on the telegraph pole on the right side of the intersection."

The following is her recollection of the miserable experience of "identifying the deceased":

I got on a rickshaw right away and found the telegraph pole on the right at the intersection of Wenzhi University. When I looked up, the notice read: "By the order of commander-in-chief Chiang Kai-shek, communist criminal Luo Yinong was executed immediately. Songhu Garrison Commander Qian Dajun." It was stamped with an official seal and date and time. I froze there for a long time. It turned out my husband was murdered yesterday. I had to find the execution ground and his body. I hope this is just a nightmare.

I dragged my heavy legs into the road where Wenzhi University is located. In the drizzle, I discovered a small pasture on the right side of the road with a pool of blood in the middle. I quickly approached it for a closer look. On the grass next to the pool of blood, there was a paper sign pasted on a bamboo pole, which read "communist criminal Luo Yinong", and a neatly folded handkerchief. My eyes darkened, my legs softened, and I fainted. Someone pulled me up. I noticed a few pedestrians around. My right hand was inside the pool of blood. I took off my black cheongsam, picked up the sign and handkerchief, rolled it up together with the clothes, and asked the pedestrians whether they know where the body was moved.

A man led me forward. There was a loess grave in front of a bush on the right side of the road. He told me it was there and left. I saw a bunch of green grass on the grave, a new grave. Is my husband in the grave, I asked myself. There was no sign around it. Could it be that the charity hall buried him in a seaport coffin out of good heart? I believed I should go back to report it first before making any discovery. I took the same rickshaw back to the hotel to look for Gu Shunzhang, but he was gone. So I had to return to the Shanghai Academy of Fine Arts. I was overwhelmed with grief, but I couldn't wail.

On the morning of April 23, Zhou Enlai sent Yang Qinglan, who was working at the Central Secretariat, to inform me that the Shanghai Academy of Fine Arts was dangerous and I should immediately move to Wang Yizhi's place. When he came to visit me at Wang's place, I made some requests to

Revolutionaries

the central government, first to give me a pistol to kill the traitor who sold my husband; second, to check whether he was buried, if he was buried hastily, a proper burial should be arranged; third, to send me to Moscow to study revolutionary theory. Zhou Enlai consoled me that he trusted my determination, but I never knew how to use a pistol, so I mustn't do it myself. The organization would take care of the traitors. He told me to consider the other requests done, that he would conveyed them to the central government. Within a few days, Yang Zhihua came and took me to her place to live. She told me that Qu Qiubai had gone to Moscow to prepare for the Sixth National Congress of the CPC and she happened to have time to keep me company for a few days.

Not long after I moved to her place, about the beginning of May, the Central Committee sent a comrade (I never asked his name), who had arranged the coffin and clothes. He brought four workers, and asked to lead me to the road of Longhua Wenzhi University. We found the new loess grave. I checked again for signs around it, but there was still nothing. So, I signaled the workers to dig. They took out the seaport coffin, opened the cover and the surrounding wooden boards. It was the body of my man.

The body was decaying, the face swollen and deformed, and there was a big hole on his head. The brains spilled onto the pillow made of a light red woolen vest, full of maggots. The body, in a dark grey robe, was tied with a thick rope; the right leg was bent, and I bought the elastic band on his socks. I asked the workers to untie the rope, carry his body into the newly transported coffin, and put in lime. There was no way to put on him newly bought clothes, so we closed the coffin after we covered the body with them. The body reeked, unbearable for the workers if they did not close it soon. Next, we carried his coffin to the pre-arranged coffin spot in the Anhui Hall. The comrades sent by the Central Committee explained to me that we had to pretend to he was a native of Anhui so that the coffin could stay there. Dizzy, I never saw what was written on a small wooden board nailed between the head of the coffin...

After liberation, it was not until the party organization went through some trouble that Luo Yinong's coffin was recovered. According to Comrade Li Qiang, an agent in the Central Secret Service, after Luo's demise, it was an underground party organization that collected his corpse, buried it in the wasteland, and put up a little monument. Subsequently, it was Li Qiang and others who secretly transported it to Shanghai Jiangwan Public Cemetery and buried it together with Su Zhaozheng (a famous worker leader and one of the early leaders of the CPC. He died of illness in Shanghai in 1929 at the age of 44) and Zhang Xiyuan (martyr, Deng Xiaoping's first wife, who died in 1929 at the age of 24). At that time, to hide the real names of the martyrs, the graves were inscribed *Grave of Yao Weichang and Bi Jue* and *Grave of Zhang Zhoushi.*

Twelve years after his sacrifice, in the International Children's Home in Ivanovo, the Soviet Union, a teacher pointed to a photo on the wall and explained to a teenage Chinese boy: "This is your father, Luo Yinong. He was an important leader of the CPC." Then she looked at him again, and concluded, "You are the spitting image of him."

This Chinese boy is Luo Xibei. That was the first time he saw how his father looked. Before that, he only knew that his father was a hero. From birth, the child was sent to his mother's hometown of Jiangjin (formerly in Sichuan Province, now in the Chongqing Municipality) to live with his grandmother. It was not until he was sent to the Soviet Union that he learned about his father's past.

Meanwhile, there was another child named Zhao Shige studying in the Soviet Union. One day his teacher led him to a wall, pointed to a photo that read "Zhao Shiyan" and said: "This is your father. He was one of the CPC founders. He used to lead the labor movement in Shanghai. The reactionaries arrested and murdered him."

Zhao Shige was 13 years old at the time. When his mother Xia Zhixu gave birth to him, his father had already died, so in fact he was a posthumous child.

His father Zhao Shiyan was arrested on July 2, 1927, a stormy day. According to the address provided by the traitors, KMT detectives broke into the secret residence of Zhao Shiyan at 190 Zhi'anfang, North Sichuan Road. His pregnant wife and mother-in-law were there that day. With enemies ambushing the house, the women were extremely anxious. At this moment, the mother-in-law saw from the window that Zhao Shiyan, who had returned from work, was walking towards home. She desperately raced to the window and pushed down a pot of flowers to warn him. However, heavy rain prevented him from noticing the secret signal. He kept running towards the house.

Zhao Shiyan did a work-study in France in 1920. In February 1921, he received a letter from Chen Duxiu, requiring him to form a communist group in Europe at once with Zhou Enlai and others. The Paris Group, including him, Zhou Enlai, Chen Gongpei, Zhang Shenfu, and Liu Qingyang, was one of the eight communist groups when the CPC was founded. Early in the morning of the April 12 coup, Zhao Shiyan heard gunshots from home, and was certain that something went wrong. He immediately raced to the Shanghai Federation of Labor Unions in the Huzhou Hall. On the way, the fleeing worker picketer informed him that the headquarters of the Federation had been occupied by the enemies. He immediately bypassed their sight, came to a contact point near the picket station and met with Guo Bohe, secretary of the Zhabei District Committee of the CPC. In response to the rapidly changing situation, they decided to launch an emergency strike to protest against the KMT's atrocities of repression.

On April 13, Zhao Shiyan and Zhou Enlai held a workers' denouncement meeting on Qingyun Road in the Zhabei District, regardless of the danger. Tens of thousands of people marched to the headquarters of the Second Division of the 26th Army to petition and protest, demanding immediate release of the arrested workers and return of workers picketers' weapons. The frantic KMT army had been well prepared for that. They fired at the protesters. It was a rainy day. The moment bullets were fired, blood flowed into a stream on Baoshan Road.

The situation soon deteriorated. All the activities of the CPC had to go underground. Leaders such as Zhao Shiyan were faced with extremely harsh challenges, being likely get arrested and shot to death at any moment. However, as one of the CPC founders, he remained fearless and continued to work relentlessly. He said at the district committee: "The CPC is a party that fights. Without it, there is no party. We must fight as long as the party exists. Inevitably, we have to face death along the way. This is what we revolutionary communists have signed up for. To build a new China, to give a bright future for our children, there is nothing we cannot give up."

Young as he was, Zhao Shiyan was an experienced revolutionary fighter. There are many legendary stories about him. For example, once on his way to attend a meeting, he noticed a spy stalking him, and he could not get rid of him. As he was anxious for a solution, a young man who was dressed exactly like himself walked towards him. When the young man approached him, he whispered: "Hide in the restaurant over there. I will deal with the spy." It was not until then that he discovered that it was Xia Zhixu (a female comrade) from the district committee that came to cover for him. Though having dodged the danger, he didn't understand why she came to his rescue. Xia Zhixu, who later married him, confessed that she often heard Li Dazhao sing his praises, thus had a favorable impression about him and she volunteered to cover him.

"Ha-ha...you are too kind!" They fell in love and married as a revolutionary couple.

However, soon after they got married, he was arrested at home. At first, his true identity was not exposed, but he was found to possess over 30,000 silver dollars, a considerable amount.

The adversaries brutally tortured him but obtained nothing. He was also betrayed by a traitor. The 30,000 silver dollars was the party's property. Zhao's family were safekeeping it without touching a penny. When his identity was exposed, they laughed at him for being an honest man. Zhao Shiyan responded to the money-greedy reactionaries: "You will never understand what the communists want!"

"What exactly?"

"What we want is the happy life for the working class and a beautiful country tomorrow."

"Foolish. How stupid!" The reactionaries burst into laughter. They naturally couldn't understand the lofty pursuits and ideals of the communists.

On July 19, 1927, 17 days after his imprisonment, the villains received an order of immediate execution from Chiang Kai-shek, who had just learned Zhao's identity. After breakfast, he was summoned out of the cell. He was aware that the end was coming. He calmly tidied up his outfit, buttoned up, and strode as if going to a banquet. Once out of the cell, he raised his arms, shouting, "Long live the CPC!" and "Down with the reactionary warlord Chiang Kai-shek!", among other slogans.

The executioners were agitated and screamed: "Behead him! Now!"

Revolutionaries

Zhao Shiyan, a hero and son of the party, died. His blood dyed the ground red.

Another 26-year-old loyal revolutionary died in Shanghai.

1927 was a particularly memorable year in the history of the Chinese revolution. That year Chiang Kai-shek betrayed the revolution and brutally suppressed and massacred Chinese communists and the masses. Within three days after the April 12 tragedy, statistics show over 300 people were killed, over 500 arrested, and over 5,000 missing.

Ah, blood was flowing on the street.

Huangpu River and Suzhou River turned red, extending to the horizon and merged with the setting sun.

In Shanghai,

In Nanjing,

In Wuhan,

In Beijing,

In Guangzhou...

Blood flew into a stream, the blood of the revolutionaries, of the communists, of Li Dazhao...

CHAPTER FIVE

―――

The Higher the Position, the Greater the Risk of Death —No Regrets

PEOPLE OF TODAY, WHEN CRITICIZING HISTORY, OFTEN PRETEND to be smart and experienced, talking foolish, and out of historical context. It is childish and ignorant.

After the April Twelfth Counter-revolutionary Coup, the Central Committee of the CPC sent Li Lisan, Chen Yannian, and Nie Rongzhen to Shanghai, obviously after key considerations: Li Lisan was one of the outstanding leaders of the Chinese labor movement and Shanghai was the place with the most workers, who were the principal force in armed uprisings and needed his leadership at critical moments; Chen Yannian, an outstanding leader in Guangdong Province, the heart of the National Revolution, and son of Chen Duxiu, had fought side by side with Zhou Enlai. During the most difficult times of the revolution, Chen Duxiu sent his boy to work in the harshest environment. The situation was of great urgency; Nie Rongzhen came also because of the needs of military struggle and armed uprising. As the representative of the Comintern and primary liaison for the formation of the CPC, Grigori Voitinsky was also sent to Shanghai, obviously to offer guidance.

As per the *Resolution of the Central Committee on the Work in Shanghai*,

Revolutionaries

a special committee composed of Li Lisan, Chen Yannian, Zhao Shiyan, Zhou Enlai, and Voitinsky was established in the city to lead the work there.

Shanghai was a paramount base camp in the early days of the CPC. After the founding of the CPC in 1921, two prefectural party committees were first set up, one in Shanghai and the other in Beijing. Li Dazhao was in charge of Beijing and Chen Duxiu Shanghai. Qu Qiubai, Li Lisan, and Deng Zhongxia all served as leaders of the Shanghai Prefectural Party Committee. The scope of work in Shanghai was not only the city proper, but also Jiangsu Province, Zhejiang Province, and Anhui Province. Revolution in Jiangsu and Zhejiang always revolved around Shanghai, thus a considerable number of Jiangsu-Zhejiang natives were among the early leaders of the CPC. We mentioned before a large number of outstanding revolutionaries from the Zhejiang Provincial First Normal School, who later grew into the backbone and leaders of the party organization in Shanghai. Certainly, Jiangsu also had three outstanding men from Changzhou, Zhang Tailei, Yun Daiying and Qu Qiubai, who have inspired many youths in Jiangsu and Shanghai to embark on the revolutionary road. This kind of revolutionary phenomenon where one man inspired an entire zone has occurred in Hunan, Guangdong, Beijing, Shandong, and Hubei. It was unique in the history of the Chinese revolution.

Li Lisan, Chen Yannian, Nie Rongzhen, and Grigori Voitinsky came to Shanghai because on the one hand the central government paid great heed to the work in the city, and on the other a major adjustment was made to leadership composition there. In the early history of the CPC, this kind of major adjustment happened as the revolutionary situation changed. Sometimes, the frequency of occurrence was as high as once in one or two months or less in a region. It was both what the revolution needed and the result of lacking leadership at that time. Complex and cruel revolutionary practices tested the abilities of every revolutionary at all times. What I particularly admire is that the vast majority of communists never complained about the party's decisions but obeyed unconditionally. Many comrades, who had been the core leaders of the party a year before, might become merely a person in charge of the most basic party organizations the following year. Deng Zhongxia, Yun Daiying and others have shared this experience.

The Higher the Position, the Greater the Risk of Death—No Regrets

Let's take a look at Chen Yannian:

The 28-year-old CPC leader in the Shanghai region had previously succeeded Zhou Enlai as Secretary of the Guangdong District Party Committee.

In Guangdong, his inability to speak Cantonese at the beginning made it difficult for him to get close to workers and farmers. So, he worked diligently to master the dialect and actively devoted himself to them. He was often seen pulling a rickshaw with the drivers. At that time, in order to disparage the communists, the *Hong Kong Business Daily* ran news about it, ridiculing this communist cadre as rickshaw boy. When he learned about it, he was not angry, but delighted. He told the revolutionary comrades around him that it was never a shame for communists to do that job, but an honor, because it was the party of the working class. There was nothing wrong with it.

He quickly opened up a new prospect. In less than two years, the number of party members increased from a few hundred to over 5,000, which was solid proof to his capability.

When the May Thirtieth Movement broke out in Shanghai, the Canton-Hong Kong strike in Guangdong to administer moral support for Shanghai lasted 16 months. It was a glorious chapter in the Chinese labor movement and even the international one. And this was the fruit of the leadership of Chen Yannian and other revolutionaries.

Chen Yannian and his younger brother Chen Qiaonian, in the short two decades of their lives, had hardly benefited from their father's great reputation. On the contrary, they were challenged with endless hardship and peril.

They had both were born and grown up in their hometown, Anqing, Anhui Province. It was not until his father returned from Japan in 1915 that the family moved to Shanghai and lived in a small brick-wood building at 21 Jiyili, Songshan Road, in the French Concession. At that time, their life was a struggle. His wife, Gao Junman, was seriously ill. He had to attend to two teenage boys. Most importantly, Chen Duxiu was ambitious. He was busy running a magazine, but there was often insufficient funding. Despite help from friends, life for his family was still difficult. That year, *New Youth*, which he edited, came out, bringing infinite light to the Chinese revolution.

Revolutionaries

But for his family, Chen Yannian had to take his younger brother to school while working part-time to make ends meet and cover tuition. They used to starve and had to take care of their sick mother. Regardless, Chen Yannian managed to read all kinds of new books and periodicals eagerly, including his father's *New Youth*. Chen Duxiu was paternalistically domineering at home. The boys feared him and disliked him a tad, but they admired his articles. For example, Chen Yannian was excited by the inaugural statement of *New Youth*:

Youth, like the early spring, like the morning sun, like the budding flowers, like the new blade, is the most precious period of life.

With great interest in the French language, Chen Yannian became good at it. So, after the May Fourth Movement, when work-study programs in France quickly swept across China, he told his father about his inclination to join them. Chen Duxiu nodded immediately. "Great. I am supportive of this decision." Chen Duxiu, who was helping a group of young cadres pursue advanced studies in Europe, also showed support for his son. And when he proposed to take the younger brother along, Chen Duxiu pondered and approved it. "It's better. Go together, return together, take care of each other. Better than staying with me."

So, at the beginning of 1920, the two boys joined the team to study in France and became members of the revolutionary youth, including Cai Hesen, Zhao Shiyan, Zhou Enlai, and others.

In 1922, Chen Yannian, together with Zhou Enlai and Zhao Shiyan, founded the Communist Party of the Youth of China in Europe among the work-study students in Europe. That fall, he was introduced to join the Communist Party of France by Ho Chi Minh (called Nguyễn Ái Quốc at the time), a member of the Communist Party of France and then-leader of the Communist Party of Vietnam. Soon, the CPC officially accepted the members of the communist group in Europe and the comrades who joined the Communist Party of France as CPC members, and formed the European Branch of the CPC, of which Chen Yannian was a leading member. His younger brother Chen Qiaonian was also a member of Communist Party of the Youth of China. In 1923, as instructed by the Central Committee of the CPC, 12 young Chinese Party members were transferred from France to the Soviet Union, where they would study Marxism and the experience

The Higher the Position, the Greater the Risk of Death—No Regrets

of the Russian Revolution at the Communist University of the Toilers of the East in Moscow. By this time, Chen Yannian and Chen Qiaonian had grown to be two of the best.

In the summer of 1924, Chen Yannian returned to the motherland half a year earlier than his younger brother. After half a month stay in Shanghai, he was assigned to Guangdong and began his revolutionary practice.

On April 15, 1927, he secretly returned to Shanghai. Less than three months later, he was killed in Longhua by KMT reactionaries on July 4. As one of newly sent leaders of the Shanghai CPC, every day he saw his comrades-in-arms and compatriots butchered one by one, group by group by the reactionaries.

However, his arrest and demise still came too suddenly, too tragically.

From April 16 to 18, Shanghai established a Secret Service Committee headed by Li Lisan. In May, Zhou Enlai, Luo Yinong, and others left Shanghai for Wuhan to attend the Fifth National Congress of the CPC. Chen Yannian, who remained in Shanghai, had been dealing with the KMT's reactionary forces' frantic massacre of communists and revolutionaries in Shanghai. Original party organizations and labor unions were either killed or suffered loss of contact; offices and rendezvous points of the central government and party organizations were destroyed; the remaining places were in danger all the time. As the primary person in charge of the Shanghai CPC, he had to handle various emergencies on a daily basis while connecting the disconnected party members and organizations. The complexity and dangers of this kind of task were self-evident. Once he discovered several party organizations together on one street, which was perilous, he set out to prepare a relocation at once. It was an arduous task for him, a foreigner in the city. The slightest carelessness might expose them to the enemies.

The day had finally come:

On the morning of June 26, 1927, according to the new instructions of the Central Committee of the CPC, he was appointed Secretary of the Jiangsu Provincial Party Committee. Wang Ruofei (his classmate in France, who died in a plane crash in 1946) sent by the central government announced the appointment. At 104 Hengfengli, Shigaota Road (now 90 Hengfengli, Shanyin Road), the meeting was held, where the CPC learned that the traffic man, who used to deliver messages to the provincial party committee, had been arrested. Wang Ruofei was vigilant. After a quick speech, he ended the meeting.

At around 3:00 p.m., Chen Yannian, the newly appointed provincial party committee secretary, deeply concerned about the security of the provincial party committee, returned to Hengfengli with other committee officials, including Guo Bohe, Huang Jingxi, Han Buxian, and others. They first inspected the surrounding outside. It was all quiet. They therefore entered the two-story building of the provincial party committee at 90 and started discussing and analyzing work. But within half an hour, a group of reactionary military police came and besieged them. "Hurry, jump out of the window!" To cover the escape of other comrades, Chen Yannian used tables and chairs as a weapon against the enemies who broke in. In the end, outnumbered, he was arrested.

Chen Duxiu's son was arrested. This was shocking news for both the CPC and the KMT. Both the CPC and Chen Duxiu's friends were trying to rescue him, but Chiang Kai-shek's made exacting terms: Chen Yannian was required to quit the party and Chen Duxiu to surrender, which the father and son would never agree to.

On July 6, Chen Yannian was secretly murdered at the Fenglin Bridge in Shanghai, at the age of 29.

Guo Bohe and Huang Jingxi, members of the Standing Committee of the Jiangsu Provincial Committee of the CPC, were arrested and died together. Secretary-General Han Buxian chose betrayal. We have introduced Guo Bohe before. Huang Jingxi, two years older than Chen Yannian, was a revolutionary from Jiangdu, Jiangsu. He used to be businessman, joined the KMT in his early years and joined the CPC after being introduced by Yun Daiying and Liu Chongmin. In 1925, during the cooperation period between the KMT and the CPC, after he was elected as Executive Committee member of the KMT Jiangsu Provincial Party Department, Luo Yinong transferred him to Shanghai. Prior to the third armed uprising, regardless of the danger of reactionary military police slaughtering pedestrians on the streets, he disguised himself as a businessman, accompanied by his wife, who pretended to a wealthy lady, driving a car or taking a rickshaw to transport weapons and ammunition, thus his title of "captain underground transportation" among comrades.

The Higher the Position, the Greater the Risk of Death—No Regrets

At the beginning of April 1927, he followed Hou Shaoqiu to Nanjing at tremendous risk to engage in underground work. Before the April 10 tragedy, Hou Shaoqiu entrusted him back to Shanghai to report on the situation in Nanjing to the party organization. When he returned to Shanghai, the April 12 massacre was taking place. As instructed by the party, he replaced Hou Shaoqiu, who had sacrificed his life, to preside over the operation of the reorganized KMT Jiangsu Provincial Party Headquarters. Those were bloody days. He took his wife and children to live with Chen Yannian's family, forming close friendships. With common ideals and as comrades on the same side, they were arrested and killed on the same day.

According to the military police, when they made the arrest of Chen Yannian, Guo Bohe, and Huang Jingxi, the three men fought them for more than an hour until they were exhausted, severely injured. In prison, despite temptation and cruel torture, Wang Jingxi's revolutionary beliefs were never shaken. On the evening of June 29, he wrote a last note to his beloved wife, mother, and comrades in a filthy and dim cell. "I firmly believe my upcoming death is worthwhile. It awakens people to understand that revolution is necessary for China. I die a happy man, especially when I die for the revolution. Comrades, keep moving forward and never be discouraged."

The three martyrs Chen Yannian, Guo Bohe, and Huang Jingxi died heroically. This is the nature of a true revolutionary.

In less than a year, Chen Yannian's younger brother also sacrificed his life heroically a few days after he became the leader of the Jiangsu Provincial Party Committee of the CPC. Those were dark days for the CPC.

Chen Qiaonian was four years younger than his brother. When he moved to Shanghai at the age of 13, Chen Duxiu homeschooled him. But then he followed his brother to France and the Soviet Union. Until he returned to China, Chen Duxiu hardly managed his education. Certainly, as the general secretary, Chen Duxiu dedicated most of his energy to the cause of the party. It was an era of complexity and changes. There was an imbalance between the weak political party and the powerful Chen Duxiu, which resulted in the criticism and attacks at him from inside and outside, which almost suffocated him. Before the start of the Northern Expedition,

Revolutionaries

he and Li Dazhao repeatedly discussed cooperation with the KMT, led by Sun Yat-sen.

However, Sun Yat-sen abruptly passed away while Chiang Kai-shek, ambitious to the bone, who opposed the CPC, usurped the power; Chen Duxiu assumed that he could use Wang Jingwei's power to counterbalance Chiang Kai-shek, but soon Wang Jingwei betrayed the revolution, leaving him helpless; when he wanted to look for power against KMT, he received wide criticism from comrades in the party. After the April 10 tragedy in Nanjing and the April Twelfth Counter-revolutionary coup in Shanghai, his residence in Shanghai and the organs of the Central Committee of were utterly destroyed by Chiang Kai-shek. Moreover, the central authorities that had just moved to Wuhan was sold overnight by Wang Jingwei.

This was not the most fatal. The deadly blow was that the members of the CPC suddenly became targets to be slaughtered by of both old and new warlords. The brutality and reports of casualties left Chen Duxiu sleepless and in tears. At this moment, his eldest son Chen Yannian also appeared on the long list of deceased CPC mainstays. In addition, what devastated him most was the loss of Li Dazhao, who co-founded the party with him. Li Dazhao was arrested on April 6, 1927, and murdered on April 28 by Manchurian warlord Zhang Zuolin, who was in collusion with the imperialists. There were another 19 revolutionaries hanged in Beijing with him.

"The reactionaries may hang me, but they can never kill the greatness of communism.

Communism will prevail in China!" This was his indignant statement before the execution.

Chen Duxiu and Li Dazhao were comrades-in-arms fighting side by side on the road to communism. When the second son Chen Qiaonian returned to China, the Central Committee of the CPC appointed him to the party organization in Beijing, which Dazhao led, as the organization minister. He was only 23 years old at the time.

Young as he was, he was competent and outstanding and became Li Dazhao's right-hand man. At the Fifth National Congress of the CPC in 1927, the young man was elected as a member of the Central Committee, serving as the Deputy Minister of the Organization Department of the

The Higher the Position, the Greater the Risk of Death—No Regrets

Central Committee of the CPC to lead its daily operation, substituting for Minister Li Weihan.

On August 7, 1927, the Politburo of the Central Committee of the CPC convened a particularly important meeting regarding the prevailing situation and that within the party, criticizing and correcting Chen Duxiu's right-leaning mistakes. He was removed from the party's leading position while a new interim Politburo was re-elected with Qu Qiubai as the head. At the meeting, Mao Zedong proposed the important revolutionary inference that great heed must be paid to military affairs in the future, and that the awareness that political power is seized through armed struggles must be built. As a representative of the younger generation of the CPC, Chen Qiaonian ruthlessly criticized his father's mistakes at this meeting.

Since the preparation to found the CPC in Shanghai in early 1920, Chen Duxiu was the leader and key man of the CPC; after the August 7 meeting, his influence within the party gradually diminished. Subsequently, his second son, Chen Qiaonian, was sent to Shanghai as the Minister of Organization Department of the Jiangsu Provincial Party Committee.

When he came to Shanghai to take office, the Secretary of the Jiangsu Provincial Party Committee was Deng Zhongxia. Before Wang Ruofei became the Secretary, four different people had been in the position. The first Secretary, Chen Yannian, was arrested shortly after taking office and killed by the foes a week later. Zhao Shiyan took over the job at once, but within a week, former Secretary-General of the Jiangsu Provincial Party Committee, Han Buxian, who was captured together with Chen Yannian, sold out Zhao Shiyan. Zhao Shiyan was murdered 17 days later.

In Shanghai, the Jiangsu Provincial Party Committee, whose scope of work extended beyond Shanghai and surrounding areas to Nanjing, the nest of Chiang Kai-shek, had always been the paramount local organization of the Central Committee of the CPC. Therefore, the work there was quite essential. After Zhao Shiyan's demise, Wang Ruofei served as acting secretary.

In August 1927, Deng Zhongxia served as Secretary of the Jiangsu Provincial Party Committee, and Wang Ruofei, Xiang Ying, Chen Qiaonian, and Liu Bojian as members of the Standing Committee.

In January 1928, when Deng Zhongxia was transferred to Guangdong

Revolutionaries

Province as Secretary, Xiang Ying took over the baton from him as acting Secretary of the Jiangsu Provincial Party Committee, with Chen Qiaonian as Minister of the Organization Department, Wang Ruofei as Minister of the Propaganda Department, and Li Fuchun as Minister of Military Affairs.

As the new Minister of the Organization Department, Chen Qiaonian, against the extreme difficulty of the semi-nonfunctioning Provincial Party Committee, dealt with adversaries ingeniously, despite personal danger. He was at the forefront of the struggle, making secret contacts and restoring the organization, so that the Jiangsu Provincial Party Committee organs and party organizations under their jurisdiction were enabled to resume work. Unfortunately, on February 16, 1928, when he was secretly presiding over a ministerial meeting of various district committees at the Embroidery Girls' School on North Chengdu Road in the concession, they were besieged by enemies, because the traitors leaked the information. Chen Qiaonian and several cadres were arrested. Once again, the committee suffered a heavy blow.

Chen Qiaonian was escorted to the Shanghai Longhua KMT Songhu Garrison Headquarters Detention Center the following day. None of the arrested managed to walk out of there. He was brutally tortured and coaxed to surrender, but nothing worked on him.

One night in early June 1928, a horrible gunshot sounded by Shanghai Fenglin Bridge. This time it was Chen Qiaonian, a 26-year-old member of the Central Committee of the CPC and Minister of the Organization Department of Jiangsu Provincial Party Committee, that enemies' bullets pierced through. Along with him, there were two other martyrs shot to death: Zheng Fuhe (sacrificed his life at 24, from Zhuji, Zhejiang, former chairman of the Shanghai Federation of Labor Union committee), Xu Baihao (sacrificed his life at 29, representative of the Second and Fifth National Congresses of the CPC, former Central Supervisory Committee member, and famous labor movement leader).

Chen Duxiu was strict with his two sons to an incredible degree. He did not allow them an easy life, but forced them to be independent. As a result, the two brothers lived entirely on their part-time jobs. They often starved. His wife couldn't bear to see them suffer and wanted to take them home.

The Higher the Position, the Greater the Risk of Death—No Regrets

He stifled the idea, scolding: "This is woman's soft nature. Although kind, it may lead to negative results. You have to allow the teenage boys to spread their wings on their own."

But as a parent, a father must love his sons, especially when his two sons were also important revolutionary comrades. Chen Duxiu was devastated by their death.

After they died, Chen Duxiu, who was nearly 50, often wept in silence.

Around 1927, especially in those days after the Chiang Kai-shek reactionary group created the April 10 tragedy and the April Twelfth Counter-revolutionary coup, the central organs suffered multiple devastating blows. The Jiangsu Provincial Party Committee in Shanghai suffered the worst destruction among the provincial and district-level party organizations across the country at that time. The overlap of the Jiangsu Provincial Party Committee and the central party organizations and cadres made it almost the prime target of frantic attacks by anti-revolutionary forces. The enemies understood that to completely destroy the CPC, the Jiangsu Provincial Party Committee must be eliminated first.

Sometime after the April 10 tragedy and the April Twelfth Counter-revolutionary coup, the Chiang Kai-shek reactionary group took action to kill communists and revolutionaries. When arrested, as long as one was proved related to the CPC and the revolution, they were murdered. The Chiang Kai-shek side would rather kill them all than to let one escape.

Liu Bojian was a student who studied in France on a work-study program in 1920, and during which he embarked on the road of revolution. When he returned to China in 1926, he was sent to the Northwest Army of the KMT as Director of the General Political Department. After the failure of the Great Revolution, he accepted the CPC's arrangement to the Jiangsu Provincial Party Committee, under the alias Wang Danian, where he served as Minister of Propaganda. Soon, Li Fuchun took over his position while he went to study in the Soviet Union. He returned to China in 1930. Next, he served as Secretary-General of the Chinese Revolutionary Military Commission and Executive Member of the Soviet Republic of China government successively. In 1931, he led and commanded the Ningdu Uprising as Director of the Political Department of the Red Army. When

Revolutionaries

the Red Army marched north to resist Japanese aggression, he and Chen Yi stayed in the base in southern Jiangxi. Unfortunately, he was captured and killed on March 21, 1935.

Marshal Nie Rongzhen had such an impression of him: "Comrade Bojian was a senior party member and famous revolutionary from the work-study period in France."

"We studied, worked, and engaged in the labor movement together in France and Belgium; then we studied together in the Soviet Union; in 1926 when he returned to China, we fought side by side in the Central Soviet Area, our friendship growing stronger. Of the many poems I have read, I keep a fading memory of most. Only his *A Walk in Fetters* has always been fresh in my head. It has been constant encouragement to me."

Liu Bojian wrote the poem *A Walk in Fetters* in prison, which marshal Nie particularly admired. When he was arrested on March 4, 1935, enemies paraded this wounded man, but in the face of torture and humiliation, he held his head high and stood upright, exhibiting the indestructible faith of communists and revolutionary soldiers. That day, he wrote the poem titled *A Walk in Fetters*:

> *Paraded through the street in fetters*
> *I faltered and faltered.*
> *Citizens lined up for a gaze*
> *That would never shame me*
>
> *Paraded through the street in fetters*
> *They clanged and clanged.*
> *Citizens all looked surprised*
> *I was instead at peace.*
>
> *Paraded through the street in fetters*
> *Dignified appearance I was making*
> *Imprisoned as about to be*
> *Yet worth it for the workers and peasants' liberation*

The Higher the Position, the Greater the Risk of Death—No Regrets

The episode of *A Walk in Fetters* in the popular grand musical and dancing epic *The East is Red* was based on his poem.

The History Museum of the Chinese Revolution collected a letter he wrote from prison to the sister-in-law of his wife Wang Shuzhen. Liu Bojian and Wang Shuzhen were married in Shanghai in 1927. Subsequently, due to busy revolutionary tasks, they seldom spent time together. He never expected that she would sacrifice her life earlier than him in the guerrilla zone in western Fujian. Unaware of the tragedy, he wrote to her sister-in-law with concern for his wife and children from prison:

I am still alive but detained in the First Army Headquarters of the Dayu Cantonese Army. What will happen next is unclear. Regardless, I am ready to die for the cause. I live for my country of China, and will die for it, too. No regrets.

I live for my country of China, and will die for it, too. What a magnificent oath!

His wife never got to see his last note, but she was fighting against the enemy in a rain of bullets. Well-aware of the danger, she forced herself to give her third son Liu Xiongsheng, who was less than four months old, for adoption to a local family surnamed Huang.

After they got married, they raised three sons, the eldest Liu Husheng, the second Liu Baosheng and the third Liu Xiongsheng. Before they left for the Central Soviet Area, the couple first entrusted their eldest son to their sister-in-law. Thereafter, the boy never saw his real parents again and was forbade by his aunt since childhood to have any contact with other children nor talk to others about his family (to avoid being kidnapped by the enemies). In 1938, the party organization located him and sent him to Yan'an. It was not until then that he handed over the two family letters (sewn in a close-fitting garment) that his father had sent to his aunt from prison to Comrade Zhou Enlai, who cherished them greatly and kept them by his side until the founding of the PRC.

Liu Bojian had his second son fostered by an old lady surnamed Guo during a battle before he was taken captive. Because his troops were

Revolutionaries

marching in a hurry, he put the boy in a bamboo basket. With the soldiers, he went over the mountains and into the bamboo forests, taking turns carrying the basket. When they came to a river, he gave the bamboo basket cradling the child to an old lady surnamed Guo, who was waiting for them. He said to her: "If I die, my son will be your grandson." She was a local boat owner. To protect the child, she changed his name to Zou Fensheng. It was not until after the founding of PRC that the party organization found him based on the letter that was written by the father from prison and kept by Comrade Zhou Enlai. That year, Liu Baosheng was 14 years old.

Concerned about the future of his three children, Liu Bojian wrote to his relatives at the last moment of his life, exhorting two things:

1. I am sure you would feel devastated and attempt to rescue me when you received my previous letter. I need neither of those from you. You must not go to Mr. Yu nor brother Deng Baoshan to come to my rescue. Although we three are close friends, they took care of my wife in Shanghai while I was abroad and who urged me not to make risky moves in the revolution, they would never understand my struggle for the survival and liberation of the Chinese nation. When we met in Shanghai, Deng expressed sympathy for me, saying it was not time yet to do what I was doing. I am willing to take risks to save China while suffering personal harm. Never bother them to rescue me, to help me. It would put them in an awkward position. I shall bear it myself. In particular, keep the trivia of my imprisonment a secret in the north and make sure Mr. Ma'er never finds out (referring to Feng Yuxiang, noted by the author) This will do me no good, but infinitely insult me and deprive me of my revolutionary personality. This is paramount. Keep it in mind. (the more people know it, the worse).

2. Xiongsheng has been entrusted to a Hu family in Huangyin, Zhi Creek, Xinquan County, Fujian one month after his birth; Baosheng was fostered this year on a merchant boat travelling between Ruijin, Huichang, Yudu, and Ganzhou. There is a man named Luo Gao from Ji'an, in his twenties, who was born in a family of tailors. He took care of Baosheng. The boat is owned by Lai Hongda from Wuyang, Ruijin. He is a little more than 50 years old and has been on the boat for decades. He is honest and known to most of the

The Higher the Position, the Greater the Risk of Death—No Regrets

merchants in Ganzhou. His wife is called Guo Jiangu, his son Lai Lianzhang (I don't remember exactly), and his daughter-in-law named Liang Zhaodi (Zhaodi meaning "may a son is born"). They adore Baosheng, so I trust them to raise him. I am poor, so I only covered a few months of his living expenses, which is yet still enough time for you to find them within this year and pay future expenses so that he doesn't starve.

I have dedicated myself to the Chinese revolution, thus there is not a penny to my name. I am sorry for the trouble I have caused you, raising three children of mine. I heard that my home in Sichuan was searched and all the money confiscated. Everyone died there. It's been eight years since I last contacted them. I am fully devoted to the Chinese nation, thus no love to spare for my family or anyone. Please try to understand and don't reprimand me for leading a poor life.

After high school when they turn 18, send the children to work in factories. Before full independence, persuade them not to get married. It's never too late to do that in their thirties, so that they don't burden themselves with parenting tasks early.

Reading the family letter of martyr Liu Bojian, in which his three boys were orphaned, brought me to tears, tears of sympathy and of respect for the noble qualities of this revolutionary.

From June 1927 to early January 1935, during which the Jiangsu Provincial Party Committee of the CPC was ordered by the Shanghai Central Bureau to terminate all activities, it underwent seven or eight destructive losses. In the process, several cadres, who were all elites in the early days of the CPC, sacrificed their lives.

Today, we can only, with reverence, look up to these stars glimmering in the sky.

Luo Dengxian, former secretary of the Jiangsu Provincial Party Committee and member of the Provisional Politburo of the Central Committee, was also a member of the Politburo of the Sixth National Congress of the CPC. He was merely 28 years old when he died.

In Shanghai Longhua and Nanjing Yuhuatai Revolutionary Martyrs Memorial Halls, there are photos of Luo Dengxian: short hair, thin face,

Revolutionaries

big ears, sharp eyes, a typical image of a proud worker. He was a native of the South China Sea. In the early years, he was employed at the Taikoo Shipyard in Hong Kong. He was a CPC member developed by Deng Zhongxia, Chen Yannian, and Zhou Enlai from workers in Guangdong and also a warrior who charged to the front during the Guangdong-Hong Kong strike. In 1927, he grew into a worker leader of the Guangzhou Uprising. Red Guards of Workers under his direct leadership played the dual role of an invincible army and a sharp knife to the heart of enemies in that uprising.

In 1928, the central government transferred him from Guangdong to Shanghai, where served as Secretary of the Jiangsu Provincial Party Committee for eight months, one of the longest among all of its Secretaries after 1927. Next, he was transferred back to Guangdong Province by the Central Committee to serve as Secretary. After the September Eighteenth Incident, the CPC appointed him to the Northeast as the representative of the provincial party Committee in Manchuria.

Two years later, Luo Dengxian returned to Shanghai again and served as Secretary of the Shanghai Executive Bureau of the All-China Federation of Labor Unions. In March 1933, a traitor sold him out as he was attending the National Seamen's Conference in Shanghai. He was imprisoned. When his identity as a CPC high-ranking official was exposed, he was immediately escorted from Shanghai to Nanjing. Trying to coax out information failed on him, so torture was imposed: breaking his legs and whipping his genitals. Soong Ching-Ling went to visit him in prison in spite of the threat from the KMT, and made attempts to rescue him. Chiang Kai-shek was afraid that a long delay may result in trouble, so he secretly ordered him to be executed at once.

On August 29, 1928, he was escorted to the Yuhuatai execution ground. The executioner asked about his last words. He sneered and said: "My personal death is nothing to be regretted. The unliberated Chinese people and the unfinished duties will be."

Luo Dengxian, a leader of the labor movement and outstanding revolutionary military strategist, was merely 28 years old when he died.

Next, allow me to tell the story of Xu Baoye, another Secretary of the Jiangsu Provincial Party Committee.

When he was transferred from the position of Secretary of the Xiamen

Municipal Party Committee to Shanghai as Secretary of Jiangsu Provincial Party Committee, he created the alias Bao'er in order to prevent the enemy from destroying it again.

Xu Baoye, born in Thailand in 1900, was first named Xu Jinhai, probably because his parents wanted him to become a wealthy businessman among the expatriates. But his father, who esteemed traditional Chinese culture, moved the entire family back to his hometown of Chenghai, Guangdong Province when he was seven. He was enrolled in a private school from childhood, and later in the Chenghai Middle School, which offered modern education.

In 1919, after high school graduation, he experienced the May Fourth Movement and understood the meaning of national salvation. That year, hearing that Principal Cai Yuanpei of Peking University was organizing the recruitment of students to study abroad in France, he was washed over by waves of excitement. Right away, he signed up and changed his name to Xu Baoye, which means ambitious and aspiring.

In the exam in Shantou, the young man from Chenghai ranked third, thus qualified as a publicly-funded student to study abroad in France.

In France, he met a group of talents in the early stage of the Chinese revolution, such as Zhou Enlai, Cai Hesen, Xiang Jingyu, Chen Yi, Li Fuchun, Deng Xiaoping, and others. They shaped the thoughts of this young man from Chenghai, who used to believe in science and industry to save the country. At that time, the doctrines of Marxism and communism were sweeping Europe, especially among progressive students studying in France. As a student of philosophy and law, Xu Baoye it was more convenient to study *The Communist Manifesto* and *State and Revolution* in depth than common people.

In 1922, when Zhou Enlai and others established the Communist Party of the Youth of China in Paris, Xu had already transferred from the University of Lyon to the August University in Göttingen, Germany, to continue his study of philosophy and military science. Among the revolutionary ranks, he was one who had studied abroad for the longest time (11 years), obtained the highest diploma (dual-degree PhD), and the best mastery of foreign languages (able to speak English, German, French, Russian, and Spanish). On October 10, 1923, he met a Chinese student

Revolutionaries

who was a military officer with a steady manner named Zhu De. He took Zhu De to be a trustworthy big brother. Under his introduction, Xu joined the CPC. Zhu De himself was the person in charge of the party branch of those studying in Europe. It was Zhou Enlai who secretly introduced him to join the CPC—his public identity was as an executive member of the KMT branch in Germany.

Next, Xu Baoye joined other progressive overseas students such as Zhu De to perform revolutionary activities, which displeased the German government. In early 1925, Zhu De left for the Soviet Union and Xu Baoye was deported by the German government. He went to Vienna to continue his PhD studies. The following year, after he obtained a dual-degree PhD in philosophy and law, and he was dispatched to Moscow to teach the Chinese classes in both the Communist University of the Toilers of the East in Moscow and Moscow Sun Yat-sen University, which specialized in training revolutionaries while he served as a Moscow magistrate.

After the September Eighteenth Incident in 1931, he returned to China at the request of the Communist International. In this way, after 11 years abroad, with two PhDs in philosophy and law and teaching qualifications at both Communist University of the Toilers of the East in Moscow and Moscow Sun Yat-sen University, this red professor secretly reunited with his motherland.

To conceal his revolutionary identity, he made a special detour back to Chenghai to reunite with his family. When he finally saw his son, who had grown to as tall as his shoulder, and his wife Ye Yanping, who had been caring for the elders and managing the home, he fell into a whirlpool of emotions.

After only half-a-month stay at home, the party organization sent him to Xiamen to form an underground party organization.

To stay inconspicuous, he took off his suit and disguised himself as a sailor, first arriving in Singapore by ship and then transferring to Xiamen. What he didn't expect in the trip to Xiamen was that the party comrades who received him doubted his identity owing to the grim situation in Xiamen. In desperation, he suggested: "I heard that Xu Zezao, my second younger brother is working here. He can testify for me."

The Higher the Position, the Greater the Risk of Death—No Regrets

"This person you speak of seems to be comrade Xu Yihua. He used to work in the Provincial Party committee, but now he has been transferred to Xiamen as our Propaganda Minister."

"Call him!" It had been 11 years since he had seen his younger brother. He missed him dearly.

"Bro! It's really you! My man. How I have missed you." After a short while, a young and energetic man appeared, took a big stride forward and embraced Xu Baoye.

He was Xu Yihua, a CPC member, Xu Baoye's second younger brother, who he called Xu Zezao.

It was a touching moment that the two brothers, both CPC members, reunited in a strange land after 11 years.

However, despite his dispatch to Xiamen by the Central Committee of the CPC, the Xiamen party organization had to contact the Central Committee of the Soviet Area to verify his identity as Secretary of the Municipal Party Committee. It was a long and complicated process, because Chiang Kai-shek was sparing no effort to exterminate communists in Jiangxi, which made the situation in the Soviet area extremely critical. In addition, Longyan in Fujian was also a key target for exterminating communists. The underground communication between Xiamen and the Soviet area was rather unstable, so for half a year he could only work as an assistant there.

When his identity was officially confirmed, he at once devoted himself to party building and the armed struggle against the enemies in Xiamen to make up for the lost time. His competence had been fully utilized during his employment as Secretary of the Xiamen Central Municipal Committee of the CPC. In the two years before he was ordered to leave the city in June 1934, he not only restored the Xiamen party organization during the white terror, but also developed 17 branches in the city with over 150 party members. The number of party members in over 10 counties and cities in Southern Fujian, which Xiamen Central Municipal Committee was affiliated to, had grown to nearly 1,000. It was this force that powered the armed struggle in Xiamen and southern Fujian, thus effectively cooperating with the struggle in the central revolutionary base in the Soviet area.

Revolutionaries

Next, he came to Shanghai. The revolutionary situation was far harsher than he expected.

As Secretary of Jiangsu Provincial Party Committee, he could only meet with one party comrade at a time as a considerable number of traitors had penetrated almost every key organization and liaison line of the Central Bureau of the CPC and Jiangsu Provincial Party Committee. The was the so-called cellular tactic that the KMT authorities implemented at that time.

The tactic was effective, causing serious damage to the party organization. Any CPC suspect that the KMT secret service noticed would be arrested and detained. Secret agents would coerce and bribe them to betray the CPC. Under severe torture and special coaxing, many with a weak will became traitors and became the enemy's weapons in the cellular tactic against the CPC. They were ordered to directly search for the surviving organizational personnel, or to return to the organization, pretending to continue the revolution, like cancer cells injected inside the body. These "cancer cells" did great harm and destruction to the party organizations, endangering the lives of comrades, because the traitors were disguised as more Marxist than the true revolutionaries; since underground parties generally made single-line contacts, some traitors pretended to be some secretary newly appointed by the central government or a superior authority, fooling both subordinates and leaders. The slightest carelessness could have the party organization completely destroyed.

It was under this circumstance that Xu Baoye was appointed Secretary of the Jiangsu Provincial Party Committee. The Central Committee specially appointed Yang Guanghua, former Secretary-General of Jiangsu Provincial Party Committee, as his contact in Shanghai. Yang Guanghua, also known as Zicai and Zhou, a native of Hubei, joined the CPC in 1927 and offered assistance the formation of the Honghu Underground Party Organization. He once served as a party representative in the Workers and Peasants Revolutionary Army led by He Long and Secretary of the Interim Provincial Party Committee of the CPC in Western Hunan and Hubei. Later, he was transferred to the Shanghai Mutual Aid Association. In March 1934 he was appointed Secretary-General of Jiangsu Provincial

The Higher the Position, the Greater the Risk of Death—No Regrets

Committee of the CPC. The central government decided to send this man to assist Xu Baoye in rebuilding Jiangsu Provincial Party Committee for his firm revolutionary stand.

Yang Guanghua knew enemy activities in Shanghai better than Xu Baoye, a newcomer. He suggested that the new Jiangsu Provincial Party Committee leaders implement the plan that one person holds the information of only one location, meaning that Yang Guanghua only knew where the Propaganda Minister lived, the Propaganda Minister only knew where Secretary Xu lived, Secretary Xu only knew where the Organization Minister lived, and the Organization Minister only knew where Yang lived. But the enemies were cunning. Knowing that a new Secretary of the Jiangsu Provincial Party Committee of the CPC had come, they had traitors planted in the CPC to trap Yang Guanghua and Xu Baoye.

One day, a defector surnamed Gong suddenly visited Yang's residence, announcing himself as a member of the Shanghai Central Bureau of the CPC, who would like to meet the new Secretary of Jiangsu Provincial Party Committee to deliver messages from the Central Bureau. It was a trick to extract the information of Xu's residence location. Thanks to the implementation of the one person one location system, Yang had no idea where Xu Baoye lived. When this visitor left, he immediately contacted Gao Wenhua, a superior of the Shanghai Central Bureau of the CPC.

But Gao was not sure whether the visitor surnamed Gong was an authentic contact sent by the central government.

They could only keep a close contact and observation on him without making any hasty moves.

Another day, a stranger suddenly came to Yang's residence. After matching the secret signal with Yang, he hurried Yang. "I am with the secret service. Gao sent me to tell you to leave this place as soon as possible. Take nothing and leave with me, now!" Yang followed the agent. Soon, he met Gao, who then took him to a printing office in the French Concession. At this time, a worker-like man explained to Yang. "Gong is suspicious. Your residence has been exposed. When the Central Bureau ordered you to leave there, Gong suggested Xinjiang Hotel. And that exposed him. Central Secret Service had long known that the hotel was where enemies were

Revolutionaries

ambushing and arresting our underground party members. Ergo, although we can't judge whether Gong has turned against us yet, necessary measures must be taken."

At the time Secretary Xu Baoye was in danger every second, but he kept working in secret. With his rich experience and strict organizational discipline, he tried his best to minimize the loss in the unexpected event. This environment was testing him as well as all revolutionaries.

"The organization isolated Gong, but he managed to escape." One day Gao told Yang the news.

"Isn't this more dangerous?" Yang was vigilant.

"Therefore, we believe that he will soon contact the enemy so as to launch another attack on Secretary Xu. And judging from the intelligence we have, Secretary Xu has been exposed, except he was adroit enough to make himself untraceable. You must alert him of this situation as soon as possible. Make sure he acts cautiously."

Yang did as told.

One day, a man dressed up as a shop assistant showed up in front of Yang with an extremely nervous look. "Gao may be dangerous. Follow me to a new place right away."

Yang couldn't tell if he was true or false, so he followed the man.

When he arrived at a new address, Yang saw Gong. He was appalled, but maintained a calm posture. "What are you doing here? I heard that you are under protection, not allowed to go out." He deliberately continued the sarcasm, "Should something happen to an important comrade like you in the party, it will be a great loss."

Gong made a sour face. "True. It is difficult for me at the moment. I have also lost contact with the Central Bureau, without a place to live. Do you think you can arrange me a temporary stay at the Jiangsu Provincial Party Committee, so that I can figure out who is the contact with the Central Bureau?"

Busted! Yang's heart skipped a beat. He thought to himself, "He has betrayed us. He wants to use me to find the Jiangsu Provincial Party Committee, then the Secretary, and more."

What danger! Yang immediately came up the countermeasures. "I have also lost contact with the Central Bureau. Besides, something happened to

The Higher the Position, the Greater the Risk of Death—No Regrets

Gao. We are no longer living in the Provincial Party Committee. It is here today and there tomorrow. Well, it's time that I should go to the rendezvous point. Wait for me here, and when I have the new address, I will inform you right away."

With that said, Yang raised his leg to leave. "Wait," Gong dragged Yang's sleeve, "One moment. I will write you an address. Once you have the new address, find me at this place at once."

"Sure!" Yang was even more certain that Gong had completely betrayed them. How shameful!

The "red team" was to make a move. This was a special operation team that Zhou Enlai organized to eliminate traitors. It was affiliated to central Secret Service.

The action to eliminate Gong was more complicated than planned, because the support behind him was the KMT intelligence unit—the Central Bureau of Investigation and Statistics.

The "red team" acted. Yang first wrote a note to Gong. "The Central Bureau is looking for you. Please go to Qianji Hotel on Sima Road. Book a single room in the name of Xiong Guohua on September 15. Someone will come to you."

Gong was fidgeting as he read the note. Sly as always, he replied. "I am in a bad situation. I shall send someone else to meet with people from the Central Bureau."

Xu Baoye and others could tell Gong's fear and his eagerness to make the KMT proud. Therefore, they instructed Yang to write another note. "Leaders of the Central Bureau will not meet with anyone else. Go yourself or the meeting will be cancelled." Gong couldn't fight the argument. It had to be himself.

"OK, agreed!" The traitor finally took the bait!

Xu Baoye and others reported it to the "red team" promptly.

That night, two secret agents slipped into Qianji Hotel. The registration book disclosed that Xiong Guohua was in room 34 on the second floor. They snuck upstairs and were invited inside once Gong correctly confirmed their contact password. Immediately, bullets were fired and the hotel was in total chaos.

The agents took the opportunity to vanish into the night.

Revolutionaries

Xu Baoye and the "red team" jumped to the conclusion that their mission was successful too soon. Unexpectedly, Gong, who took three bullets, escaped death and survived. The Central Bureau of Investigation and Statistics arranged him to be admitted to Renji Hospital for treatment, where police were deployed to guard his safety.

What next? This defector has already held the information regarding Secretary of the Shanghai Central Bureau of the CPC, Secretary Xu Baoye, and the basic situation of Jiangsu Provincial Party Committee. Once the badly injured Gong regained consciousness, he would definitely cause irreparable loss to the Central Bureau and the Jiangsu provincial party committee.

The situation was pressing. A new plan must be drawn to eliminate him at once.

What plan? "We storm him." Xu personally sorted out the plan with the person in charge of the "red team."

Around 3 p.m. on September 26, visiting hours at Renji Hospital were open. Four "red team" members disguised as family of the patient, holding flowers, went straight to the closed ward.

"Hey, visiting card first." The guards stopped them.

"Sure. Here they are." Two pistols were aimed at the guards' chest. Instantly, they raised their hands in fright.

Simultaneously, other "red team" members cut off the telephone line in the hospital, and raced straight to Gong's ward.

"You...?" Before Gong could react, the noise of gunshots filled the ward.

Gong died on the spot. Mission succeeded. By the time a legion of police and plainclothes spies arrived in the hospital ward, "red team" members were long gone.

The killing of Xiong Guohua stirred up a sensation in Shanghai for a while. It hit the arrogant KMT reactionaries hard.

Secretary Bao'er was therefore relatively safe for the time being. The Jiangsu Provincial Party Committee of the CPC, which had suffered repeated destruction, resumed operations.

Xu Baoye, alias Bao'er, spent three thrilling and tense months in Shanghai as Secretary of the Jiangsu Provincial Party Committee. In

The Higher the Position, the Greater the Risk of Death—No Regrets

September 1934, due to the arrest of the Secretary of the Xinyang County Party Committee, the underground party in Henan Province was basically unable to perform any activities. When the Central Committee learned about the stagnation, Xu Baoye was appointed to be the new Henan Provincial Party Committee Secretary.

This time he used Liu as another alias. However, during this trip to central China, he failed to escape enemy's radar. When he met with the head of a local party organization, he was sold out by a native traitor, and arrested in the rendezvous hotel.

His identity was totally exposed. The enemies imposed the harshest torture on him in an attempt to extract the core intelligence of the Central Committee of the CPC. Ten bamboo sticks were inserted into his fingernails one by one.

He never gave them a word of information until he was tortured to death. He died of severe injuries in a cell at the age of 35.

Ye Yanping, his wife far away in their hometown, never knew where her husband was! Even after the founding of the PRC, she still hadn't found out about his whereabouts. No one knew who Xu Baoye was. Comrades who had worked in Provincial Party Committee only knew a secretary named Bao'er, who was not there long and only made single-line contact, and that it was an alias. As a result, nobody knew Xu Baoye after the founding of the PRC. Ye Yanping, from her hometown in Chenghai, waited for him all her life, from a young lass to a seriously ill old lady in 1982. It was not until her dying days that she asked to look for her husband. The local government and party organizations was startled by her request. As a result, finding her husband became a major task for party organizations in several provinces and cities.

In 1985, it was finally confirmed that Xu Baoye was Bao'er. Guangdong Province officially confirmed him as a revolutionary martyr and held a grand memorial. However, the woman who had been waiting for her husband for 52 years failed to attend. A few months later, she passed away and was reunited with her man after half a century.

His name is also listed in the Shanghai Longhua Martyrs Memorial Hall and Nanjing Yuhuatai Martyrs Memorial Hall to be forever remembered.

There were more like him, whose names were rarely known after

Revolutionaries

their heroic sacrifices for the revolution. Soon after he left Shanghai to take the position as Secretary of the Henan Provincial Party Committee, the new Jiangsu Provincial Party Committee, which was rebuilt less than three months before, was destroyed again. Its Secretary, Minister of Organization, and Minister of Propaganda were arrested altogether. Thereafter, its activities came to be fully suspended.

The Zhejiang Provincial Party Committee had a similar fate to the Jiangsu Provincial Party Committee. The two provincial committees were united into one Jiangsu and Zhejiang District Committee. After their separation in June 1927, all key leaders of the Zhejiang Provincial Party Committee were sent to Hangzhou from the Shanghai Central Bureau.

As adjacent cities, many of the early Marxists active in Shanghai came from Hangzhou.

After the April Twelfth Counter-revolutionary coup in 1927, the revolution in Zhejiang faced an extremely complex and urgent situation. From April to July, KMT reactionaries arrested over 400 communists and revolutionaries in Ningbo and Hangzhou alone, and killed 117 people. By the end of 1927, in Zhejiang a total of 1,805 people were arrested and 932 killed. However, the white terror never intimidated the Zhejiang communists. Under the leadership of the Central Committee of the CPC in Shanghai, they continued to fight resolutely against KMT reactionaries. However, the fighting environment at that time was extremely dangerous, especially during the period from June 1927 to April 1929, 10 Provincial Party Secretaries and Acting Secretaries were successively replaced, of whom eight died. Their average age was less than 30, the youngest 21, the oldest 36. Since they all died young, later generations hardly know most of their names. For example, Wang Jiamo was the youngest of the nine Provincial Party Secretaries, only 21 years old when he died. After his demise, his corpse was transported back to his hometown in Xiangshan, near the city of Ningbo by his mother herself, and buried in the foothills of Dakeng, outside the west gate of Dancheng.

Zhang Qiuren, another Secretary of the Zhejiang Provincial Party Committee, was a senior communist. This good comrade, considered capable by Mao Zedong, good at propaganda, and popular among the masses came from Zhuji in Zhejiang Province. He was born in a peasant

The Higher the Position, the Greater the Risk of Death—No Regrets

family in 1898 and came to Shanghai as early as 1920, where he got acquainted with Chen Duxiu, Li Dazhao, Yun Daiying, and others, and soon became one of the earliest members of the CPC. In 1926, he left for Guangzhou to replace Shen Yanbing as Editor-in-chief of *Political Weekly*. At that time, he resided in the same building with Mao Zedong and Yang Kaihui, and they formed a profound revolutionary friendship. He not only gave lectures at the Guangzhou Peasant Movement Workshop that were hosted by Mao Zedong, but also served as a political instructor at the Whampoa Military Academy. He, Yun Daiying and Xiao Chunü were also regarded as the "Three Outstanding Men of Guangzhou." They were influential young revolutionaries back then.

On March 17, 1927, KMT rightists began the purge in Guangzhou, massacring communists and revolutionaries. Whampoa Military Academy put CPC member Zhang Qiuren on the wanted list. Having received instructions from the CPC, he left Guangzhou promptly, first for Wuhan, and then, with the central authorities, back to Shanghai, where he worked in the Propaganda Department of the Central Committee of the CPC with Deng Zhongxia and others.

In September 1927, the central government decided to send him to Hangzhou as Secretary of the Zhejiang Provincial Party Committee. He had just married Xu Jingping, a female member of the Communist Youth League, at the time in Shanghai, but he never hesitated about the mission. Right away, he took his newly-wed wife to Hangzhou. Before leaving, he, who had a full estimate of the situation, said to those around him: "I believe my end awaits in Hangzhou. But to complete the task of rebuilding the Zhejiang Provincial Party Committee, I must go!"

On the first day in Hangzhou, Wang Ruofei announced the decision within the Zhejiang Provincial Party Committee on behalf of the central government. The next day, a formal meeting was convened to announce the establishment of a new Provincial Party Committee headed by Zhang Qiuren.

The third day was his first time to work outside the office since he became Secretary of Zhejiang Provincial Party Committee. For better cover, he deliberately wore a suit and came with his wife to the West Lake, ready to meet with party comrades. However, he noticed two stalkers,

Revolutionaries

whom he couldn't get rid of. He had no alternative but to stop. As the stalkers approached, he recognized them as two reactionary students from the Whampoa Military Academy who knew him.

"This is bad." He whispered to his wife, trying to lose the stalkers, but the two reactionary students of Whampoa Military Academy shamelessly prevented him from leaving.

"What do you want?" He was agitated.

"Mr. Zhang, relax. We just want to invite you to give a speech!" They showed no sign of letting him go. With rich experience in fighting against the enemy, he had a premonition of upcoming trouble.

"We must get rid of them!" He quickly blinked to his wife, and spoke in English: "We are in danger. Stay calm. Don't panic. Take the pillowcase and leave, now!" Next, he made an unexpected move. He kicked off his shoes, took off the suit, and jumped into the West Lake next to him.

"Hey!" The two men stood at the lakeside in total panic, not sure what to do. It turned out they couldn't swim, and Zhang Qiuren knew about it since Whampoa Military Academy.

He stayed underwater for a long time–during which he took care of an extremely important matter: he buried a list of Zhejiang organizations and party members hidden in his undergarments in the mud at the bottom of the lake.

"Hurry! Get the boat here!" The two reactionary students called in plainclothes secret agents lurking near the West Lake and borrowed a boat. Together, they fished him out of the water, tied him with hemp rope, and paddled to the lakeside.

The wife managed to escape while the enemies were panicking. She swiftly returned to Huaxing Hotel, where they were staying, packed up key documents, and left the danger zone.

Zhang Qiuren was detained in Zhejiang Military Prison and quickly sentenced to death. At that time, a young cellmate discovered that the man on death penalty kept learning every day. Out of curiosity, he asked: "As someone about to die, why are you still learning?"

Zhang Qiuren replied, smiling. "Communists live every single second for the party. I cannot engage in a revolution here in prison, so I must study every day. I can't sit idle, can I?"

The Higher the Position, the Greater the Risk of Death—No Regrets

These words inspired the young man, who then swore an oath to follow his example. He persisted in studying in prison for three and a half years and became a well-known economist in China. He was the famous Xue Muqiao.

On February 8, 1928, before execution, the prison authority wanted to verify his identity. When asked about his name, he struck the table and rose up. "Fucking Zhang Qiuren!" Next, he leapt a few steps forward, grabbed the inkstone on the table, and cast it at the judge. It was total chaos. The executioner pushed him out of the door and promptly killed him. He was only 30 years old when he died.

There were multiple Zhejiang Provincial Party Committee secretaries, just like him, who had been performing underground party activity in Shanghai for a long time, then were sent to Zhejiang and died heroically.

Today, at the entrance of the Zhejiang Revolutionary Martyrs Memorial Hall in Yunju Mountain in Hangzhou is a giant slab of granite engraved with the striking last words of the revolutionary martyr Qiu Guhuai: "Comrades, when victory falls, please don't forget us!"

Frankly, how can we ever forget their honorable names?

However, in the cruel years of struggle, many of our dedicated party members died with their names unknown. Even where they were killed has never been found.

As I have mentioned above, less than half a year since Bao'er left Jiangsu Provincial Party Committee, all three principal leaders of the new Jiangsu Provincial Party Committee were arrested, leaving it suspended for years.

I am aware that in Shanghai Longhua Martyrs Memorial Hall and Nanjing Yuhuatai Martyrs Memorial Hall, there are still quite a considerable number of heroes whose names are rarely known to the public.

They are the unsung heroes who sacrificed their lives for the revolution.

CHAPTER SIX

—

Intrigues, Defectors, Wrong Routes: the Reign of Terror

I WROTE THE LAST CHAPTER WITH A LEADEN HEART BECAUSE OF THE massive deaths of the CPC members in Jiangsu Province and Zhejiang Province, including the two outstanding boys of Chen Duxiu. They were all so young. It was unbearable to look back.

They should have survived. They died heroically, but mostly too suddenly and a little bafflingly. At unimaginable moments, they were gone in ways that were inconceivable. It never should have happened.

While grieving, I intend to figure out what caused their deaths. It was the rain of bullets that killed heroes at war. There is no question about why they died. The battlefield itself is a matter of life and death. However, in the underground work shrouded in white terror, they became revolutionary martyrs for only two reasons: intrigues of the enemy and betrayal of comrades. And as the CPC grew stronger, there was another explanation for their tragedy: the wrong routes.

The blood of revolutionaries who died because of them flowed in streams.

I find it difficult to suppress the grief within.

After the April 10 incident and the April Twelfth Counter-revolutionary Coup in 1927, the KMT reactionary group headed by Chiang Kai-shek, in an attempt to strangle and shatter their will of the revolutionary struggle, implemented the policy of "better kill all the communists and revolutionaries than have one slip away." However, they failed. Chinese communists never lost their revolutionary determination. Instead, they acted swiftly, launching armed uprisings in cities and villages throughout the country. In the manner of quid pro quo, they fought a life-and-death struggle with the KMT reactionary group. Over 100 armed uprisings and riots, such as the Nanchang Uprising, the Autumn Harvest Uprising, and the Guangzhou Uprising rained down on the enemy's burning arrogance.

Faced with endless revolutionary attacks, some KMT masterminds like Chen Lifu proposed Chiang Kai-shek one trick: to coax some communists to betray the CPC. Soon, they issued the so-called "Law of Communists Turning Themselves In." Upon its release, there were immediately voices calling it a major threat to the CPC. Some with a weak mind and little faith in revolution wavered. Consequently, some arrested communists were coaxed and shamelessly became traitors to the revolution. Some even took the initiative to surrender. Therefore, when we read biographies of the revolutionary martyrs, we will inevitably notice that many of them were arrested and killed because traitors betrayed the revolution. Repeatedly, I have heard party historians conclude that behind every martyr always stood a traitor.

And the fact is behind a group of revolutionary martyrs stood one traitor, meaning one traitor alone could have a group of revolutionaries killed.

From Chen Yannian, who was appointed Secretary of Jiangsu Provincial Party Committee in June 1927, to successor Bao'er (Xu Baoye), over 20 party secretaries were killed. All their deaths were ascribed to the same traitors, who sold them out. For example, the most central figures in the organization, like Kong Er, the Provincial Party Secretary, Xu Xigen, Minister of Organization, and Han Buxian, Secretary General, surrendered to betrayal. The consequences were easy to picture.

One traitor alone from the provincial party committee was enough to destroy the entire organization, and then to pose a threat to organizations of the entire region.

And a traitor in the highest organizations of the CPC would cause even greater damage. From 1921 to 1933 from the founding of the CPC,

Intrigues, Defectors, Wrong Routes: the Reign of Terror

Shanghai was basically where the highest organizations and leaders of the CPC were located. Under the white terror, all the CPC's work was done secretly underground. However, right in the heart of the party, there was Gu Shunzhang, an alternate member of the Politburo and leader of intelligence, who defected to the enemies.

Gu Shunzhang was known as the most threatening traitor in the history of the CPC.

In 1931, the Gu Shunzhang Incident occurred—

In April that year, Gu Shunzhang, an alternate member of the Politburo of the Central Committee of the CPC and person in charge of the Central Secret Service, escorted Zhang Guotao and Chen Changhao, who were then persons in charge of the Central Committee of the CPC, to Wuhan. With a wealth of experience in the secret front, Gu accomplished the task perfectly. They arrived safe and sound. Zhang Guotao recalled it as "an absolutely safe trip."

However, Gu Shunzhang made a mistake. Allegedly, he lingered on the streets of Wuhan for a hooker. For a while, he was broke and went on stage to perform magic tricks in Hankou People's Theme Park under the pseudonym Hua Guangqi. Unexpectedly, a traitor in the audience recognized him, and reported it to the head of the KMT Party Affairs Investigation in Wuhan.

On the evening of April 24, he was captured.

Soon after his arrest, he defected, but he made a condition to his captor, the Wuhan agent Cai Mengjian, that he would only talk to Chiang Kai-shek, or give them nothing. The reason why he demanded that was first to get full immunity from Chiang Kai-shek and second to prevent information leakage during the process. He knew the presence of an undercover CPC member at the KMT secret service headquarters in Nanjing, the legendary Qian Zhuangfei (an early CPC member, Zhou Enlai personally had him infiltrate the Central Bureau of Investigation and Statistics as a confidential secretary to its leader Xu Enzeng. He died in 1935).

The story about Gu Shunzhang's betrayal has been told in many films, TV series, and novels. It is truly thrilling:

Cai Mengjian, the Chief of the Wuhan secret service who captured

Revolutionaries

him, disregarded his repeated requests that no telegram be sent to Nanjing in order to take more credit. Instead, he promptly sent six consecutive telegrams to Nanjing.

It was April 25, a weekend. Six top-secret telegrams sent from Wuhan to Central Bureau of Investigation and Statistics Secret Service Headquarter, which hung the plaque that read Zhengyuan Industrial Co., at 305 Nanjing Zhongyang Road, eventually fell into the hands of Qian Zhuangfei, secretary of Xu Enzeng, Head of Central Bureau of Investigation and Statistics Secret Service.

Here is a brief introduction to Qian Zhuangfei. He was a native of Huzhou, Zhejiang, and a medical student. He married classmate Zhang Zhenhua after graduating from Beijing Medical School in 1919. Both of them joined the CPC and were directly under the leadership of Li Dazhao. After the Northern Bureau of the CPC was totally destroyed in 1927, Qian's family moved to Shanghai. The party organization arranged for him to enter the newly established intelligence unit directly led by Zhou Enlai— the Central Secret Service, which consisted of four departments: General Affairs, Information, Operations, and Transportation. Chen Geng, Li Kenong, Li Qiang, and Gu Shunzhang were respectively their early heads. Qian Zhuangfei and Hu Di, who he befriended in Beijing (a martyr who died in 1935, and former director of the Scouting Department of Protection Bureau in the Soviet Area) joined Central Secret Service together. Qian was admitted to the KMT Shanghai Radio Training Course with flying colors. For his extraordinary talent, Xu Enzeng, Head of the Secret Service thought highly of him and invited him to be his secretary. After the establishment of the Central Bureau of Investigation and Statistics, Qian followed Xu to Nanjing. Next, he made use of his position to obtain a lot of information about the plan to wipe out communists, thus providing highly valuable intelligence support for the CPC army's fight against the atrocity.

Next, allow me to describe one shocking event that happened on the night of April 25. When the confidentiality officer who sent the telegram left, Qian immediately started to crack the six top secret telegrams. "We captured Dawn. He surrendered. Should Beijing be quickly crippled, all central organs of the CPC can be wiped out in three days."

Damn! He was trembling as he picked up the decoded telegram. He

176

Intrigues, Defectors, Wrong Routes: the Reign of Terror

knew Dawn was Gu Shunzhang. The man has defected. It was not impossible for all the central organs of the CPC to be wiped out within three days. The betrayal of an alternate member of the Politburo of the Central Committee who was in charge of Secret Service was a fatal blow to both the central organs and the leaders of the CPC in Shanghai.

Against everything, Qian sent an emergency warning to the Central Committee of the CPC in Shanghai via a confidential telegraph. Then, he rang the bell to summon in his son-in-law Liu Qifu, who was also undercover at the Secret Service headquarters, and sent him to Shanghai overnight to report the urgent news to Li Kenong and Zhou Enlai.

After breakfast on April 26, Xu Enzeng, head of the Central Bureau of Investigation and Statistics Secret Service, came to the office, exhausted. Qian calmly placed a pile of documents and telegrams on Xu's desk, and left the Secret Service headquarters on the excuse of taking a rest.

At that time, the anxious Qian Zhuangfei was not sure whether his son-in-law had found the leader of the Central Secret Service in Shanghai, nor whether the central government had received his emergency warning. As he contemplated, he decided, regardless of danger, to go himself to Shanghai at once, because he had learned that Gu Shunzhang would be escorted to Nanjing by secret agents from Wuhan on the afternoon of the 27th.

In fact, both his message and his son-in-law reached Zhou Enlai and Li Kenong in time, who were in charge of intelligence work.

In Shanghai on the 26th and 27th, thrilling battles were fought on the inconspicuous streets, piers, and stations quietly. And every minute counted.

At about 3 p.m. on the 27th, the vehicle that escorted Gu Shunzhang pulled in at 305 Zhongyang Road, Nanjing.

"This is your organization?" Gu Shunzhang, gazing around the house plate, asked in surprise. Then, he stomped his feet and shouted: "I'll be damned. Qian Zhuangfei of the CPC has infiltrated you all this time."

"What? Qian Zhuangfei? Ca-ca-capture him! Im-Immediately!" Xu Enzeng stammered, collapsing to the ground as soon as he heard the words.

Qian Zhuangfei had already gone far away.

From April 28–30, it was chaotic in Shanghai. On wide and narrow

Revolutionaries

streets, in alleys, at piers, inside and outside stations, there were police cars, officers, armed forces, and agents in plainclothes everywhere. They searched every inch of the addresses Gu Shunzhang offered, but gained little. This was the result of the Central Committee of the CPC acting swiftly and decisively under the leadership of Zhou Enlai. And naturally, it should be credited to Qian Zhuangfei, who delivered the valuable information at critical moment.

However, after all, Gu had too much information about the core organs of the CPC and the underground party in Shanghai. Despite the swift and meticulous action of Zhou Enlai, Li Kenong, and others, not all organs and party members could be hidden.

For example, soon, enemies shot Yun Daiying, who was detained in the Nanjing KMT Military Prison.

And Gu personally led the secret agents to Hong Kong and arrested Cai Hesen, one of the top leaders of the CPC at the time. Next, the British authorities in Hong Kong extradited him to the Guangdong warlord. In the Guangzhou prison, Cai Hesen was tortured, limbs nailed to the wall and chest poked with a knife. The unyielding man was shot at only the age of 36.

Also, it was Gu Shunzhang, who had established many communication lines and trained contact persons of the CPC's fundamental organizations in Shanghai, Wuhan, and other places. And central leaders like Zhou Enlai couldn't possibly know all of them, thus saving everyone while Gu sold all of them out to KMT secret agents.

Additionally, Gu was also familiar with the nature of the CPC organizations and personal habits of the CPC leaders. Based on the knowledge he imparted to them regarding the CPC, KMT agents captured Xiang Zhong, then General-Secretary of the Central Committee of the CPC. After Xiang was arrested, he defected as well, which dealt a huge blow to the CPC. Fortunately, the KMT authorities in Shanghai did not buy the information he offered, but shot him two days after the arrest.

Furthermore, from his arrest to his death in 1935, Gu Shunzhang trained a legion of competent agents for the KMT to suppress and massacre CPC members. These agents, who held confidential information regarding the CPC, murdered many CPC members and revolutionaries...

Intrigues, Defectors, Wrong Routes: the Reign of Terror

Gu Shunzhang was therefore labeled the most dangerous enemy of the CPC. In 1931, the Central Committee of the CPC issued a special notice to assassinate him, an unprecedented move in its history.

In fact, since the Counter-revolutionary coup launched by Chiang Kai-shek in 1927, there must have been more traitors within the CPC. Gu Shunzhang was never the only one. They betrayed countless CPC leaders and revolutionaries.

When I was writing the stories of about Peng Pai, it happened to be the May 1, 2019, Labor Day. So, I couldn't help but go back to 98 years ago when a revolutionary led his students to sing the Labor Day Song he wrote himself—

What's the date today?
May 1st, the Labor Day,
The Anniversary of the strike by International Workmen's Association.
The most sacred is labor
The time for the social revolution has come.
Brothers and sisters,
Please remember the word labor always.

It was Peng Pai who wrote the song. This young master of a rich family in Haifeng, Guangdong, was a revolutionary who firmly believed in communism. He established the first county-level Soviet power in his hometown and allocated family-owned land and property to farmers. For that, Qu Qiubai praised him as the first fighter of the Chinese peasant movement.

In 1924, Peng Pai created the first peasant movement workshop in Guangdong. Two years later, Mao Zedong served as its director. He introduced Peng Pai to the students at class. "He is the king of our peasant movements."

On August 30, 1929, Peng Pai was killed by reactionaries in Longhua, Shanghai, at the age of 33. The next day, the Central Committee of the CPC immediately issued a declaration, commenting on his life. "His image as a revolutionary fighter has long been deeply rooted in the hearts of the laborers and peasants across the country. He has become the most cherished

Revolutionaries

leader of the broad masses. Everyone knows Peng Pai of Guangdong. Everyone knows this leader of the Chinese peasant movement!" Indeed, he was the famous leader of the peasant movement in the early days of the CPC. Someone once concluded "that he was a dreamer, that he lived for his dreams, strove to realize them, and eventually died for them."

However, such an outstanding peasant movement leader died at the hands of traitors. How tragic!

It was on August 24, 1929, that Peng Pai was captured. As a member of the Politburo of the Central Committee of the CPC, Secretary of the Central Agricultural Committee and Secretary of the Jiangsu Provincial Military Commission, he was in a meeting with Yang Yin, an alternate member of the Politburo of the Central Committee of the CPC and Minister of Military Affairs, on the 2nd floor of 12 Xinzha Road Jingyuanli District. Renegade Bai Xin, Secretary of the Military Commission, sold him out, thus he was arrested. On August 30, he, Yang Yin, Yan Changyi, Xing Shizhen, and others were killed in Longhua Prison. Zhang Jichun was released on bail for being a student of Whampoa Military Academy, and survived.

This betrayal led to disastrous consequences, the death of essential military leaders. The name of Peng Pai is widely known but that of Yang Yin, Minister of Military Affairs, is not. This man, who came from the same place as Sun Yat-sen, set his mind from a young age to be a revolutionary to fight for happiness for the country and the people, inspired by Sun Yat-sen's revolutionary ideas. Yang Yin joined Tongmenghui (the Chinese Revolutionary Alliance, a secret society set up by Sun Yat-sen and others) early. When Sun Yat-sen was elected as the interim president of the Republic of China, Yang Yin was the presidential guard. He followed Sun Yat-sen through ice and fire, and developed excellent military skills.

In 1922, he joined the CPC. Next, he resolutely resigned from an official position of the national government and embarked on the road of revolution, organizing labor movements in various parts of Guangdong, which revitalized revolution in that city.

After the May 30 Tragedy in Shanghai, Yang Yin, Deng Zhongxia, and others organized the massive Canton-Hong Kong strike, which earned them a fine reputation. Then, he was sent to Shanghai to lead the labor

Intrigues, Defectors, Wrong Routes: the Reign of Terror

movement and armed uprising. The big fish of local gangs in Shanghai had already heard of him, and attempted to rope him in multiple times. As a revolutionary, he would never collude with them.

When Chiang Kai-shek launched the April Twelfth Counter-revolutionary Coup in Shanghai in 1927, he was in Guangzhou. KMT reactionaries stationed in Guangzhou were frantically suppressing and slaughtering Chinese communists, and reactionary military police besieged his residence, but he was long gone.

In fact, he was ordered to hide somewhere else, planning the Guangzhou Uprising with Zhang Tailei, Ye Ting, Yun Daiying, Ye Jianying, Nie Rongzhen, and others.

After the uprising, a Soviet government was established in Guangzhou, with Zhang Tailei as the Acting Chairman and Yang Yin as member of the Elimination of Counterrevolutionaries Committee. On the second day of its establishment, Zhang Tailei died. Yang Yin kept leading the Red Guards with Ye Jianying, Yun Daiying, and Nie Rongzhen in fighting the reactionary warlords.

In 1928, he went to Moscow to attend the Sixth National Congress of the CPC. At the First Plenary Session of the Sixth Central Committee, he was elected as an alternate member of the Politburo of the Central Committee, an alternate member of the Standing Committee of the Central Committee of the CPC, and Minister of Military Affairs of the Central Committee of the CPC.

After the meeting, he once again worked in the Central Committee of the CPC in Shanghai, leading military struggles in various provinces in harsh underground fights.

On August 24, 1929, when five people, including him and Peng Pai, were having a meeting, Bai Xin sold them out, and all were arrested. Merely one day later, they were extradited to the KMT Shanghai Public Security Bureau by the Xinzha Police Station. Cunning enemies, certain that the CPC would do everything possible to rescue them, conducted a hurried interrogation and escorted them to KMT Songhu Garrison Command.

Expectedly, the sudden arrest of Peng Pai, Yang Yin, and others deeply concerned Zhou Enlai. The plan to hijack the prisoner van was hatched and implemented the next day. However, the heavily guarded prison van

Revolutionaries

suddenly changed its course. There was no chance to rescue them.

"Regarding our rescue:

1. Try to avoid having all five of us executed;

2. If this fails, you have to sacrifice An and Kui, and try to rescue the remaining three who hold no critical information." This was a letter Yang Yin and Peng Pai jointly wrote to the Central Committee via a secret prison channel. An was Peng Pai's code name, and Kui was Yang Yin's. Certain that rescue was hopeless, Yang Yin left the last note to the organization. "We are well here. Don't be sad because of our death. Please take care!"

On August 30, four captives, including Yang Yin and Peng Pai, were pushed out of the cell and headed to the execution ground. "A person who has attained enlightenment has no regret in life!" As he stepped out of the prison gate, Yang Yin, who feared no death, marched forward in fetters, as if to a new battlefield...

The revolution was not only a battle of life or death with the rivals, but also a test of the values and faith of the revolutionaries. It was when being leaders of Central Committee of the CPC or the persons in charge of the Jiangsu Provincial Party Committee that Peng Pai, Yang Yin, Chen Yannian, Zhao Shiyan, Deng Zhongxia, Xu Baoye, and other revolutionaries were arrested, betrayed, and murdered. Their revolutionary sentiment was noble and loyal, which left future generations an invaluable spiritual legacy. However, there were also those in high positions in the party, who failed to resist the temptation or withstand torture and became shameful renegades.

The Jiangsu Provincial Party Committee had successively lost several secretaries because one traitor sold out a group of communists and had them arrested, among whom more defected, which led to another arrest of more communists and the destruction of the rebuilt committee.

After the arrest, the Secretary of Jiangsu Provincial Party Committee under the pseudonym Kong Er shamelessly defected, not only causing damage to the committee itself, but also affecting the Shanghai Central Bureau...

Kong Er's real name was Zhao Lin, a native of Tianjin. He used to be an aspiring youth, but when the enemies imprisoned him and forced him to choose between defection and death, he surrendered. He knelt on his knees, begging the prison guard to spare his life, thus becoming their

Intrigues, Defectors, Wrong Routes: the Reign of Terror

lackey. In their words, he was a bomb to be put back within the Communist Party and detonated at any time.

After his defection, the Secret Service released Zhao Lin back into the CPC. He kept playing the role of provincial party committee secretary who connected the Shanghai Central Bureau and Jiangsu Province. In addition, he strove to leave an impression of a more passionate and determined revolutionary on party comrades.

In and out of the meetings, he put more emphasis on discipline and safety than before, thus creating an image of stronger vigilance than all previous provincial party committee secretaries towards comrades in the committee.

But a series of incidents broke out. At around 9 a.m. one day, the police of the Ministry of Industry of the Public Concession, according to a secret report, arrested Li Menong, Minister of Propaganda of the Jiangsu Provincial Committee of the CPC, and his subordinate Wang Tiemin, who were engaged in underground propaganda, near Jing'an Temple Road.

At about 12:30 the next day, the interim organization of the Jiangsu Provincial Party Committee located at 677 Changping Road was, all of a sudden, besieged by a legion of military police. Over ten essential cadres of the Jiangsu Provincial Party Committee, including Yang Yilin, a member of the Central Bureau of the CPC, Zhao Lin, Secretary of Jiangsu Provincial Party Committee, and Zhang Ziyun, Liu Guixiang and their wives, leaders of its Organization Department, were arrested on the spot. They also searched and found a great many Chinese, English, and Russian materials regarding communist movements. The real identity of Yang Yilin was Huang Wenrong, Minister of Organization of the Shanghai Central Bureau, and Zhang Ziyun was actually Li Shi, former Secretary of the Manchuria Provincial Party Committee and then-Minister of Organization of the Jiangsu Provincial Party Committee.

Within two days, the key organs of the Jiangsu Provincial Party Committee were totally destroyed. The Central Committee of the CPC was deeply concerned, but at the time, it didn't know why it happened. Three days later, after some investigation, several comrades, including Zhao Lin, were released.

But peculiarly, Li Menong, Minister of Propaganda of the Jiangsu

183

Revolutionaries

Provincial Party Committee, was not released, but escorted to Nanjing. His real name was Li Shaoshi, as recorded on the list of martyrs. He was the brother-in-law of Lian Chengzhi. He was a passionate revolutionary and excelled at poetry. On the way to Nanjing, he composed a sonorous revolution poem:

> *I am eternally loyal to my country, more lasting than the universe.*
> *I shall die no ordinary man, but a hero smiling on the execution ground.*

This romantic and poetic revolutionary never surrendered in prison, even though his feet were broken and his lungs injured. He leaked no word harmful to the organization. He was one typical example of communists' infinite loyalty to the party and their heroic spirit. After the full outbreak of the War of Resistance Against Japan, he was released as a political prisoner. During Mao Zedong's trip to Chongqing for negotiations in 1945, he arrived in that city first, as Zhou Enlai's English secretary, yet publicly known as a journalist for Xinhua Daily. One day, he came across the KMT army while sending Liu Yazi home on behalf of Zhou Enlai. He was shot to death, at the age of 39.

The destruction of the Jiangsu Provincial Party Committee this time hit the Shanghai Central Bureau of the CPC hard again.

The Shanghai Central Bureau of the CPC was established after the Provisional Politburo of the Central Committee of the CPC withdrew from Shanghai to the Soviet area in 1933. The Central Committee of the CPC decided to set up a representative organ in Shanghai to guide and lead the work of parties in White Area (KMT-controlled area during the Second Revolutionary Civil War, 1927–1937), including Shanghai, on behalf of the Central Committee, and contact the Communist International. The full name was set as the Shanghai Central Bureau of the CPC, and Shanghai Central Bureau for short.

Since it led the Jiangsu Provincial Party Committee on behalf of the Central Committee in terms of organizational form, yet on the other hand, Shanghai Municipality was under the jurisdiction of the Jiangsu Province, positions were overlapped when the Central Committee appointed the primary leaders of the Jiangsu Provincial Party Committee. One may

Intrigues, Defectors, Wrong Routes: the Reign of Terror

be Minister of Organization of the Jiangsu Provincial Party Committee and holding a position in Shanghai Central Bureau at the same time, but other leaders of the Jiangsu Provincial Party Committee knew nothing about his/her position in the Shanghai Central Bureau. This kind of cross-functionality happened because of the particular CPC Shanghai organizations and the CPC Jiangsu organizations. On the other hand, it also achieved mutual supervision and support.

However, the first detonation of Zhao Lin, a time bomb hidden in the CPC, within the Jiangsu Provincial Party Committee this time caused the first tremendous damage to the Shanghai Central Bureau since its establishment.

The time bomb was promptly cleared. The new Shanghai Central Bureau decided to form the provisional Jiangsu Provincial Party Committee, with Zhao Liren (alias Zhao Yueshan, Zheng Yulong, and Hei Dahan) as its Acting Secretary. But the party organization in Shanghai was already in chaos. The defection of an essential figure arrested had inevitably caused a new round of great destruction of the CPC organizations.

In late June 1934, KMT police in Shanghai arrested Zhou Guangcheng, chief commander of the British American Tobacco Strike Committee, at Maoxingfang, Fumin Road. This man failed to withstand the harsh torture and declared his separation from the organization at once. Moreover, he was eager to make his collaborators proud. He exposed the CPC organization and related party members that he knew to be secret agents, which triggered a shocking and malignant event.

On the evening of June 26, the police arrested Li Wenbi, Zhang Wenqing, head of the All-China Federation of Labor Unions, and Zheng Yulong, Secretary of Jiangsu Provincial Party Committee, at the Liaozhou Corner of Kangnaotuo Road in the public concession. At 8:00 p.m., in another residence, Li Zhusheng, Secretary of the Shanghai Central Bureau, alias Yu Qiquan, Li Yueying, and Wang Chen were arrested. At around 9:40 p.m., the concession police captured Liu Zhigang, Chairman of Shanghai Federation of Labor Unions, at 74, Huaiyinli, Wuding Road. At about 10 p.m., Li Dezhao, Head of the Secretariat of the Central Bureau, alias Lin Ziming, was apprehended. At 11 p.m., the central liaison officer Wu Bingsheng was seized.

Revolutionaries

At 1:30 a.m. on the 27th, the police arrested party members of the Shanghai Central Bureau, including Li Jinfeng, Chen Zaige, Wang Gensheng, and others at 12 Changkangli, Kangnaotuo Road.

At that point, the Shanghai Central Bureau had completely fallen into the danger of extreme passiveness.

What was worse was that under these circumstances, the arrested Shanghai Central Bureau Secretary Li Zhusheng, Jiangsu Provincial Party Committee secretary Zheng Yulong, Wu Bingsheng, Qin Manyun, and others had successively turned against the revolution. They joined the Secret Service and launched even more frantic blows to devastate the CPC. At once, Shanghai was shrouded in overwhelming anti-revolutionary haze. Plenty of communists were either arrested or slaughtered.

Blood flowed in streams.

Li Zhusheng's defection not only led to the arrest of many comrades, but also jeopardized the security of the revolutionary front in the Soviet area.

This was one more devastating blow that the Shanghai Central Bureau suffered.

However, Chinese communists in Shanghai never gave up on the revolution. Regardless of the difficult environment, they exhibited the best loyalty and persistence. Although they had repeatedly taken heavy blows from KMT, they re-ignited the revolutionary flame from a pile of ashes.

Huang Wenjie took over as Secretary of the Shanghai Central Bureau and performed an arduous restoration. Particularly, new revolutionary forces had been developed in the cultural and intellectual circles, thus forming a revolutionary left-wing cultural alliance, whose revolutionary activities were rather frequent for a while. It intimated the KMT authorities. They made a move, training approximately 30 agents in the Secret Service to infiltrate Shanghai. They were called red hat agents, because they read about Marxism-Leninism, and progressive books and periodicals, seemingly passionate about the revolution. They disguised themselves as revolutionaries to blend in with the left-wing cultural ranks and the CPC's fundamental organizations.

On February 19, 1935, the KMT Secret Service, which believed that the time had come, suddenly launched another attack on the new

Intrigues, Defectors, Wrong Routes: the Reign of Terror

organization of the CPC in Shanghai. From that night to the early morning of the 20th, round-up operations took place in both the public concession and the French concession to outflank the CPC's secret headquarters and other venues located on Foxi Road. Twenty-six people were arrested and piles of documents confiscated.

On the same night, police officers from the Xinzha Police Station of the Ministry of Industry in the Public Concession raided 11 Anshunli, Shanhaiguan Road and arrested Chen Zhesheng and his wife Chen Lin. Chen Zhesheng was actually Tian Han, an executive member of the left-wing General League of Culture. Police also apprehended Wang Zhizhong at 56 Guangxingli, Wuchang Road, and Chen Zhichao at 47 Dexingli. Wang Zhizhong was Ouyang Jixiu, also known as Hua Han or Yang Hansheng. He was Secretary of the Communist Youth League of General League of Culture and Secretary of the Cultural Committee of Shanghai Central Bureau.

This evening, the police in the French Concession captured another essential figure in the CPC, a man who claimed to be Zhu Ziming and his companion Li Yuemei. Zhu Ziming was in fact Zhu Jingwo, then Head of the Propaganda Department of the Provisional Shanghai Central Bureau. Meanwhile, they broke into 1 Sanxinfang, New Yong'an Street, and apprehended Fang Ziping, his wife (who was surnamed Xie), and Fang Ziguo. Fang Ziping was Xu Dixin, a big fish in the CPC's cultural circles.

Wang Fuzhi, Li Wenmin, and Li Guanglin of the Secretariat of Shanghai Central Bureau of the CPC were also captured. Among them, Li Guanglin was the alias of Huang Wenjie, Secretary of the Shanghai Central Bureau.

One organization after another was taken down. Revolutionaries and communists were imprisoned.

On the night of the 18th, in the pouring rain KMT agents escorted a group of communists to Nanjing as key criminals, including Huang Wenjie (a native of Xingning, Guangdong, former secretary of provisional Shanghai Central Bureau, who died in 1939 at the age of 37) and Zhu Jingwo (a native of Yin County, Zhejiang Province, Minister of Propaganda Minister of Jiangsu Provincial Committee of the CPC, who died in the Southern Anhui Incident in 1941 at the age of 40), Du Guoxu, Tian Han, and Yang Hansheng. These revolutionaries, like warriors on the battlefield, chanted

Revolutionaries

The Internationale and their self-written poems along the way:

A worrier all my life,
Yet, calm as a prisoner today.

—This was Tian Han singing.
And Xu Dixin joined him loudly.

Unity is like a rock,
Fighting spirit is like fire.
I growled at the jailer,
I lost track of time in prison.
Sticks and shackles,
One after another.
When final victory is won,
No regrets at all.

Under extreme difficulty, it was the relentless efforts of the revolution-aries that kept the flame of communism from extinguishing in the Shanghai Central Bureau of the CPC, which had suffered multiple damages...

And none of the renegades who sold out their comrades for their own survival and turned their back against the revolution ended well—

For another kind of blood and fire in the long history of the Chinese revolution, we have to go back in time—

In the history of the CPC, two mistakes had caused tremendous dam-age to the Chinese revolution around 1930: one was Lisan's left-leaning, and the other Wang Ming's route. These two mistakes differed greatly in nature. The former led more to the loss of revolutionary forces in the course of urban armed struggles, while the latter hurt the revolution as a whole. Li Lisan's left-leaning had severely reprimanded and criticized party comrades, but Wang Ming's route tolerated no different voices within the party, and ruthlessly attacked those who held other opinions or even decapitated them.

Apparently, the protagonists of these two mistakes were Li Lisan and Wang Ming. Despite his mistake, Li Lisan was still a loyal proletarian

Intrigues, Defectors, Wrong Routes: the Reign of Terror

revolutionary and famous leader of the Chinese labor movement; Wang Ming was not.

Li Lisan was a tank (his nickname among party comrades) revolutionary leader with endless revolutionary passion and unwavering revolutionary determination. In the end, slandered as a senior agent who colluded with foreigners during the Cultural Revolution, he suffered injustice and committed suicide.

He was a native of Hunan and was ambitious from childhood. In middle school, he gave himself a pen name: Youguozi (a man who worries about the fate of his country). On a photo with a classmate, he wrote *We are meant to be heroes, you and I. We may not succeed but be ambitious. This is not arrogance but self-encouragement.* These words perfectly summarized what kind of person he was. He criticized himself in the second half of his life. "Those words fully exhibit my arrogance when I was young. It got me in trouble a lot. And my mistakes are directly related to it. How I regret not having been humble." The Central Committee later called him a man who obeyed the truth, humble and sincere, who had the courage to criticize himself and learn from past experience, who could see the big picture, adhere to principles, and act candidly when redressing his grievances.

In 1917, Mao Zedong, who was six years older than him, put out a friend-seeking notice in Changsha, which ended with him making three and a half friends. The half was Li Lisan. Mao's friend Luo Zhanglong wanted to introduce to him Li, who was new to Changsha as a student, and he agreed. So, one day they met at the Provincial Library. During the meeting, Mao exhibited great eloquence like a teacher, while Li never said a word, like a pupil, thus Li left Mao with the impression that he was half a friend.

During the May Fourth Movement, Li Lisan went to Beijing and entered a preparatory class for a work-study program in France. In October, his father sold 16 acres of land inherited from his ancestors and financed him 200 silver coins of tuition. Thereafter, he set out from Shanghai to study in France, thus embarking on the revolutionary road.

Li Longzhi was his original name. For his loyalty and righteousness, he held high prestige among the students studying abroad in France. And he has always had progressive and avant-garde ideas—

Revolutionaries

I am a duckweed with broken stems,
Wandering as far as the wind takes me.
To estuary of the Huangpu River,
To the bank of Xiang River,
To the north,
To the south,
And to the west today.
I breathe the air of freedom,
I pay homage to the goddess of liberty.
I sing the song of freedom
I ring the bell of liberty
To awaken the poor compatriots,
From their deep sleep...

This was a revolutionary poem Li Lisan wrote in the early days of his stay in Europe. He left his classmates an impression of a candid, open-minded, resolute, but impatient man. He was a man of action, never hesitant or sloppy. Regarding the old world, reactionary warlords and shameless politicians, he always preferred more aggressive words, such as overthrow, topple, and kill, which demonstrated his will to fight. However, when there was disagreement and aggressive behaviors among the students studying abroad in France, he often adopted a moderate manner. Unlike those who advocated struggle led by Cai Hesen, he insisted that the work-study program in France be the way out for Chinese students, as did Zhao Shiyan, Chen Yannian, Liu Bojian, and Chen Gongpei, with particular emphasis on the necessity of learning from workers. He sought employment as a worker in a French factory, where he had a first-hand experience of French workers' enthusiasm for the revolution, and joined the Communist Party of the Youth of China in Europe initiated by Cai Hesen and Zhou Enlai, as the first group of CPC members.

In the fall of 1921, the French government deported 104 Chinese students, including Li Lisan, Cai Hesen, Chen Gongpei, and Chen Yi, back to China for their participation in protests against the deportments.

"France doesn't want them, but I do!" In Shanghai, Chen Duxiu was excited to see the returning youth, Li Lisan, Cai Hesen, and the others.

Intrigues, Defectors, Wrong Routes: the Reign of Terror

He kept Cai Hesen to work in the Central Organ of the CPC and sent most of the others to work for the labor movement across the country. Li Lisan was sent to the Anyuan Coal Mine, which was close to his home, to engage in the labor movement. Thereafter, he grew to be an outstanding leader of Chinese labor movements. In the Anyuan strike, under Mao Zedong's leadership, he and Liu Shaoqi fought side by side and earned a fine reputation. After the victorious strike, his name appeared in the lyrics of the strike song.

> *Too numerous to be listed are the workers' sufferings.*
> *Yet, there are rarely heroes in the world.*
> *One is Mr. Li Longzhi. He studied abroad in France and returned.*
> *Only twenty-four years old. He came from Hunan, lives in Liling.*
> *From Changsha to Pingxiang, he came to rescue us out of hell.*

The workers greatly espoused him. Next, he was appointed to lead the labor movement in Wuhan, which he did with excellence. When the May 30th Movement broke out in Shanghai, he was Chairman of the Shanghai Federation of Labor Unions and one of the six figures that the reactionaries wanted to eliminate the most.

As a revolutionary backbone that matured from the labor movement, Li Lisan quickly improved his political status within the party in the background of Shanghai where urban armed struggle was the central task of the revolution. Especially after the April Twelfth Counter-revolutionary Coup, the revolutionary team was massively crippled, likely to be wiped out. In order to reverse Chen Duxiu's right opportunism, Li Lisan, known for leading workers' armed riots, gradually became one of the core leaders of the Central Committee of the CPC after the Sixth National Congress of the CPC. At that time, the revolutionary situation was urgent, coupled with the incorrect guidance from the Communist International.

In response to the fear of some, he pointed out: "Is the revolution really at a cul de sac? No, not at all. Obviously, none of the problems of the Chinese revolution have been resolved. Instead, the imperialists are still fiercely oppressing us, the feudal forces still alive, and the lives of the broad masses more painful than before. Can this go on? Even without the Communist Party, I assume that people like Hong Xiuquan and Yang Xiuqing will rise up and rebel. Long-term rule can never be built on white terror, so objectively the revolution is inevitable. We cannot just sit idly by and wait for the outbreak of a world war and a world revolution. If we do nothing, we will be nothing when it happens. Fruit is ripening on the trees. Sitting under them will never harvest them. That is laziness. Get the ladders and climb, harvest the fruit!"

After the August 7 Meeting, quite a few comrades in the party believed that the darkest hour had passed and that a new revolutionary climax would come. The decision-maker of the Central Committee of the CPC were youths in their thirties, especially Li Lisan, who was bold and active. It was the time that they could easily go astray to revolutionary adventurism. And it happened that the Communist International was going against right-leaning. Under these subjective and objective circumstances, Li Lisan published *Preparing to Establish a Revolutionary Power*, advocating that establishing a revolutionary power would become the central task of the strategic route, that it should be established in one or several provinces first, and that as long as a massive workers' struggle breaks out within the industrial zone and the political center, a revolutionary climax would ensue.

Next, he successively published a series of articles on the journals of the Central Committee of the CPC, such as *Preparing to Establish a Revolutionary Power and Leading the Proletariat, Conditions to Seize the Power of One and Several Provinces, Chinese Revolution and World Revolution*, and *On the Revolutionary Climax*. As if a battle bugle was being sounded, he issued a combat order to the whole party and all revolutionaries to seize power.

At the time, the Central Committee of the CPC headed by Li Lisan was very frantically absorbed before the revolutionary climax, but the desperation was impractical to Chinese revolution and caused greater losses: the Shanghai strike turned out a fiasco again, unlike the May Thirtieth Movement, which mobilized over 800,000 labor union members. Moreover, the Jiangsu Provincial Party Committee, which was assigned specific tasks, exhibited resistance to the Central Committee's order. Li Lisan was irritated. He appointed himself as the Secretary of the Jiangsu

Intrigues, Defectors, Wrong Routes: the Reign of Terror

Provincial General Committee and took over its leadership. Seniors He Mengxiong and Lin Yunan stood up to oppose him and suffered his severe criticism and suppression. There was a huge split between the superiors and the subordinates. The KMT Secret Service made use of the internal division of the CPC to repeatedly damage the central organs of the CPC and various district organizations in Shanghai. A large number of CPC members were arrested, raining heavily on the revolutionary flames in Shanghai, the center of the revolution.

The strike in Shanghai failed. Li Lisan left for Nanjing to organize a soldiers' riot. It came out even worse: not only did it fail, but party organizations and the key leaders the CPC were exposed. The enemy launched an immediate counterattack and damaged the organs of the Nanjing Municipal Committee of the CPC. A total of over 100 key and grass-roots individuals in charge were arrested. Most of them were killed. Party organizations in Nanjing suffered the sixth major destruction in history. The Wuhan riot had the same fate. The revolutionary forces in Wuhan were weak, only over 300 people and 150 workers' red guards. However, they still launched the uprising according to his command. Eventually, armed reactionaries suppressed them. Sixty communists were arrested and 36 killed.

The damages to the revolution that Li Lisan's left-leaning risk-taking caused extended beyond the cities. It also led to the failure of the Red Army's forcible attack on the cities. For example, in the battles against Changsha and Wuhan, a great many of Red Army soldiers were killed.

The lost lives of countless communists on the city streets and the loss of blood of front-line Red Army soldiers awakened Li Lisan and the Central Committee of the CPC. Within the CPC, timely measures were taken to correct mistakes. However, at this very moment, the young CPC took more seriously incorrect guidance: the intervention of the Communist International and Wang Ming's usurpation of the supreme power of the Central Committee of the CPC. This was more devastating than Li Lisan's left-leaning risk-taking.

Shanghai was unusually cold around New Year's Day in 1931. The roaring north wind lifted the waves on the Huangpu River into the air.

In the early morning of January 7, He Mengxiong, a member of the

Revolutionaries

Standing Committee, put on a coat and hurried from home to the secret meeting venue of the Central Committee of the CPC at 6 Xiudefang, Wuding Road (now 14 Lane 930, Wuding Road).

In the wind and snow, he looked sullen, but his fighting spirit was undiminished. There was always unyielding fortitude on his face. This was the kind of person he was. And comrades in the party have always seen him as a fighter who never gave up.

"Yes, I am a fighter since the day I joined in the revolution," He Mengxiong constantly reminded himself. However, recently, he was depressed and discouraged. First, since he was the first in the party to oppose Li's left-leaning risk-taking, many comrades held grudges against him; second, his wife passed away, leaving behind two children, a five-year-old and a three-year-old. But these were not the most important. As a professional revolutionary, what pained him the most was that since he accepted the appointment and came to Shanghai in the summer of 1927, there were many disagreements in views and decision-making within the party and among the central leadership.

He missed the days in the north. Sometimes, he sauntered down memory lane. It used to be great, he thought, even if tomorrow death might come, there was a clear line between friends and enemies. It was either reactionary warlords and capitalists or dear friends of the workers.

"Friends, long time no see. I am so happy to be here with you!" As follows was his speech at the workers club as one of the leaders of the Beijing Underground Party.

The topic of my speech today is "Who is the worker's friend." Buddies, don't get me wrong: a friend can be anyone, an acquaintance, or even the villains who destroy the workers' organizations. But the definition of the friend I speak of today is different. I believe anyone who has great enthusiasm for the labor movement, who is willing to sacrifice his status or even life for the benefit of workers, who never retreats regardless of the pain, who has no personal agenda, who does not deceive workers, is a worker's friend.

Among them, the most famous in the world is Marx. Every foreign worker knows him. He went to college. He saw workers' suffering. He was dedicated to the social revolution. He found ways to give the workers a better life. He

Intrigues, Defectors, Wrong Routes: the Reign of Terror

wrote books, good enough to be the bible of the workers' revolution.

    ...

    Buddies, recognize the true friends. In short, respect and support whoever is willing to sacrifice time, money, and even life for your benefit, because they are your friends!

He Mengxiong was high-spirited and vigorous in those days. This hot pepper-loving Hunan native was born to fight. He had clear goals. Especially after following Li Dazhao, from directly participating in the May Fourth Movement to contributing to the first early organizational construction of the Communist Party in Beijing, he had been arrested three times. Every time he was released from prison, his revolutionary will was more determined and his struggle experience richer. Later, he and other revolutionaries such as Li Dazhao and Deng Zhongxia ignited much revolutionary tinder in Changxindian, in the city of Tangshan (where he was Secretary of Tangshan Municipal Party Committee), Tianjin, and other places. It was these real struggles that made him better understand the significance of the practicality of revolution.

When he was appointed to the Jiangsu Provincial Party Committee in August 1927, it was at a critical moment of severe destruction. He came to Shanghai with his wife, Miao Boying, the first female communist in the history of the CPC (who died at the age of 30 in Shanghai Renji Hospital in 1929 due to overwork for the revolution), and has been working there ever since.

This newcomer seemed not quite compatible with the political environment in Shanghai. So he chose the countryside to engage in revolution. By faking marital quarrels, he "escaped home" three times to Huai'an in northern Jiangsu Province to organize the peasant movement there. He rebuilt the party organizations in four counties and personally commanded the armed riots there. Although they failed in merely three days, he learned a lesson about the errors in the plan he made for the first peasant movement in Jiangsu, and drafted the *Resolution Regarding Jiangsu Province Accepting the China Issue Resolution* at the February Meeting of the Communist International Executive Committee, which was subsequently approved by the Jiangsu Provincial Party Committee. In this *Resolution*, also known

Revolutionaries

as the *May Resolution* in the history of the CPC, he sharply criticized the putschism of the Central Committee. It was the first time that someone made such harsh criticism of the Central Committee as a party member and in the name of a provincial party committee. Thereafter, his reputation for stubbornness spread.

During that period, the work of the Jiangsu Provincial Party Committee, especially the rural revolutionary movement that He Mengxiong and Li Fuchun led, achieved positive outcomes and summed up many useful experiences in rural work. As He Mengxiong pointed out, "Scattered guerrilla warfare that separated itself from the masses and failed should be opposed, but it must be explained that the form of rural struggle differs from that of the city. It could easily evolve into armed conflicts. The conditions of a city riot did not apply to that in the countryside. Instead, rural armed forces could only adopt guerrilla warfare, which was by no means a local struggle separated from the masses, but a united fighting area for combat. Divided armed forces came together to surround the enemies, so that scattered battles converged into a total battle." This was a summary of the rural revolutionary struggle under the historical conditions of 1927. It was rooted in the strategic thinking of the land revolution of Chinese peasants, which was perfectly consistent with Mao Zedong's experience of encircling the city with the countryside when he established the Jinggangshan revolutionary base.

He Mengxiong was a revolutionary with independent political opinions and ideas about the struggle. Because of this, the Jiangsu Provincial Party Committee, after he took office, made unprecedentedly outstanding achievements. The results convinced Xiang Zhongfa, General Secretary of the CPC at the time, to announce that the Jiangsu Provincial Party Committee was outstanding and the strongest provincial party committee in the country. But soon, the central government "reformed" it as central leadership directly and concurrently assumed its leadership and that of Shanghai. It appalled many comrades.

Next, because of various reasons, the central government halted the "reform," but made a bigger move. It disbanded the Jiangsu Provincial Party Committee. Except for two original provincial party standing committee members, all the others were transferred to Shanghai for labor movements.

Intrigues, Defectors, Wrong Routes: the Reign of Terror

He Mengxiong was no exception. He was assigned to the West Shanghai District Committee.

And he was not alone. Yun Daiying and Deng Zhongxia received the same result. So as a stubborn man, he publicly argued against Li Lisan at the Central Committee meeting, and wrote directly to the Central Committee, stating his opinions again and again.

He was almost expelled from the party due to the influence of Li Lisan's left-leaning risk-taking. However, he soon discovered that the new head of the provincial party committee was even more poisonous than Li Lisan. And that was Wang Ming.

"Why was I dismissed from my post?" He Mengxiong, who had only become Secretary of Central Shanghai District Committee for several days, suddenly received a notice from the provincial general committee that he had been dismissed. For this early revolutionary of the CPC, what mattered was not the dismissal but what he had done wrong to deserve it.

In the small chamber of the district party committee office, the stubborn He Mengxiong drafted the famous *Political Position Paper* of over 20,000 Chinese characters with the most loyalty to the party and the country. In the name of a senior party member, he expressed his theories and strategic propositions of the Chinese revolution based on his long-term research. The problems he mentioned were truly important theoretical and practical problems that the CPC was challenged with at the time. At the end of the *Political Position Paper*, the young the CPC fighter could not hide his indignation. "I have dedicated myself to the proletarian revolution, to the party for a decade. Every day I am at the forefront. It pains me that at this very moment I am not there fighting tooth and nail with the class enemies. This is my voice that the party must hear."

However, the central government, represented by Wang Ming, merely ignored his dedication and loyalty to the party. They showed no regard for his opinions. At this time, He Mengxiong received *Notice No. 96* issued by the central government, which informed him of an emergency central meeting to be held. He mistook it as an invitation to discuss his *Political Position Paper*. He raced to the meeting venue, excited.

He was fully confident on the way to the venue, because at the central meeting held at the end of 1930, the central government issued the

Resolution on the Issue of Comrade He Mengxiong, which acknowledged that his opinions are generally correct and cancelled the punishment towards him. Instead, his submission was published.

It was a rare resolution made specifically for one comrade in the party. The issue of He Mengxiong was obviously a major one in the party at the time.

However, when he arrived at the meeting, he realized he had mistakenly judged it. Xiang Zhongfa, General Secretary of the CPC, suddenly announced that the meeting was the Fourth Plenary Session of the Sixth Central Committee approved by the Communist International. He Mengxiong and others voiced their objection as soon as they found out it was not as what the notice described.

Chaos pervaded the meeting. Zhang Jinbao, then general executive committee member, recalled the meeting like this: "When I arrived there, many had come. I remember there were 30 to 40 attendees, including Wang Ming, Bo Gu, Wang Jiaxiang, Xiang Zhongfa, Zhou Enlai, Qu Qiubai, Shen Zemin, Shi Wenbin, Chen Yu, Chen Yuandao, Gu Shunzhang, Xiao Daode, Xu Xigen, Luo Zhanglong, Zhang Wentian, Wang Fengfei, Xu Lanzhi, Yuan Naixiang, Wang Kequan, He Mengxiong, Shen Xianding, Xu Weisan, Yu Fei, Han Linhui, international representative Pavel Mif, and others. Xu Bing was the interpreter. From the composition of the attendants, it was easily seen that Wang Ming was playing a trick. He invited those who share the same opinions to attend it. According to the notice of this emergency meeting, Tang Hongjing, six-time member of the Central Committee and Manchu Provincial Party Committee was supposed to come but he stayed in the hotel. Nobody was sent to take him to the meeting venue. Thus, one less vote. In addition, there was a conflict before the meeting: a party leader of the railway suddenly broke into the venue and accused loudly, "Why am I not notified to attend this meeting? I assume he should attend it especially when he found out about this secret place. Maybe Wang Ming deliberately prevented him from joining us. He was forcibly thrown out."

It was too chaotic to continue the meeting. At last, they had to vote on the legitimacy of the so-called Fourth Plenary Session of the Sixth Central Committee. The result was 19 to 17. Wang Ming had two more votes.

Intrigues, Defectors, Wrong Routes: the Reign of Terror

Obviously, He Mengxiong and the others did not approve of the rigged meeting agenda. However, with the support of Pavel Mif, a representative of the Communist International, Wang Ming forced his way to become the de facto supreme leader of the CPC.

The Fourth Plenary Session of the Sixth Central Committee on January 7, 1931, which changed what the meeting was originally about, had a huge impact on the CPC organization in Shanghai: on the one hand, Wang Ming, who represented the Communist International, took over the leadership of the central government of the CPC, kicking his predecessor Qu Qiubai aside; on the other, those who opposed Li Lisan's left-leaning risk-taking, such as He Mengxiong, were slandered as rightists who were against the central government (they actually only opposed Wang Ming).

Then, something incomprehensive to many party comrades happened. "What happened to Daiying and Zhongxia today will happen to us tomorrow!"

"No, we have to stop this abnormal and wrong route."

Lin Yunan and Li Qiushi were indignant after He Mengxiong conveyed to them the principles of the central conference, because they were both comrades-in-arms of Yun Daiying. Their dear friend and young Chinese leader was locked in the enemies' prison with an uncertain fate (Yun Daiying had not been killed yet). They were both core leaders engaged in the student movement in Wuhan with Yun Daiying during the May Fourth Movement, and also were CPC members in its early days. They had firm revolutionary beliefs and rich experience in struggle. They cared as much for the fate of the country, of the party as He Mengxiong. And they were especially disgusted with Li Lisan's left-leaning risk-taking and Wang Ming's practice, which broke away from the reality of the Chinese revolution.

"What they are doing is wrong. We should express how we feel to all party comrades. Involve everyone to help our party correct the mistakes and never make them again."

"Indeed. Let's write a Letter to Comrades!"

"I'm on board!"

Therefore, on January 8, the 18 CPC members who opposed the Fourth Plenary Session of the Sixth Central Committee, including He Mengxiong,

Revolutionaries

Lin Yunan, and Li Qiushi, co-published *Letter to Comrades within the Party*.

It was a huge slap on Wang Ming and Pavel Mif, the Communist International representative.

On January 13, Mif attended the cadre meeting with the theme Anti-Fourth Plenary Session as Communist International representative. The atmosphere could not be more tense. Mif waved his fists, pointed at He Mengxiong and others, shouting: "You are anti-Communist International representative, anti-party!"

"Opposing the Fourth Plenary Session of the Sixth Central Committee the Communist International approved is opposing the Communist International!"

Accusations came one after another. Senior CPC members like He Mengxiong were never afraid of Mif's accusations. As a result, the struggle within the party intensified.

It led to the occurrence of the Oriental Hotel Incident in Shanghai from January 17 to 18, 1931.

The Oriental Hotel in old Shanghai was located at the southwest corner of Hankou Road and Zhejiang Road. The house number was at 222 Sanma Road, which is 613 Hankou Road today. It was a medium-sized western-style hotel, a relatively stylish hotel in Shanghai at that time. It was built in 1923 and had 110 rooms. Since it was a popular, a group of famous cultural figures rented out a few rooms in this hotel to escape the surveillance of enemies and prepare for the first National Congress of the Chinese Soviets. Underground party organizations took full advantage of this spot and regularly gathered there to study and discuss the current situation, to exchange information, and to convey the spirit of the party. The first days were uneventful. However, after the Fourth Plenary Session of the Sixth Central Committee of the CPC, it was no longer a peaceful spot.

On the 17th, some CPC cadres who agreed to oppose the Fourth Plenary Session that Wang Ming and Mif controlled—mainly the CPC members from the former Jiangsu Provincial Party Committee were ready to meet there to discuss related issues. None saw it coming that around 1:40 p.m., many police surrounded the hotel. Then, they ambushed Zhongshan Hostel, Huade Road Primary School, and other places, arresting a total of 36 communists and Left League members. This was the shocking Oriental

Intrigues, Defectors, Wrong Routes: the Reign of Terror

Hotel Incident in Shanghai.

The enemies captured 36 people, including high-ranking CPC cadres like He Mengxiong, Lin Yunan, Li Qiushi, Ouyang Li'an, Yun Yutang and well-known Left League members such as Rou Shi, Yin Fu, and Feng Keng in one action.

Subsequently, they brutally shot 24 communists, including He Mengxiong, Lin Yunan, Li Qiushi, Yun Yutang, Rou Shi, Yin Fu, Hu Yepin, and Feng Keng secretly on the grass in the backyard of the detention center of the Longhua KMT Songhu Garrison Headquarters...

Today, they are known as the Twenty-Four Martyrs of Longhua. Their deaths are one of the biggest regrets for the Chinese communists. The surviving revolutionaries became desolate every time they thought of them—

It was the first massacre, a secret slaughter, of revolutionaries on such a large scale since the April Twelfth Counter-revolutionary Coup; allegedly, it was a reporter of the *Red Flag* that sold them out, but it seemed impossible that an ordinary journalist could have that many communists on different fronts arrested altogether according to the rules of the underground party. So who exactly betrayed these revolutionaries?

What was more infuriating was that on the second day after He Mengxiong and the others were arrested, Wang Ming accused him of being a right-leaning opportunist against the Fourth Plenary Session at the Shanghai activist meeting. On the third day of his imprisonment, his five-year-old son and three-year-old daughter were taken to prison along with their nanny. When the prison underground party branch consulted the party organization on how to rescue them via a secret channel, Wang Ming not only showed no sympathy at all, but informed the prison party branch that they were all rightists, thus forbidden to have any association with the party organization, meaning not to rescue them. It was a dagger stabbing them in the back.

On the contrary, He Mengxiong, Lin Yunan, and Li Qiushi, who were locked up in the same cell, were still deeply concerned with the party, the country, and the people. Under extreme difficulty in prison, they were trying the figure out how to correct the leaf-leaning opportunism route in the party. Together, they wrote a letter to the Communist International:

Revolutionaries

1. Opposing international representatives was not opposing the Communist International;

2. How the international representatives handled the problem does not conform to China's national conditions. Mif ignored the presence of a legion of cadres with both ability and integrity in China, and made the mistakes of dogmatism and sectarianism by merely taking a handful of henchmen as the only source of cadres to reform the CPC. Revolutionaries, such as He Mengxiong, with utmost loyalty to the party, entrusted this letter to a neighbor cellmate named Huang Liwen at the last moment of their lives. On the freezing night of February 7, 1931, along with other revolutionaries, they were brutally killed by the enemies on a wild grass ground less than 400 meters away from the prison...

That year—

Lin Yunan was 33;

He Mengxiong was 33;

Li Qiushi was 28;

Long Dadao was 30;

Ouyang Li'an was 17;

Yun Yutang was 29;

Luo Shibing was 35;

Wang Qingshi was 24;

Cai Bozhen, age unknown;

Wu Zhongwen (Wife of Cai Bozhen) was 28;

Duan Nan was 23;

Li Wen (Wife of Yun Yutang) was 21;

Rou Shi was 29;

Hu Yepin was 28;

Yin Fu was 21;

Feng Keng was 24;

Fei Dafu was 24;

Tang Shiquan was 26;

Tang Shilun was 24, brother of Tang Shiquan;

Peng Yangeng was 35;

Liu Zheng was 31;

He Zhiping, age unknown.

Intrigues, Defectors, Wrong Routes: the Reign of Terror

... (There are still two martyrs whose names are unknown.)

Longhua, a place of lofty morals for thousands of years. The heroes died but the dream continues.
Inside the walls, peaches bloom, outside, blood is shed, equally brightly-colored.

In 1933, Zhang Kaifan, then Secretary of the West Shanghai District Committee of the CPC, was arrested and imprisoned in the same cell where He Mengxiong was locked up. He heard the story of the Twenty-Four Martyrs of Longhua and composed this poem, filled with regret. He wrote it on the cell wall to motivate the comrade-in-arms to fight.

The Twenty-Four Martyrs of Longhua were a tragedy. It was not only a crime committed by KMT reactionaries, but also a disastrous result of Li Lisan's left-leaning risk-taking and the Wang Ming route. It is a historical lesson that the CPC should always remember.

Fortunately, at the Seventh Plenary Session of the Sixth Central Committee of the CPC in 1945, as presided over by Mao Zedong, the *Resolution on Certain Historical Issues* acknowledged that over 30 important party cadres, including Lin Yunan, Li Qiushi, and He Mengxiong had greatly benefited the people, that they had a good relationship with the masses, that they were arrested by the enemies but never surrendered and died heroically, and that their proletarian heroism deserves to be remembered always.

Marshal Chen Yi once commented on He Mengxiong, saying that he was his direct leader of the national revolutionary movement in China-France University in Beijing. He especially admired his heroic spirit of struggle. With great respect, he said: "Mengxiong had a checkered life. But his aim has never wavered. Instead, he has repeatedly asked to work for the party. He was a true hero."

He Mengxiong's parents died when he was a child. He grew up with his elder brother. During the May Fourth Movement, he was a brave warrior when he rescued 32 students from Peking University. That was the first time he was arrested. In 1920, he led seven work-study mutual aid team members to parade on the street. The second time he was arrested, he

Revolutionaries

went on a hunger strike for seven days before he was released. For that, he was called the first juvenile leader imprisoned for the May 1st Movement in China; in 1920, on his way to Irkutsk, Russia to attend the Far East Conference, he was arrested by reactionary warlords when he reached Heilongjiang. In 1924, reactionary warlords blacklisted him and Li Dazhao. This is what this young communist had endured.

> *Once a lowly official was arrested in Jiangzhou. Today I am a prisoner at Heilongjiang.*
> *I have travelled thousands of miles to Amur, calm and shall never fail the ambition.*

He Mengxiong composed this poem on the prison wall after his arrest in Heilongjiang. He was a rare CPC fighter whose revolutionary momentum never diminished after countless hardships. His wife Miao Boying, the first female CPC member, fell ill from fatigue. Before she died, she held her husband's hand, deeply concerned. "When I'm gone, who is going to shield you from adversity in the future?" Her words brought him to tears.

He suggested: "Let's have faith in the party!" As a revolutionary couple in the early days of the CPC, this was how they bid farewell, holding hands tightly.

As a senior cadre of the early CPC, He Mengxiong suffered repeated attacks and discrimination after he expressed different opinions to the organization based on the principles of party character. However, he was never discouraged. His loyalty and passion persisted. When he was imprisoned, his identity had been fully exposed. Moreover, the traitors informed the enemies of his experience of exclusion within the party. They attempted to sway him. "There is factionalism going on in your party. For that, someone sold you out. A person as capable as you, why bother to work for a party that doesn't trust you?"

He replied confidently, "There are indeed shortcomings and mistakes in our party, but they can be overcome via struggle. Your argument is pointless. The CPC is not like the KMT. You are anti-people. We are righteous. The more we fight, the stronger we get. It is you that factionalism is eroding. You are hopeless. You expect the CPC to lose because of some

Intrigues, Defectors, Wrong Routes: the Reign of Terror

shortcomings and mistakes. But that is wishful thinking. The KMT will eventually perish, and communism will prevail!" This was He Mengxiong, a man of strong faith.

The spirit of these communist martyrs will always shine and illuminate the way forward for future generations...

CHAPTER SEVEN

The Flower of Life Blooms

WHEN I WAS LITTLE, I READ *REMEMBER IN ORDER TO FORGET* BY LU Hsun (Lu Xun). I only knew that he was the author and I didn't feel the grief and indignation about the murder of those mentioned in the essay by the enemies. Now, I do. For Lu Hsun, they were like burning flames that empowered him with inspiration. Therefore, when these ambitious, energetic, and capable youths were suddenly murdered, he was infuriated. Grief and indignation haunted him for two years. It was a rare thing for this writer, who was brave and good at fighting. So, this literary fighter wrote the following words of indignation (selections):

> I have long wanted to write a few words in memory of the several young writers, not for another purpose, but because for the past two years, grief and indignation have haunted me and they still do. I want to take this opportunity to get rid of the sorrow, and cut myself some slack. To put it bluntly, I am going to forget them.
>
> Two years ago, the night of February 7 or 8 in 1931, was when our five young writers were murdered all together. At that time, newspapers in Shanghai were afraid to report it, or perhaps unwilling to, or disdained to. There was only one article in the Art News that vaguely described it.
>
> ...
>
> But in China, writing was prohibited everywhere at that time. The ban was tighter than canned food. I remember that Rou Shi returned to his

hometown at the end of the year. He stayed there for a long time. When he returned to Shanghai, his friends reprimanded him. He complained to me that his mother was blind and wanted him to stay for a few more days. How could he leave? I understand it was the love of the blind mother for her son and the vice versa. When Beidou was first created, I wanted to write a little about him, but I couldn't. I had to choose a woodcut of Mrs. Kollwitz (Käthe Kollwitz, German artist), called Sacrifice. *It was a mother tragically sacrificing her son. Only I know that Rou Shi deeply treasured it.*

Among the four young writers who were killed at the same time, I had never met Li Weisen, and Hu Yepin only once in Shanghai. We had a brief exchange of words. I knew Bai Mang better. We once exchanged letters and submitted manuscripts together, but none could be found today. They must have been burned by the night of seventeenth. I didn't know that Bai Mang was also arrested. However, the Petöfi Sándor Poem Collection *was there. I skimmed it, and found nothing, except four lines of translation next to the Wahlsprush:*

Liberty and love
These two I must have
For love, I will
sacrifice my life;
For liberty, I will
sacrifice my love.
On the second page, Xu Peigen was written, his real name I suspect.

Two years ago today, I hid in the inn, but they were escorted to the execution ground; today of last year, I fled to the British concession amidst the sound of gunfire, and they were already buried in the ground that nobody knew; today of this year, I sat in the old apartment. People were asleep, including my wife and children. I felt unspeakable weight again that I had lost good friends, and China had lost good young men. I calmed down in grief and indignation. But my habit pulled me out of it and I wrote the words above.

I have to keep writing, but there is still nowhere to write in China. When I was young reading Xiang Ziqi's Ode to Bygone Days, *I used to wonder why he only wrote a few lines. The ending came shortly after the beginning. However, now I understand.*

The Flower of Life Blooms

It is not that the young write in memory of the old. In these thirty years, I have witnessed the blood of many youths clot and pile up, burying me underneath, suffocating. I can only write a few essays, as if digging a small hole in the soil and catching a breath. What kind of world is this? The night is long, the road too. I might as well forget them and leave them be. But I am certain that even if it is not me, there will always be a time to remember them in the future and speak of them again.

He wrote this essay two years after the death of the Twenty-four Martyrs of Longhua on February 7–8, 1933. It took him two days to finish it, only a few thousand Chinese characters. He suffered tremendous grief and rage. He used to say that in those years, he witnessed the blood of many youths clot and pile up, burying him underneath, suffocating. This was the brotherly sympathy of a literary revolutionary fighter to the proletarian revolutionaries.

Yin Fu, whom he described in his works, was an important member of the Left League and revolutionary poet of significant influence in the 1920s and 1930s. He received enthusiastic care and guidance from Lu Hsun when he was alive. He invited Lu Hsun to write a preface for his anthology of poems *Urchin Tower*. In the preface, Lu Hsun concluded that Yin Fu was not only a poet, but first of all a revolutionary fighter.

Indeed, that was true. It took some time for this intellectual from a petty-bourgeois family to become a revolutionary fighter. Yin Fu's real name was Xu Boxing. He had three older brothers and two older sisters. The eldest brother was a senior KMT officer, an intellectual who studied abroad in Germany, and former-head of KMT aviation. He once tried to have his younger brother follow his path, but Yin Fu chose a different one and secretly joined the revolution. Their mother saw what was happening but never stopped him. She only warned him to be careful. For that, Yin Fu was grateful to the woman, and composed the poems *Maria of the East-to Mother* and *To Mother*.

Yin Fu was only 21 when he died, but he had already become an influential poet and a determined revolutionary. In 1923, this 13-year-old teenager was admitted under the name Xu Bai to Shanghai Minli Middle School, which was next to Pudong High School. Here, he began

Revolutionaries

to participate in the revolutionary movement and joined the Communist Youth League. During the April Twelfth Counter-revolutionary coup, the 17-year-old was betrayed and imprisoned for three months, and almost shot dead. Thanks to his brother, a senior KMT officer, he was released on bail.

"Stop this nonsense! Study and nothing else!" Once he was released from prison, the brother reprimanded him angrily, "Hear this. The situation is about to change. You will suffer a lot if you continue to make trouble."

Yin Fu tossed a question back at his brother, "Going to change? Into what? How do you know?"

The brother could not leak the information regarding how Chiang Kai-shek planned to deal with communists, to Yin Fu, who was in favor of the communists. So, the brother could only order him without giving any explanation. "None of your business! Don't go anywhere. Just stay by my side!"

He put Yin Fu under house arrest and sent him to their hometown in Xiangshan, Zhejiang Province, to prepare for the college entrance examination. Shackled as he was, he never gave up the pursuit for revolution. He composed poems, looking forward to returning to the fiery revolutionary movement. Meanwhile, he took this opportunity to learn English, German, and Russian, and reached the level where he could translate. It laid the foundation for him to translate much Russian revolutionary literature in the future. At that time, he was following Shanghai's revolutionary literature publications. He wrote a long poem *Before Death Falls* and mailed it to *Sun Monthly*. It was admired by the famous poet Jiang Guangci and the literary theorist A Ying, who later recalled, "I was immediately excited. It was so full of revolutionary passion. The cover letter showed he was a comrade, so I couldn't help but write to him and invite him to meet me in Shanghai. Soon, in a pleasant mood I shared the news with Guangci, Meng Chao, and other comrades."

Yin Fu came to Shanghai as scheduled. He was young, good-looking, tanned, medium-sized, and short-haired, as Lu Hsun described in *Remember in Order to Forget*. When A Ying talked with him, she discovered that he spoke in a low voice, as if in a clandestine meeting, and each sentence was concise, but sincere. "He had the simple and modest style of the revolution, but his verses are burning flames. He is a totally idealistic revolutionist," commented A Ying.

Thereafter, Yin Fu officially become a part of the revolutionary literary and art front. He was recruited as a member of *Sun Monthly*.

In the autumn of 1928, during a revolutionary activity, he was arrested by secret agents who were undercover in Tongji University. He was imprisoned again. His eldest brother was studying in Germany. It was his sister-in-law who came to bail him under the condition that he had to return to the hometown in Xiangshan. His siblings saw him as a child lacking discipline. Sending him back to the hometown was a punishment. However, he was totally dedicated to the revolution. Neither the beautiful hometown scenery nor the long distance could extinguish his enthusiasm and fighting spirit.

Simultaneously, he reflected on his inner non-revolutionary character, as he analyzed himself in *Notes Preceding the Urchin Tower*. "My life, like that of many intellectuals in this era, is a process of contradiction and battle. Tears, laughter, sorrow, joy, excitement, disappointment... a series of positive and negative emotions make up my life curve. The times need me to be more advanced, more sound." His desire for revolution was stronger, as he chanted in the poem *Return*. "Come back! My enthusiasm. Burn in my chest, the madness of youth, the passion of revolution! I am hungry for them, infinitely! Come back! My enthusiasm, to the days of my life that have passed!"

He later contacted the organization, shouting in *When I Wake Up*: "When I wake up, the sky smiles, the bird chirps, your cute nickname... only when you exist, my life glows."

At the end of 1929, with the help of his sister, Yin Fu left Xiangshan and returned to Shanghai. This time he was cut off from his family and became fully dedicated to the revolution. From then on, a revolutionary poet illuminated Shanghai...

Words written by blood,
Lie diagonally on Nanjing Road,
This unforgettable day—
Polishes every year...

Revolutionaries

...

I am the beginning of a rebellion,
I am the eldest son of history,
I am a storm petrel,
I am the spike of the times.

May 30 will be shackles of revenge,
May 30 will be iron railings to imprison the enemy,
May 30 will be sickles and hammers,
May 30 will be cuffs and cannonballs!

...

His *Words of Blood* became a declaration of war for students and workers to commemorate the May 30th Movement on the streets of Shanghai.

Let the dead be dead!
Their blood is not shed in vain,
They lie on the street, smiling,
As if sincerely to us, nodding
Their blood paints a map
Dying red villages and towns
They died gloriously,
It is no time to shed tears.
At us, the enemies are aiming,
Don't raise our hands!

...

"Let the dead be dead" depicted the clear-cut stand of a young revolutionary. At this time, Yin Fu was no longer someone who merely stood on the shore of the revolution shouting slogans. He was weaponized with revolutionary poetry, leading proletarian fighters to fight in the streets—

Today,
We must hold the red flag high,
Today,

The Flower of Life Blooms

We are ready!

Fear no tank, no cannon,
Our great team is the Great Wall!
Fear not decapitation, nor shooting, nor imprisonment,
The blood of our youth will never run out!

...

We are those who can't be killed,
We are those who can't be fooled,
We liberate our class,
We charge into battle, selflessly

...

The 20-year-old Yin Fu's *May First Song* not only became a clarion call for the Shanghai citizens to commemorate Labor Day and fight, but also broke through the style of lyric poetry of the May Fourth Movement period. He created a battle anthem with a sonorous rhythm, sophisticated artistic creation, bold and unconstrained, and full of proletarian revolutionary passion. It was his personal peak. Together with the works of other revolutionary literary and art workers, it mobilized the masses and motivated the revolutionaries.

It was at this moment that Yin Fu entered Lu Hsun's circle. Under the pen name Bai Mang, he translated Hungarian revolutionary poet Petöfi Sándor's glorious poem, which is widely popular among young people, *Liberty and love, These two I must have; For love, I will sacrifice my life; For liberty, I will sacrifice my love.* He came to Lu Hsun with the translated manuscript.

As Lu Hsun concluded, Yin Fu was more of a revolutionary warrior. In July 1927, the 19-year-old man was arrested and imprisoned for the third time because he joined in a strike at a silk factory. He had nothing on him when he was released after imprisonment for some time. He borrowed a long gown from a friend and went to visit Lu Hsun. In front of Lu Hsun, he confessed embarrassingly. "It was my third time in jail. I am released on my own. My brother bailed me out the first two. I had to pay the price of losing my freedom. I didn't notify him this time. I prefer freedom."

Revolutionaries

Lu Hsun laughed wildly when he heard it. He liked this young fellow also from Zhejiang even more. However, it was the last time they met. Lu Hsun offered some financial help to Yin Fu, who was penniless at the time.

Yin Fu was imprisoned for the fourth time when he received a notice from the organization saying there was a meeting at the Oriental Hotel. Soon after he sat down with other comrades, armed enemies broke in and arrested him. He was never released again but killed in the hell of Longhua. He once composed a song called *Longhua in Dreams*, describing it as one of devil and blood.

Rou Shi, who was also in Lu Hsun's commemorative essay together with Yin Fu, was his student. Lu Hsun particularly favored him. As he wrote, when he went out with Rou Shi, Rou Shi always looked after him as if he were his father, fearing that he would trip and fall. In short, he was extremely careful and caring. Lu Hsun was grateful for all of them. Therefore, when he heard that Rou Shi was killed, he suffered as if he lost his own son. He wrote a biography for Rou Shi, a rare move in his career. The friendship between the two was so strong that, as needed by the revolution, Rou Shi would use Lu Hsun's name when he could not publish any essays under his pen name. Later, those were included into Lu Hsun's works, which Lu Hsun did not object, another evidence to their strong friendship.

Precisely because of that, Rou Shi's death devastated Lu Hsun tremendously.

Rou Shi, born in Ninghai, may have had a strong mind, which explained why he and Lu Hsun hit it off. Of course, this could also be ascribed to his revolutionary experience before he met Lu Hsun.

Rou Shi used to be called Zhao Pingfu. When he was 16 years old, he was admitted to the Zhejiang Provincial First Normal School. It was in 1918. The young man walked out of the mountains for the first time. He took a boat from Ningbo Port, first Shanghai and then to Hangzhou. The first time he was far away from home, he visited three major cities, especially Shanghai and Hangzhou, which opened his eyes to the wider outside world. When he attended Zhejiang Provincial First Normal School, it happened to be the heyday of this Zhejiang revolutionary crucible. Especially because of the four key figures of the New Culture

The Flower of Life Blooms

Movement in the school, Chen Wangdao, Liu Dabai (who later lectured at Fudan University, the lyrics writer of its university anthem, died in 1932), Li Cijiu, and Xia Mianzun (who died in 1946 due to persecution by the Japanese invaders), Rou Shi was baptized by the May Fourth Movement in his sophomore year. He just wanted to study hard but as he witnessed the dismissal of his respected principal Jing Hengyi and the four key figures, the expulsion of Shi Cuntong, editor-in-chief of the progressive publication *Zhejiang New Wave,* he had a new understanding of education to national wealth and strength, to individual happiness.

However, in those days, like most youths, who on the one hand, accepted progressive ideas, and on the other, were impeded by old forces like their families and the society, he suffered restraints on his pursuit. Rou Shi attended college in the provincial capital. In order to keep him at home, his family arranged an arranged marriage for him. This put him in a contradictory situation. It went against his life pursuit as a revolutionary fighter. Many of his works and poems revealed his pain of fighting to break away yet having failed. Many in the May Fourth Movement period had similar experience, including Lu Hsun, Mao Dun, Chen Duxiu, and others.

This kind of pain and struggle haunted the youths of that era for a lifetime—

Live happily,
Die without regret,
Calm down! Don't forget the meaning of life,
And the value of yourself!

Rou Shi motivated himself with his own poems and reminded himself: "You should know your own worth and love. You should fly high and travel around the world... You should climb the Himalayas and look down on the vastness of the Pacific. From now on, may you understand the changing times, understand life and death, and understand their significance!"

It is believed anger breeds poets, depression nurtures writers. Rou Shi became more interested in literature in this state of mind, using it to release his agony from inside.

In 1925, he took his novella collection *Madman* to Peking University

Revolutionaries

as an auditor, where he had another leap in his life. It was there that he met Feng Xuefeng and Lu Hsun, who taught classes there. Listening to Lu Hsun lecture was the greatest pleasure of his life, obliterating all the agonies.

That year, the May Thirtieth Movement in Shanghai had a huge impact and influence on his ideology. A progressive young man, he was determined to become a revolutionary. It was in this wave of anti-imperialist revolutionary struggle that he published *Fight*, a famous battle poem which earned him fame. Ninety-five years have passed, let us re-read it and immerse ourselves in the fighting passion of those extraordinary years—

Dust and sand disperse the clouds in the sky,
Dust and sand bury the flowers on the ground;
The sun sobs on the gray hills,
The children race towards the ancient forest!
...
Real men, wake up,
Bombs! Pistols!
Daggers! Poison arrows!
Ancient and modern weapons lie in front of us,
Demons and soldiers from above,
Come together to help mankind fight,
Fight!

Sparks everywhere,
Blood floods,
Bones are piled into mountains,
Meat rots in fertile fields,
The house of blessing for future generations,
It is built by the moon-lit lake

Oh! Fight!
Even if my heart's ripped out!
Even if my head's chopped off!
May the beautiful mountains and rivers,
Stay beautiful!

The Flower of Life Blooms

Oh, fight!
Charge forward,
Fight!

The year when Rou Shi was in Beijing, he had the most ideas and wrote the most works, including novels, poems, one-act plays, and prose, at which he excelled. In those days, he had a kind of Byronesque heroic pursuit, which fit his personality: monosyllabic on the outside but passionate on the inside. He often suffered insomnia in the dark of night, when he exhibited the most passion. It was during the sleepless nights that he completed many works. "In the dark night he pursued light. It was the best time of his burning flames of revolution," commented his friends.

In 1926, Rou Shi returned to his hometown of Ninghai to run a school, and later was promoted to be the director the county's education department. And the Ninghai Middle School, which he was managing, gradually became the base camp of the Ninghai Revolution. Unfortunately, under the influence of the left-leaning route within the party, a "riot" destroyed the school and his plan to save the country with education in his hometown.

The failure of a revolution in his hometown shattered his dream of opening up local culture. The cruel reality enlightened him that the only way out for the revolution was to overthrow the reactionary rulers.

"The white horse tied in front of the gate was screaming in the morning breeze. The sound moved the thinking sword on the wall!" Rou Shi left his hometown again. And this time he didn't come back...

His destination was Shanghai. As a revolutionary ready to fight, he officially became a fighter beside the giant Lu Hsun.

It was early autumn of 1928. The sweet scent of Osmanthus flowers had permeated Shanghai. Lu Hsun was living at 23 Jingyunli, Hengbang Road, Zhabei District. When they met for the first time, Rou Shi humbly presented his manuscript, *Death of the Old Times*, and elaborated his creative motives and the revisions to his mentor. Lu Hsun immediately hit it off with this fellow Zhejiang native. Back in Beijing, he had heard of this literary youth from Ninghai. Lu Hsun encouraged him as he received the manuscript. That elated Rou Shi to the fullest. He was unable to sleep at

Revolutionaries

night, so he wrote to his family far away with the delightful news:

> *I have submitted three volumes of novels to Mr. Lu Hsun for review. Mr. Lu Hsun is a well-known writer today. If I am good enough to earn his praise and have the works published with his endorsement, my future is going to be beyond promising.*

Apparently, Lu Hsun's encouragement stirred up a surge of emotion in him. Coincidentally, as 23 Jingyunli, where Lu Hsun lived, was close to Baoshan Road, where there were noisy pedestrians and neighbors' children, soon there was a house available for rent at 18 Jingyunli. Lu Hsun decided to take it. He invited his third brother, Zhou Jianren, who was an editor at Commercial Press, to move in with him at number 18. Worried that Rou Shi and other young people had no place to stay, he also accommodated them in the newly vacated number 23. Rou Shi jumped up joyfully when he heard the news. What moved him even more was that Lu Hsun also provided them meals at his place.

Rou Shi was eternally touched and grateful. In his diary, he wrote, "When I feel unusually disturbed, dining with Mr. Lu Hsun calmed me. His perseverance, clear thinking, eruditeness, and rational speech, all humbled me. His kindness, comical jokes, and deep criticisms of the society, delights me and teaches me more." Lu Hsun also helped him publish his *Death of the Old Times* in the magazine *Flow*.

Lu Hsun's support undoubtedly opened up major opportunities for Rou Shi to embark on the road of revolutionary literature and art. Soon, Rou Shi learned that his pal Feng Xuefeng escaped to Shanghai, wanted by KMT reactionaries in his hometown of Yiwu, Zhejiang Province. He introduced this talented and knowledgeable young literary theorist to Lu Hsun.

"Great! Invite him for a meeting." Lu Hsun was excited when he heard the name Feng Xuefeng. "I have read his translation of Russian literature. *Flow* published it. He is talented."

When Rou Shi broke the news to Feng Xuefeng, the young man from Yiwu, who later became an essential literary and artistic leader of the CPC, shouted with excitement.

The Flower of Life Blooms

Their meeting formed a bond between Feng Xuefeng, a Chinese communist and Lu Hsun, a cultural giant. Lu Hsun particularly adored the talented young man and regarded him as another true confidant. Lu Hsun's wife Xu Guangping knew her husband best. She called Feng Xuefeng the person who understood him best in China. In the winter of 1933, Feng Xuefeng accurately and comprehensively described Lu Hsun to Mao Zedong for the first time when he was transferred to the Soviet area as Dean of the Academic Affairs of the Party School of the Central Committee of the CPC. From then on, Mao Zedong had an emotional resonance with Lu Hsun. And Rou Shi was undoubtedly the bridge to that. Rou Shi became a true Chinese Communist under the introduction of Feng Xuefeng. Thereafter, the two of them lived with Lu Hsun as his students and as the link and bridge between him and the Chinese revolutionary camp. They three were close teacher/students/comrades-in-arms fighting side by side on the cultural front. In particular, Rou Shi and Lu Hsun became more and more inseparable over time. Lu Hsun admitted that Rou Shi was "The only person in Shanghai who not only he could confide himself in, but also entrusted private affairs to." Agnes Smedley, a famous American journalist who interviewed Lu Hsun, once recalled: "There was a teacher named Rou Shi. Among Lu Hsun's friends and students, he might be the most capable and his favorite."

Rou Shi made Lu Hsun's daily life easier, but most importantly, he introduced many revolutionary literary and artistic youths to Lu Hsun, including Hu Yepin. And Rou Shi himself gained a stronger and more thorough revolutionary spirit and beliefs by staying close to Lu Hsun. He had completely grown into a passionate revolutionary idealist. His pen and emotion were burning with revolutionary ideals. He no longer used the love between young men and women to express revolutionary enthusiasm and yearning for communism, but nurtured the real mind of a revolutionary.

His on-the-spot record writing entitled *A Great Impression* vividly depicts the revolutionary flames burning fiercely inside him...

> *'Tis the final conflict;*
> *Let each stand in his place.*
> *The International working class*

Revolutionaries

Shall be the human race!

Surrounded by red walls, we chanted the melodious and majestic Internationale *in front of the portraits of Marx and Lenin. We, forty-eight people, stood closely and quietly, calmly and solemnly, with our hands hanging straight and our heads slightly lowered; we dreamed big, we were cheerful and excited; it was as if the sound of our singing was one beautiful cloud, wrapped in the red color of communism, carrying us to the free and equal paradise without rich and poor, without class.*

We, forty-eight people, gathered in a room like a living room and surrounded a large "I"-shaped table. It was covered with red cloth with gorgeous floral patterns. Our meeting began in a tense atmosphere.

"Comrades! The Soviet flag has been hoisted across the country!" Our Chairman made a solemn opening speech to us peacefully and gently.

We were like brothers, our organization was like a family; we spoke, talked, walked, and performed all daily activities in accordance with the secret living rules. A sister-like comrade, with beautiful posture and sweet feelings, managed the purchase and distribution of the supplies we needed, and said "Good night" to us before going to bed every night.

"Who wants an elixir?" After a long meeting, she often tossed this question at us with a smile.

To minimize the noise of moving chairs and stools, we ate standing like soldiers. Once, when a comrade was waiting for the meal, he joked: "Eating is the same as revolution; chopsticks are guns and rice is bullets. With them, we eat fish and meat; hurry up, revolution, and eat, so that hunger will be no longer!"

After dinner, when there were no meetings, or when some did not have to attend any, we would talk freely—to each other, we reported how we experienced the revolution, or ask others to report on the current revolutionary situation of the group to which they belonged. With a victorious yet gentle tone, we confided in each other.

"Which group does this comrade represent?"

It was a common question.

Comrades from the Soviet areas and the Red Army were eager to know the revolutionary situation in Shanghai.

"How do the workers, citizens, and small business owners in Shanghai see

The Flower of Life Blooms

the revolution? Do they want it? Do they know it?"

"Except for the workers, ordinary citizens, small business owners, probably because of their class, only sympathize with the revolutionary organizations and actions without direct participation," I answered.

"The work in Shanghai is important!" They exclaimed. "The revolution in the countryside is expanding day by day. The tension is increasing. Workers and citizens of Shanghai must rise up!"

There was a comrade from East Liaoning, tall and kind-faced. When we talked for the first time—we shared the floor of the same dormitory—he told me his first understanding and actions of the revolution: that the reason why he joined the revolution was not for the proletariat. He was the child of a rich landlord, but he wanted to overthrow the tyranny of government class—a term he created; he said he was from the commoner class, so he took a gun from home and tried to join the bandits with empty pockets, because bandits were the only enemy of government class. But the first time he was injured. A bullet pierced through his upper arm and out from the back—he took off his clothes and showed me the first two scars. He was injured several times (I know he had mental scars too), and the second time the back of the face, under the ears, was injured, the size of a silver coin. Meanwhile, he believed that there was no future for bandits, that he had to take further actions to overthrow feudal society, so he joined the proletarian revolutionary group.

...

The mighty, vigorous, and powerful slogans ended with one shouting and many raising their hands in the victorious closing ceremony of the meeting. We swayed slowly, anxious yet excited. Our attitude was firm and optimistic. Behind each of us, there were tens of millions of people, celebrating, shouting, and dancing with joy in the clouds, walking with us, supporting our ten major political programs, our five major resolutions, and 22 minor resolutions of the meeting. We worked hard to implement the resolutions and to accelerate the success of the revolution. There were millions of people behind us. We scattered, carrying these major revolutionary missions of the workers and peasants, and went deep into all parts of the country, into the workers and peasants of the country; our iron fists were holding fierce torches. China, burn! China, burn! We would ignite all flames of the world! Long live the success of the world revolution! We were all waiting with fire, with blood, and with death. We scattered. In our ears, it seemed as if the trumpets of victory resounded, the sound of triumphant drums echoed. The red flag dancing in the howling wind was as if hoisted on the top of our Himalayas.

This is the most intuitive, most vivid excerpt with a strong sense of the scene that I have seen so far depicting revolutionary youths talking about the revolution, joining organizations, and picturing romance together at the beginning of the last century.

On January 17, 1931, the evening before Rou Shi was arrested, he visited Lu Hsun, asking what he could do for him. Lu Hsun entrusted him to discuss with the Beixin Book Company on his behalf about a contract that was signed before. Having received Lu Hsun's copy, Rou Shi hurriedly said goodbye and mentioned that he would attend an important meeting tomorrow.

The next morning, he first came to a small café on the right side of the Yongan Company, and attended a meeting of the Executive Committee of the Left League. After that, he visited his friend Wang Yuhe for lunch. Then, he took Feng Keng, a revolutionary comrade he had always called Mei, to the Oriental Hotel for a meeting.

They entered room 31. Soon after they sat down, military police and secret agents surrounded them. Eight people including Rou Shi, Feng Keng, Lin Yunan, and Hu Yepin were arrested...

Three days later, on January 19, the Criminal Court of the Second Branch of Jiangsu High Court opened. That day, Rou Shi, who had been tortured for three days, lost his glasses yet was still in a suit with a swollen face. Feng Keng, a young female party member, had such swollen cheeks that people could hardly recognize her.

"Why are they all here?" Rou Shi couldn't hide his surprise as he saw over 30 Communists were arrested, including He Mengxiong.

How strange! It must have been betrayal from a traitor.

"Now let's begin—"

The pre-arranged court trial started to put on a show. After the judge asked the names one by one without an actual purpose, he read out the written verdict:

The defendants were found guilty of colluding in a clandestine meeting in Room 31, Oriental Hotel, 111 Hankou Road, at 1:40 p.m. on January 17, the 20th year of the Republic of China (1931), with the intent to subvert the government, violating Article 103 of the Criminal Law. The defendants also violated Article 6 of the Provisional Regulations Prohibiting Counter-Revolutions at 1:40 pm on January 17, the 20th year of the Republic of China. There was suspicion of the defendant colluding with the Communist Party. Ergo, the Chinese Public Security Bureau requested to transfer them to the Shanghai Special Administrative Region Court. Should the request be granted, all documents seized will be handed over to you...

"Come, escort the prisoners away!"

Rou Shi and others immediately protested: "We will not accept the verdict!"

"We are innocent!" The court was in chaos. The bailiffs didn't tolerate any resistance but used rifle butts and batons to intimidate them into the police vehicles parked at the gate.

Rou Shi was shackled with fetters that weighed 18 kilograms. Obviously, the enemies saw him as much a felon as He Mengxiong and others.

"You must know where Lu Hsun lives?" They wanted to get information from his mouth so as to make wider arrests.

Rou Shi sneered, "No idea at all!"

At the Songhu Garrison Headquarters Prison, Rou Shi and a younger fellow named Ouyang Li'an were locked in the same cell in the ninth room of the second lane. There were 10 people in total, six political prisoners and four military prisoners. At night, Rou Shi and the senior CPC Chai Yingtang slept on top of the bunk. Rou Shi did not have a quilt but shared that of Comrade Chai. Both fettered, they often woke up because of the freezing torture device. They had to wrap their feet with dry towels before going to bed every night...

Life in prison was extremely difficult, but Rou Shi remained optimistic. Concerned with the safety of Lu Hsun, he secretly wrote to Feng Xuefeng via secret channels from prison to inform him of the situation there:

Revolutionaries

Brother Xue:

I was escorted to Longhua yesterday with 35 accomplices (seven females). We were shackled last night, the first political prisoners to be ever shackled. The case was too big. I might not be able to get out for a while. Brother Shiwang from the bookstore would run errands for me. I'm fine now, and I'm learning German from brother Yin Fu. Please tell it to teacher; but tell him not to worry, we have not been physically tortured. The police station and the Public Security Bureau were probing his address several times, but I leaked them no information! Don't worry about me and good luck.

Zhao Shaoxiong

Zhao Shaoxiong was a pseudonym of Rou Shi in prison. In fact, if it weren't for the traitors, the true identity of many of them would not be exposed. His short letter showed that despite imprisonment, Rou Shi was still concerned with the safety of teacher Lu Hsun. This friendship is truly touching. Later, comrades of the Left League all called Lu Hsun teacher.

Rou Shi, who looked frail in appearance, was actually strong within. His fighting spirit especially resembled Lu Hsun's. They were deceived that it was a trip to "Nanjing" when he and his cellmates were abruptly escorted to the "court" on the second floor on the night of February 7, and they had to "sign the documents" one by one. When it was Rou Shi's turn, he scrutinized the "official document" and found out it was order of execution!

Rou Shi was infuriated and screamed to the cellmates: "Comrades, this is an execution order! Don't put fingerprints on it!"

"What? They are going to shoot us!"

"Down with KMT reactionaries—!"

Immediately chaos filled the courtroom. "Quickly, hold them down! Now!" Angry screams of slogans were mixed with the shouts of the armed military policemen. That night in Longhua was particularly sad and bloody...

In case of any accidents, the enemies escorted 24 Communists, including Rou Shi, to a wasteland next to the Garrison Headquarters. They loaded the guns and fired at them with a brutal inhumanity.

Alas, it was the most tragic scene in Longhua's history. There is the belief that peach blossoms in Longhua are extremely red because they

The Flower of Life Blooms

absorbed the blood of many revolutionary martyrs... Maybe it is true.

"China has lost a group of promising youths. I have lost good friends." Lu Hsun was overwhelmed with grief as he heard the news of the brutal murder of Rou Shi, Hu Yepin, and Feng Keng. Three days later, when he met with Feng Xuefeng, sobbing, he took out the mourning verse that he had just composed, "*Chanting was finished. I bowed my head. I couldn't write. The moon shines like water, upon my sweater*".

Two years later, in tears he wrote the famous eulogy *Remember in Order to Forget*.

Feng Keng, who Lu Hsun mentioned in this eulogy, was a young revolutionary woman of marked invididuality. She had a great influence on Rou Shi in his last two years, so he called her Mei.

In Lu Hsun's writings, Mei (the Chinese character for the plum-like flower wintersweet is 梅 méi) was frail, not beautiful, but indeed with a few thorns of the revolution...

Her character matched the name she gave herself, a strong young revolutionary. She was only 24 when she was killed. Her husband was Xu E. They were classmates. He was her father's student as well. She used to be called Lingmei (wintersweet on the mountains) when she was a child. Her elder brother took the two Chinese characters from the Tang poem "*Throughout four seasons grass grows by the river, in October wintersweet blooms on the mountain*." Feng Keng was her pen name after she embarked on the road of literary revolution.

Perhaps because there were too many boys in her family, she developed a boyish temper and character from childhood. She had thick eyebrows and doll-like eyes, never liked grooming but enjoyed debates. She used to quote, "Heroes protect the weak. Bullies are never heroes." After graduating from middle school, she and Xu E fell in love at their own will and together they taught in a rural elementary school in Chao'an County, a neighboring county of Shantou, her hometown. As a fan of literature, she found the evil forces of the old society at that time unbearable, so she worked hard to study and write. She once vowed: "I have to study hard, master the weapon of literature, avenge the people I love and realize my dreams." The works she created in those days exhibited a revolutionary spirit. For example, the heroine Zheng Ruolian in the novella *The Last Way*

Out broke out of the feudal family shackles and called out the innermost feelings of women's liberation "struggle for ourselves, for the masses," It was actually the reflection of her own pursuit of a new life.

1929 was a difficult year for the Chinese communists. Right after the Lunar Lantern Festival that year, Feng Keng and Xu E risked their lives to go to Shanghai, the oriental Moscow. Soon after she met with the revolutionaries from Shantou, she established contact with the Shanghai Underground Party, and joined the CPC, introduced by the famous Shantou translator and CPC member Ke Bainian, thus becoming one of the rare young female writers of the Left League. As a professional revolutionary, Feng Keng had cherished communist ideals. Holding two weapons—flyers and revolutionary literature, she roared at the dark society. She sometimes attracted massive attention in Shanghai. In revolutionary battles, she often forgot her identity as a female. For any tasks assigned by the organization, no matter how perilous, she always marched forward without hesitation. There have been many times when she, carrying revolutionary flyers, came across reactionary policemen patrolling and making body searches on the street, and she calmly dodged them, leaving her comrades in awe.

Busy as she was, she used the time on the tram and knitted a blue wool vest for her husband.

"You go out more often. You should wear it." Xu E loved his wife and comrade-in-arms deeply.

It was this wool vest that played a key role in finding the Longhua martyrs after liberation.

On December 6, 1949, a revolutionary survivor wrote an article in memory of his sacrificed comrades in *People's Daily*. It immediately caught the attention of some leaders of the central government and the mayor of Shanghai, comrade Chen Yi. Next, the civil affairs department and the public security department joined forces to search for the twenty-four martyrs of Longhua mentioned in Lu Hsun's writings. However, it was a long time ago and they were killed in secret. The search was difficult. Plus, the information collected from Longhua locals was not clear enough. Finally, employees of the public security and civil affairs departments dug up a pile of decayed bones beside a chimney behind the former KMT Songhu Garrison Headquarters. It was impossible to confirm their

The Flower of Life Blooms

identities given that there was no appearance left to check. However, there was a blue wool vest on one of the deceased remains that had not fully rotted (it is collected in the Shanghai Longhua Martyrs Memorial Hall). Afterwards, related departments asked the martyrs' relatives to identify it. Xu E recognized it at one glance. In this way, the tragedy of the Twenty-four Martyrs of Longhua was eventually confirmed...

The stories of each of the twenty-four martyrs were enough materials for a book, not only because of their sudden death, but their higher-than-ordinary revolutionary ideals and beliefs. Among them, the innocent 17-year-old boy, adorable and full of revolutionary enthusiasm as Rou Shi wrote, Ouyang Li'an, deserved most respect.

Ouyang Li'an was a Changsha native. All his family were revolutionaries. His father Ouyang Meisheng was an early CPC member. In 1958, his mother Tao Cheng published the memoir *My Family* via oral narration. This book later became a traditional red classic that all my generation knew. At the age of 17, Tao Cheng married Ouyang Meisheng, a student of Changsha Number 1 Normal School. Soon after their marriage, Ouyang Meisheng embarked on the road of revolution, and she gradually followed her husband to engage in underground revolutionary activities. They raised six children: Li'an, Yingjian, Benshuang, Zhihe, Benwen, and Shuanglin. The family scattered several times during the years of war. First, Ouyang Meisheng went to work in Hanyang due to changes in the situation and Tao Cheng took some of their children to Hankou shortly afterwards and worked as a cover for regional organs.

In 1928, Ouyang Meisheng died of overwork, and Tao Cheng took the children to Shanghai, Wuhan, Yan'an, and other places. During those days, her daughters Benshuang and Shuanglin died of illness, her eldest son Li'an was killed in Shanghai, and her fourth child Zhihe sacrificed his life in Yan'an.

Ouyang Li'an, the eldest child, was vivacious and naughty. Afraid of being scolded by his father for having caused some trouble, he followed strangers to Xiangtan and joined the army there. Later, his mother found him. Under the influence of his father, Ouyang Li'an joined the wave of revolution at a young age. He gradually became mature. When the Northern Expedition Army entered Changsha in 1926, all sectors of the

Revolutionaries

provincial capital held a welcome ceremony at the Education Conference, and he was elected as a student representative to give a speech. At that time, he was only 12. Not tall enough, he had to stand on a stool to reach the microphone. After the provincial workers picket was founded, his father took him to observe the picket training. After that, he became a secret mail boy, helping his father deliver various secret documents. In Hanyang, he played the same role, distributing the newspaper *Big River*, edited by Xiang Jingyu and Xie Juezai, to contact points in the city every day. His young age allowed him to avoid the suspicion from enemies and he grew into an excellent little red messenger.

After his father died, he left for Shanghai and continued his underground work as a messenger. Next, he was sent to study in Soviet Union and joined the party, introduced by He Mengxiong. Although he was only 16 and a particularly young member of the CPC, he had been engaged in revolutionary work for several years. After returning to China, he served as a member of Jiangsu Provincial Committee of the Communist Youth League and head of the Youth Industry Department of Shanghai Federation of Labor Unions. On January 17, 1931, he came to Zhongshan Hostel on Tianjin Road for a meeting as instructed by the organization notice. Enemies besieged the meeting venue. After he was arrested, they discovered his certificate for participating in the International Conference of the Communist Party of Young Chinese and internal party documents from his residence. Consequently, this red messenger could no longer hide his identity. On the evening of February 7, enemies' bullets took the young life of this 17-year-old...

It has been 88 years since the Twenty-four Martyrs of Longhua died. However, I recently learned from a report of Hunan media that there are still martyrs like Liu Zheng and Duan Nan, who used pseudonyms when engaged in underground work in Shanghai. As a result, for a long time after their death, no one knew where they came from, who were their family, and what their real names were. They didn't have the chance to leave any word when they were killed. It was not until 88 years later that Hunan martyrs like Liu Zheng and Duan Nan were identified and brough back to their hometown.

These were the revolutionaries who sacrificed their young lives for

The Flower of Life Blooms

the founding of PRC. They had ideals and passion, faith and loyalty, and nothing else.

Among the Twenty-four Martyrs of Longhua, there is another shocking story. The young couple, Cai Bozhen and Wu Zhongwen, who held their wedding in a prison vehicle.

There are only a couple hundred words of information about them. Especially Cai Bozhen, to this day, no one knows when he was born. What is known is that he died on the evening of February 7, 1931. His resume was also simple: he was a native of Meixian, Guangdong, participated in the Guangzhou Uprising in December 1927, and was later sent to study in the Soviet Union. After returning to China, he served as secretary of Shanghai Youth Anti-Imperialist League and of Shanghai Central Committee of Jiangsu Provincial Party Committee.

His wife Wu Zhongwen, originally named Wu Xingxian, came from Nanhai, Guangdong. She was born in 1903 and studied at the only girls' high school in the county. Inspired by the Great Revolution, she actively joined the patriotic student movement. In 1924, she came to Guangzhou and enrolled in the women's vocational school that He Xiangning ran to receive revolutionary education. In 1925, she participated in the Guangdong-Hong Kong strike led by Deng Zhongxia and Chen Yannian, working in the Ministry of Women. She joined the CPC in the same year. The following winter she went to study in the Soviet Union. In the autumn of 1928, she returned to China and worked in Fa'nan District Committee of the CPC in Shanghai, guiding the youth movement. Later, she worked in the Wusong District Committee and Zhabei District Committee, leading the women workers movement in silk factories and yarn factories. She once served as secretary of the Zhabei District Committee of the Communist Youth League. This was a female communist who put revolution first. In those years, it was rare for a 28-year-old woman to be unmarried.

I assume that they fell in love while studying together in the Soviet Union. When they came to Shanghai to work underground, it was the most difficult days of the revolution. Perhaps they, who were in love, did not have time to think about getting married. However, destined to be together, they held an unimaginably special wedding in the prison vehicle in the last moments of their lives—

Revolutionaries

On January 17, 1931, after being arrested together, two days later Cai Bozhen and Wu Zhongwen were escorted to the Longhua Songhu Garrison Headquarters. On the way from the concession to Longhua, fellow cellmates in the prison vehicle heard Cai Bozhen explaining: "Comrade Zhongwen and I told them we were husband and wife during the interrogation. We were too busy and actually never had time to think about getting married, let alone preparing a wedding."

"Alas, in that case, you have to have a ceremony."

Someone in the same prison vehicle suggested, "Our situation is complicated. Probably, we will not walk out alive. Why not hold a ceremony here? A special wedding."

"Yes, a revolutionary couple. You deserve a wedding! Come, we will be your audience."

"Great! A wedding in the prison vehicle!" All the captives there cheered, excited.

Cai Bozhen consulted Wu Zhongwen with affection.

She blushed, signaled him "Yes" with a warm look, and leaned her head on his chest...

"Okay-now the wedding of revolutionary soldiers Cai Bozhen and Wu Zhongwen begins!"

"Bowing to each other as husband and wife is replaced with a revolutionary embrace."

Amidst the cheers, they hugged each other tightly. Although the iron fetters shackled them, the couple who put revolution ahead of their romance held on to each other tightly at this moment...

"What is it? What are you doing? Be quiet." The military policemen escorting the prisoners did not know what was happening inside, and kept hitting it with rifle butts and batons.

At this moment, the prisoners, to buy more time for the newly-wed to share an embrace, chanted *The Internationale* together...

At this moment, pedestrians on the streets watched in astonishment a singing prison vehicle going away...

At this moment, Wu Zhongwen, who was nestling in her bridegroom's chest, raised a pair of teary eyes and looked up at her husband. She pressed her burning lips at his fiercely...

CHAPTER EIGHT

———

Youth Comes Gently, Leaves Too Soon...

IT HAPPENED TO BE THE 100TH ANNIVERSARY OF THE MAY FOURTH Movement when I was writing this chapter. As I leafed through the biographies of revolutionary heroes, looking at their innocent and youthful faces, the speech that General Secretary Xi Jinping delivered in the Great Hall of the People echoed in my ears. "Youth has the most energy and the most daring dreams. Since modern times, the beautiful dreams that Chinese youth have been unremittingly pursuing have always been closely connected to the historical process of Chinese revitalization. During the years of revolution and wars, the vast number of youths were full of revolutionary ideals. For national independence, for people's liberation, they charged forward and sacrificed their lives..."

Indeed, it was their dreams and vigor that encouraged generations of youth to fight and die for the country. In the years of overthrowing the old world and establishing a new China, young revolutionaries came to Shanghai with dreams, to the party, to the center of the revolution. Many of them gave up an easy life, a chance to start a family, and sometimes their studies, leaving their families and hometown behind. They came alone or in groups.

Martyr Cao Shunbiao was such a young lad. He was the youngest of the 13 victims of the "Republic Stage Incident" in Shanghai in 1932. He was

Revolutionaries

only 17 when he died. But inside him the revolutionary flame was burning no less fierce than the elders. When he was escorted from Shanghai to a prison in Nanjing along with over a dozen "felons," he learned that execution was waiting at the destination, but he never shuddered. In the dark night, he whispered to his cellmate. "I am ready to die. After that happens, please send a message to my brother, who is also a communist, that my body should be buried next to the main road. I want to be there to see the Red Army triumphantly enter Nanjing City."

This young lad from Xiaoshan was the youngest child in the family. He had three older sisters and two older brothers. At the age of 12, like his brother, he was admitted to the Shanghai Baxian Bridge Guofa School, with great anticipation for Shanghai, and then transferred to Lida Academy the following year. He joined the Communist Youth League when he was 15. He was detained for over a month when he took part in a parade for the first time. Then, he was expelled from school for reading progressive newspapers. Next, with the help of his family, he studied at the high schools of Fudan University and of Daxia University. At that time, despite his young age, he had already become an active member of the revolutionary team. His childlike appearance made it easier to distribute revolutionary and progressive newspapers. Two years later, the revolutionary situation underwent profound changes. At the age of 17, he embarked on the road of revolution, becoming one of the leaders of the Middle School Student Union.

On May 5, 1932, the national government and the Japanese invaders entered into the Shanghai Armistice. Chinese government troops withdrew from Shanghai and designated the city as a so-called "unarmed zone." However, Japanese troops were allowed to be stationed in the Shanghai concession. It aroused firm opposition from the CPC, patriots, and progressives across the country, and Shanghai citizens. To please the Japanese aggressors, the Chiang Kai-shek KMT government suppressed waves of opposition from the CPC and the progressives. Therefore, under these circumstances, the Jiangsu Provincial Party Committee in Shanghai made a decision to initiate the establishment of Shanghai People's Anti-Japanese Armistice and Northeast Army of Volunteers Aid Association through dozens of anti-Japanese groups, including the Shanghai People's

Youth Comes Gently, Leaves Too Soon...

Anti-Japanese National Salvation Association, the Shanghai Anti-imperialist League, and the Shanghai University and High School Alliance. It continued to organize and lead Shanghai people to carry out the anti-Japanese struggle. Because Wen Jize, Secretary of the Youth League branch of Fudan University responsible for this task was a busy student, the organization transferred young professional revolutionist Cao Shunbiao to the Youth Department of the Shanghai People's Anti-Japanese Armistice and Northeast Army of Volunteers Aid Association in Luhuile, Yunnan Road, as a full-time officer to help Wen Jize with daily work.

At this time, the Central Committee of the CPC decided to establish a national anti-imperialist alliance on August 1 that year. The Jiangsu Provincial Party Committee in Shanghai, based on this decision, acted immediately, and published a notice regarding the preparation of the alliance on July 2 in Shanghai's *Current News*. It announced a congress to be held on July 15 regarding Jiangsu people's aid to the Northeast Army of Volunteers against the free city of Shanghai, along with the address of the "preparatory office," inviting all citizens to join the "discussion of a national matter."

"This is bad! Why is this secret information public?" Young as he was, Cao Shunbiao had a strong sense of revolution. When he saw this announcement, he consulted Wen Jize at once.

"Exactly. A peculiar move." Wen Jize agreed that it was too dangerous. The two expressed their concerns to superiors, but never got a reply.

They didn't understand what the superiors were plotting. But they kept diligently preparing for the alliance congress. They learned that the date had been finalized on July 17, and the venue was set as West Shanghai Republic Stage (also known as the Republican Theater) at the intersection of Jiaozhou Road and Changshou Road in West Shanghai.

"This spot is easy to find. Delegates can easily locate the big clock at the crossroads. You guys should go early and set up the venue." Superiors commanded Cao Shunbiao and other staff in the preparation office.

In the early morning of July 17, Cao Shunbiao came to meet Wen Jize at the venue with plenty of flyers and banners of slogans. They discovered a few suspicious people nearby, so they hid the promotional materials and the banners in a hole in the wall. Next, they found the Chairman of

Revolutionaries

the Congress Presidium, who was an officer from the provincial party committee, and proposed that the venue be changed immediately just in case.

"Alas, I'm afraid it's too late." The person in charge of the conference replied embarrassingly as he pointed to the delegates who had arrived. "How about we send three representatives to the Public Security Bureau (PSB) and ask them to protect our venue." Cao Shunbiao and Wen Jize exchanged glances, wondering if it was a right move.

At once, three representatives were sent to a nearby PSB, but they never came back—the PSB that was about to arrest them at the venue detained them, and simultaneously deployed a large number of well-prepared armed police towards the meeting venue...

"The police are here! Quickly, evacuate..." Cao Shunbiao was not tall or old enough, but his eyes were sharp and reactions quick. The moment he noticed a group of armed police rushing towards the theater, he shouted promptly.

"The police are here! Everyone, run—" Wen Jize also signaled loudly.

Suddenly, the delegates who had arrived at the venue were in a panic. Some wanted to jump off the wall, some wanted to run to the door, but it was blocked by the police... "Step on me and off the wall!" A tall, strong man was yelling. It was Cai Jihu, a hunk. At his signal, many stepped on his shoulders and jumped out of the courtyard wall.

"Quickly! Jump!" In this way, fifty to sixty people escaped to safety. However, Cai Jihu was so exhausted that he couldn't even stand. When he was about to flee, several dark guns had been aimed at his chest...

Reactionary police apprehended a total of 88 people including Cao Shunbiao and Cai Jihu in the front yard. The next day, all important newspapers in Shanghai reported the news.

They tied the 88 captives two by two with a hemp rope and escorted them to the Shanghai PSB by truck.

After three days of "interrogation," they were transferred to the Longhua Songhu Garrison Headquarters Detention Center. About a week later, they were escorted to the KMT Military Police Headquarters in Nanjing for trial because it was deemed a major case.

Betrayed by a traitor, Cao Shunbiao was exposed. "Yes, I am one of

Youth Comes Gently, Leaves Too Soon...

the organizers of the Congress, Minister of the Youth Department, and a member of the Communist Youth League! Come after me. Release the innocent!" Aware that his identity had been exposed, Cao Shunbiao tried to protect other comrades by assuming all the responsibilities.

The verdict that they were "communist felons" was soon made, and 13 people including Cao Shunbiao were sentenced to death.

The first to be dragged out and shot was an old comrade surnamed Xiao, who was also the oldest among them. His full name was Xiao Wancai, a native of Funing, Jiangsu. His entire family of four were arrested. His daughter Xiao Ming was only 14. She was Minister of Ministry of Women of the Zhabei District of the Communist Youth League and an activist in the Anti-Imperialist League. She was first sentenced to death but her young age saved her. The sentence was changed to 18 years in prison; Comrade Xiao's eldest son was 20 years old and was sentenced 12 years of imprisonment; his wife, also a revolutionary, was granted bail, because her identity was not exposed and she was blind.

Cao Shunbiao greatly admired the old man's heroism. The night before the execution, he confided to his pal Wen Jize, who was in the same cell but did not suffer identity exposure. "Inevitably, people die for the revolution. The day I was imprisoned, I was ready for that. But I do have two regrets. The first is that I can no longer continue the path of revolution; the other is that I have never been in love during the 18 years of my life."

Wen Jize gently asked this young lad: "Have you ever loved anyone?"

He shyly confessed: "I have, a female comrade who I work with... I think she likes me back, but we never said anything. Now this will die with me."

As he revealed his secret, he gently recited the poem by Petöfi Sándor, the Hungarian poet:

Liberty and love
These two I must have
For love, I will
sacrifice my life;
For liberty, I will
sacrifice my love.

Revolutionaries

"I have to sacrifice both now!" He softly wiped a handful of tears in front of his friend...

"Cao Shunbiao! Out!" The executioner called his name.

"What are you howling out?" Cao Shunbiao rolled his eyes at the ferocious military policeman, swiftly took off his pants and overalls, handed them to his cellmates, and calmly walked out of the cell to the execution ground...

"Bang!" A criminal bullet extinguished the young revolutionary flame.

It was on October 1, 1932, that the 17-year-old lad died at Yuhuatai. 17 years later, the People's Republic of China was founded.

Alas, our young martyr, for the revolution, put a period to his life at the age of 17.

Let's take this chance to remember the names of the other 11 martyrs who were killed together with Cao Shunbiao and Xiao Wancai: Xu Qingru (25 years old), Yang Xiaoerzi (20), Xu A'san (24, also known as Pan A'er), Xu Jinbiao (24, also known as Xu Ziming), Cui A'er (43, also known as Cui Si), Zhong Mingyou (28), Qiu Wenzhi (23, also known as Qiu Wenzhi), Chen Shan (28, also known as Zeng Taigong), Chen Shisheng (43, also known as Chen Jisheng), Wang Desheng (30, also known as Wang Mingguo), Liu Rijun (30, also known as Liu Dongchen). The fact is they were all young, just like Cao Shunbiao...

On the list of martyrs in two revolutionary martyrs memorial halls in Longhua in Shanghai and Yuhuatai in Nanjing, the names of two martyrs are engraved on my heart. One is the first martyr whose portrait is displayed in Nanjing Yuhuatai Martyrs Memorial Hall. He was Jin Fozhuang. This CPC member who died in 1926 had a special identity: the first military CPC member. In 1918, he was 18 and admitted to the Baoding Military Academy, where he became a midshipman. Four years later, he served as deputy company commander in the Zhejiang Army and joined the Communist Youth League. That year, he accepted the inspection of Xu Meikun, head of Shanghai District Executive Committee of the CPC and was approved by the organization to become a member of the CPC. He was one of the three CPC members in the first party group–Hangzhou Party Group, in Zhejiang Province at that time.

Youth Comes Gently, Leaves Too Soon...

In the spring of 1924, as a CPC member, Jin Fozhuang secretly arrived in Shanghai and reported the revolutionary situation in Hangzhou to the Shanghai District Committee of the CPC. After the KMT-CPC cooperation entered the "honeymoon period," the organization assigned him to help establish the Whampoa Military Academy in Guangzhou as captain of the third student team in the first semester. During those days, he was highly regarded by Liao Zhongkai, the KMT leftist leader and party representative of the academy, and promoted as one of the five members of the KMT Special Party Headquarters of the academy. Meanwhile, he followed instructions from the CPC to actively encourage activists among the students to join the CPC. In the two "eastern expeditions," he served as the party representative and head of the 2nd Regiment of the 1st Division of the 1st Army of the National Revolutionary Army. After the "Zhongshan Ship Incident," he returned to the military academy as a military instructor. Chiang Kai-shek also thought highly of him. He used the fact that they came from the same place to repeatedly coax Jin to leave the CPC and become his right-hand man. Having consulted the organization, Jin Fozhuang took the job as Deputy Director of the staff section of the general headquarters and Chief of the third department next to Chief Chiang Kai-shek. In fact, he was keeping Chiang Kai-shek under surveillance.

From July 1926, the Northern Expedition Army swiftly marched towards Jiangsu, Zhejiang, and Shanghai. News of the victories kept pouring in. It frightened Sun Chuanfang's old warlord troops. At the end of November, the General Command of the Northern Expedition Army convened a military meeting regarding attacking Sun Chuanfang's troops in Shanghai, Jiangsu, and Zhejiang. They planned to send Jin Fozhuang to Shanghai, who was familiar with the situation in those places, to instigate a rebellion within Sun Chuanfang's troops.

On the evening of December 9, Jin Fozhuang, on a special mission disguised as a businessman returning to Shanghai, boarded the British merchant ship Taikoo from Jiujiang, Jiangxi, and sailed eastward. Along the way, he couldn't control his anxiety, because he found out when he worked by his side how dangerously ambitious Chiang Kai-shek had become. He wanted to take advantage of this trip to Shanghai and report

Revolutionaries

critical information he had collected to the CPC organization in Shanghai. Unexpectedly, when the ship anchored at the Nanjing Xiaguan Wharf on the 11th, Wang Qichang, Sun Chuanfang's Nanjing military police commander, "invited" him offshore.

On the 12th and 13th, comrades of the Shanghai Organization of the CPC were still waiting for him to come but he never showed up, so they inquired about his whereabouts with the piers along the way at once. Soon, news came from Nanjing: on the evening of the 12th, Sun Chuanfang had ordered Wang Qichang to kill Jin Fozhuang at Yuhuatai...

He was 29 that year. He was born in a peasant family in Dongyang, Zhejiang Province. In his short life, before he could make the third "close contact" with Shanghai, he was gone forever, too soon. Even his name is rarely mentioned. When I stood in front of the photo of him in the uniform of the Northern Expedition Army, his vigorous and youthful face moved me. I wondered: had he arrived in Shanghai successfully, would he have become another marshal of People's Republic of China?

Compared with Jin Fozhuang, Yu Xiusong, also a martyr, had an extraordinary "relationship" with Shanghai. He spent over ten years in the Soviet Union. In the end, he was unjustly killed in the Soviet elimination of counter revolutionary movement as he was framed by Wang Ming and Kang Sheng. He was merely 39 years old when he died. Dating back to more than 13 years (that is, 10 years in the Soviet Union from 1925 to 1935, and 3 years in Xinjiang, sent by the Central Committee of CPC, supervising the warlord Sheng Shicai's united front, and seven to eight months in prison after being transferred from Xinjiang to the Soviet Union), Yu Xiusong, before turning 26, was an outstanding revolutionary in the Red Revolution camp in Shanghai.

When he was around 24, he had already been a senior CPC member in the Shanghai revolutionary camp, because he was the youngest of the several people who were planning to establish a communist group in the city.

"From ancient times, whoever wins the hearts of the people wins the country; whoever loses their support loses the power to rule."

"From ancient times, a great man has never feared difficulty, why? The answer is strong will. In the legend, the foolish old man eventually moved

Youth Comes Gently, Leaves Too Soon...

the mountain. Old but he was 100% determined... However, Chinese youth are no less determined than he is, are they? If so, China is going to be strong, isn't it?"

"China is poor while other countries are wealthy; China is weak while other countries are strong. Why? Answer: absence of gumption... gumption is paramount in life."

These were the words of Yu Xiusong when he was a teenager. He was born in a family of *xiucai* (scholars) in the late Qing Dynasty in Daqiao Village, Zhuji City, Zhejiang Province. Influenced by his father, who was a teacher, he was diligent with his studies from childhood. There were eight children in the Yu family. As the eldest, he experienced great difficulty in learning while attending to his younger siblings.

At the age of 17, he was admitted to the Zhejiang Provincial Number 1 Normal School with flying colors. In this school full of new ideas, he was nurtured by revolutionary ideas and Marxism. A teacher named Ma Yifu, the first Chinese scholar who came into contact with Marx's *Das Kapital*, was his first teacher.

In May 1919, when the May Fourth Movement broke out in Beijing, schools in Hangzhou promptly responded. By that time, Yu Xiusong had already been promoted to organizer of the Hangzhou Student Movement. On May 12, he and Xuan Zhonghua, a student leader, marched at the forefront of a parade with over 3,000 people from 14 schools in Hangzhou.

Subsequently, Yu Xiusong and others co-founded the revolutionary publication *Zhejiang New Wave* under the influence of his seniors and teachers like Chen Wangdao. On the first issue, he wrote: "In the spirit of struggle, we shall apply approaches of investigation, criticism, and guidance to promote the self-awareness and unity of the labor circles, to destroy the forces that restrain us, that exploit us, that plunder us, and to build a society of freedom and mutual aid, so that people can lead a happy and progressive life." Without a doubt, under the inspiration of the October Revolution and Chen Duxiu's *New Youth*, Yu Xiusong had begun his transformation from an anarchist to a "Bolshevik."

"Comrade Yunqin..." At the end of 1919, when he saw the news that in Beijing, Cai Yuanpei, Chen Duxiu, and Li Dazhao had launched a work-study mutual aid project, he was so excited that he wrote to his father, asking for financial support. But he addressed his father as Comrade Yunqin, which infuriated the father, who only mailed him one silver coin. Father wrote back to his "muddle-headed" son: "Four hundred million compatriots are your comrades. If everyone finances you one silver coin, the problem is solved. Why bother to ask your family for help?"

Eventually, he borrowed enough money from his friend to cover his travel expenses to Beijing. It was right after New Year's Day in 1920. He was excited. In an old coat received from his classmates, he paid to have a photo of himself taken in the photo studio as a memento. He told his friends: "I came here to experiment with my thoughts, and to spread them to all mankind, until they can share this new life of satisfaction, happiness, fraternity, mutual aid, freedom..."

It was an earlier model of work-study programs in China. However, he discovered that it failed to finance life and study through labor, let alone transform and change the entire society. He wanted to change the old world, thus withdrawing from the work-study mutual aid program. He embarked on the pursuit of another ideal life path. "I don't want to be a scholar anymore (I used to want that). I would rather be a revolutionary even though the world is against it," he screamed, swearing to the sky.

On March 26, 1920, he took a train from Beijing to Shanghai. From then on, his youthful years of outstanding contributions to the establishment of the CPC commenced.

In April, Voitinsky, representative of the Communist International, came to China, first Beijing and then Shanghai, to meet with Chen Duxiu. Yu Xiusong, as the interpreter of their meeting, witnessed and participated in the first moments of building of the CPC. In May, he, Chen Duxiu and others launched the Marxism Research Association. In August, he contributed to particularly important initial preparation of CPC building. Afterwards, in addition to leading the establishment of the Communist Youth League, he had been instructing party building in various places. This revolutionary youth was only 21 at the time, but already a mature and experienced politician—

......I arrived at Duxiu's place at 9 p.m. to give him the translation of The Communist Manifesto *by Wangdao. We talked about how translation*

Youth Comes Gently, Leaves Too Soon...

should always be accurate and meticulous, but now people make a living by translating books. Eight thousand characters on a daily basis makes the ends meet. Inevitably, they misunderstand, they fabricate. This is what happens under the private property system. I am in no place to judge those who translate books to survive.

...Too many mosquitos tonight. Not sure when I would be able to fall asleep.

—June 28, 1920

I have written five letters today.

—June 29, 1920

I am waiting for letters from my friends all day long. Every letter makes me happier. I checked the mailbox five or six times today. Nothing. There was only one post card from Zhang Fa in the afternoon. Alas, when you are in pain, everything seems painful!

I went to bed early today, but the mosquitos bit hard, keeping me awake, so I got up to finish today's diary. When I finished, it was already three a.m.

—June 30, 1920

Yu Xiusong loved writing diaries when he was young. And it was precisely thanks to his diaries that survived that we could see these many historical details in the early days of the founding of the CPC and deep down into the heart of this outstanding lad.

In the early days when the CPC was founded, various places communicated via letters. Yu Xiusong was young and good at writing. He almost became Chen Duxiu's right-hand man. In the first half of 1921, the CPC was preparing for the First National Congress. Yu Xiusong, head of the Shanghai Communist Youth League, of whom Grigori Voitinsky, Secretary of the Eastern Department of the Communist International spoke highly, was invited to attend the Second Congress of the Communist Youth International in Moscow. Therefore, in July and August when CPC held its first national congress, he was absent in Shanghai, but in Moscow.

The following year, he returned to China from the Soviet Union and received instructions from Chen Duxiu and the Central Committee of the

Revolutionaries

CPC. He was assigned to lead the establishment of the Communist Youth League in various places, and served as head of the party department in Shanghai during the cooperation between KMT and CPC. During the May Thirtieth Movement, he was one of the organizers and leaders of the strikes, responsible for convening joint meetings of the KMT district party committees to mobilize KMT members in Shanghai to engage in the anti-imperialist struggle. This youth, who joined the KMT in his personal capacity, stood with enthusiasm at the forefront of the anti-imperialist struggle and the main battlefield, exhibiting the vigor and drive of a Chinese revolutionary youth, as well as his clear standpoint.

Perhaps, it was precisely because of the vigor, the drive, the standpoint, that some revolutionary opportunists were jealous and ostracized him.

In October 1925, the Central Committee of the CPC sent him to study in the Soviet Union again. Unexpectedly, this time, the young yet experienced revolutionary never returned...

"Comrades, be strong! We are revolutionaries, and revolutionaries brave the wind and waves. We should always be ready to die for the revolution! No waves are tall enough to frighten us. Look ahead. We are going to the center of the world revolution. Our minds should be as vast as the sea, so that all difficulties are easily overcome! We will conquer the roaring waves..." Yu Xiusong made this impromptu speech when a boat of revolutionary youth were suffering from seasickness and dizziness on their way to the Soviet Union. No one, including himself, had foreseen that his future fate would unfold like raging waves ready to swallow it all—

First, Wang Ming framed him and Dong Yixiang (martyr, a native of Changzhou, Jiangsu Province, early CPC member, persecuted by Wang Ming, and unjustly killed during the suppression of counter-revolution-aries in the Soviet Union at the age of 43) as anti-party members of the Jiangsu and Zhejiang Association. It was not until 1935 after he suffered excruciating torture that he returned to his motherland. However, many changes had taken place in China. Yu Xiusong accepted the instructions of the Central Committee of the Communist Party of Soviet Union to stay in Xinjiang and handle tasks regarding the United Front. Despite his far distance from the Central Committee of the CPC, controlled by Wang Ming at the time, he never escaped political persecution. In the summer of 1938,

Youth Comes Gently, Leaves Too Soon...

he was forcibly escorted to the Soviet Union, where there was the crueler suppression of counter-revolutionaries. He understood what awaited him at the destination. Before leaving his wife, he calmly consoled his relatives: "Be strong. Don't be sad. Imprisonment is common for revolutionaries. To be a revolutionary, one must not fear death. They cannot kill all of us. The revolution will prevail!"

In this way, Yu Xiusong, an outstanding early revolutionary activist of the CPC and one of the founders of the Chinese Communist Youth League, disappeared at an unknown historical moment. It was not until decades later that his reputation was restored.

Alas, this was the youth of revolutionaries, the fate of young revolutionaries. They never feared death, never doubted their faith—

We are young Bolsheviks,
Everything is steel:
Our mind,
Our language,
Our discipline!
We were born in the flames of revolution,
We were born in the rhythm of struggle,
...
We fear no death,
We do not weep,
We want to destroy,
We want to build,
Our stand is clear,
Axe, sickle and blood...
(Poem by Yin Fu)

In fact, Yu Xiusong was not the only one full of revolutionary pride in those turbulent years. Most revolutionary youth gave their precious lives for the revolutionary cause without leaving a trace of their footprints.

There is a martyr I have always remembered. He was Yuan Zitong, a young martyr from Guizhou Province. I call him young because I learned after I interviewed people from Shanghai, Nanjing, Hangzhou that when

Revolutionaries

he died he was only 16. However, the enemies changed his age in the death sentence letter from 16 to 18...

Yuan Zitong was neither from Shanghai nor Nanjing, but Chishui, Guizhou Province. I have been to his hometown four times in the past two years. That small town was the key battlefield of the Red Army's *Four Times Crossing Chishui*. On the hill near his home, the Red Army and the KMT reactionary army fought a famous battle—the Battle of Qinggangpo. Both sides suffered severe casualties. According to the local people, corpses of both sides piled up, covering the entire hillside.

The time of his death was September 17, 1930. He was one of the victims in the famous, historical Massacre of Ten Martyrs of Xiaozhuang. Xiaozhuang was China's first experimental rural normal school, opened by educator Tao Xingzhi in the suburbs of Nanjing. Located in the hinterland of the enemies, it was actually a "cradle of young red revolutionaries" headed by the Shanghai Underground Party. Comrade Chen Yun, one of the leaders of Jiangsu Provincial Party Committee at that time, once called it the spark of revolution.

Yuan Zitong went to study thousands of miles away from his hometown because he was born rich. His two elder brothers were government officials, and one of them was a high-ranking official in the KMT army. When he was 10, his family sent him to the Dashun School run by Huang Qisheng, a famous modern educator in Guiyang, thanks to his uncle Zhang Huafeng's friendship with the Huang Qisheng. Huang Qisheng was Wang Ruofei's uncle. His progressive ideas and advanced education enabled him to have great local influence. Unfortunately, his son fell ill and died. He took the clever Yuan Zitong as his nominally adoptive son, and showed him extra love and care. Later, Huang Qisheng founded the Zunyi Provincial Third Middle School and admitted a group of progressive students. Opposed to the dark rule of the KMT, he stirred up students unrest on many occasions and was dismissed. He fled to Shanghai in order to escape the pursuit of the reactionary government. At the age of 13, Yuan Zitong followed him to Shanghai despite disapproval from his family. Interestingly, he met Wang Ruofei, a leader of the CPC, in Shanghai, and thereafter embarked on the road of revolution...

Youth Comes Gently, Leaves Too Soon...

In 1929, under the instruction of the Jiangsu Provincial Party Committee that a party organization should be set up in the hinterlands of the enemies to actively engage in revolutionary activities, Tao Xingzhi founded Xiaozhuang Normal School which became the primary revolutionary base. When Wang Ruofei, former head of the Jiangsu Provincial Party Committee, asked Yuan Zitong whether he would like to study there while making revolution, he gladly expressed his willingness. There, he soon joined the Communist Youth League and became secretary of the school's league branch. Young as he was, he was extremely devoted to the revolution. He secretly distributed leaflets on Nanjing Street in Shanghai and performed revolutionary propaganda in factories and rural areas. He always marched in the forefront and Tao Xingzhi admired him deeply. Once he and his classmate Yao Ailan led over 200 students and teachers on a spring trip to Qixia Mountain to collect plant specimens. To get rides for the children of these poor peasant families who could not afford them, he came forward to negotiate with the railway authorities, and succeeded.

When Tao Xingzhi learned of this, he wrote a poem of praise:

Born not free, yet born to be free.
Who is the revolutionary, the young man of course.

However, Nanjing was the nest of the KMT. The revolutionary activities of communists in Xiaozhuang Normal School and Youth League members soon caught the attention of KMT agents and Chiang Kai-shek. Consequently, the Nanjing KMT government suspended the school.

The moment Tao Xingzhi heard the news, he organized teachers and students to fight, setting up a student group to protest on the streets of Nanjing. This provoked the Chiang Kai-shek KMT government to "demolish the school," and "completely destroy the communist dens." It sent a legion of secret agents to hunt down communists in the Xiaozhuang Normal School, Communist Youth League members, and other revolutionaries. When Yuan Zitong was arrested for the first time, his elder brother, an officer of KMT army, personally bailed him out. He warned Yuan Zitong lividly: "Do this again and I'll leave you to die!"

Revolutionaries

He ignored the warning and kept doing intense underground revolution work. The organization often entrusted him to report to Wang Ruofei on the Nanjing situation and work progress.

"The situation is serious. Mr. Tao has also arrived in Shanghai. Why don't you stay with me for the time being?" Party leader Wang Ruofei was concerned about his safety.

"Precisely because Mr. Tao is here, the party members and league members in the school over there are exposed to greater danger. I have to arrange their safety first. Otherwise, I cannot rest my mind here in Shanghai," explained Yuan Zitong sincerely.

"Alright. Go. Come back soon!"

In this way, he embarked on the dangerous road northward again. At this time in Nanjing, danger was lurking everywhere, especially in Xiaozhuang Normal School, where over 30 people had been arrested. In order to remove the source of trouble, KMT secret agents were everywhere. When Yuan Zitong appeared on the streets of Nanjing again to contact the underground revolutionaries, snipers hiding in the dark aimed their guns at him...

He was arrested again.

"This idiot has been completely brainwashed by the Communist Party! Incurable." KMT secret agents exhausted their torture tricks in an attempt to turn the young revolutionary. However, he was loyal and defended himself aggressively in court, which provoked the executioner Gu Zhenglun, chief of the Nanjing KMT PSB, who, embarrassed and agitated, sentenced him to the death penalty.

Yuan Zitong's adoptive father, Huang Qisheng, rushed to Nanjing when he heard the news. He directly contacted Gu Zhenglun (whose wife was also his student), and implored him: "From old time's sake, spare his life. This child is still young. A rare patriot. True that he is impulsive. But a death penalty? Isn't that too much?"

"This..." Gu Zhenglun understood Huang Qisheng's prestige and power, and caved. "Have him sign a statement of repentance and declare his separation from the Communist Party on a newspaper. And he lives."

Gu Zhenglun personally took the statement of repentance for him to sign, and argued: "You are young. Choose wisely. What you have done deserves imprisonment and death sentence. Don't you know that no one comes back to life after death?"

Yuan Zitong turned his head away and replied: "I am young, but I know how to live. Some live like dogs. Some die honorably. We revolutionaries prefer an honorable death."

"Damn it!" Gu Zhenglun left with anger. Back at the office, he changed Yuan Zitong's age on the verdict from 16 to 18.

> *Dear brother:...We are in different predicaments. Some endure the humiliation, some wait and see, some march forward courageously. When one is not afraid of death, one has no more scruples. With this kind of self-sacrificing spirit, our dreams will come true.*

The cruel enemies did not spare their lives because of their young age. In August and September of 1930, the KMT gunned down the Ten Martyrs of Xiaozhuang at Yuhuatai. The youngest of them was Yuan Zitong. There was another one whose nominal age was 17. The reactionaries adopted the same trick: changing their age to legalize their death sentence.

Let's remember then ten young revolutionary martyrs (four communists and six Youth League members): Yuan Zitong (16), Shen Yunlou (17), Yao Ailan (female, 18), Guo Fengchao (female, 19 years old), Xie Weiqi (20), Ye Gang (22), Tang Zao (22), Ma Mingju (22), Hu Shangzhi (23), Shi Jun (23).

Young lives fell during the struggles, inspiring countless revolutionary soldiers who were still fighting. Having learned of the tragic death of another group of young revolutionaries a few months before his own demise, Rou Shi composed this famous poem *Boiling Blood* (excerpt):

> *Blood is boiling,*
> *Hearts are burning,*
> *In this terrible night,*
> *He died!*

> *He died!*
> *In this night of white terror—*

Revolutionaries

Our young comrades,
Gunned down,
The bullet pierced through his chest,
Fell down–their little bodies,
On the grassland,
Flowed bright red blood!
...
The red water of the Yellow River washed up on both banks,
The flag of the Soviets,
Fly over the mountains of China!
Great revolution,
Great struggle,
Our young comrades,
The captains of the young vanguards,
Died here!
...

On the blood-stained revolutionary paths, I have noticed many young "inspectors." The nature and dangers of their work were rarely mentioned in the past. A party historian explained to me: Back then, to supervise the work of local party organizations and investigate the independent performance of related party leaders in underground work, the Central Committee of the CPC had sent a group of highly loyal, young, clever and disciplined "inspectors" to related jurisdictions. They would conduct "work inspections." In addition, they were also responsible for conveying instructions from the higher-level party organization and the central government to subordinate units. In a way, in those days of underground work, they shouldered dual missions of supervising the subordinate units and responsible persons and conveying messages between higher-level party organizations and the central government and subordinate units. Thus, they were usually required to be young, energetic, swift, and disciplined. They had to be well aware of the situation of subordinate units while keeping secrets and following iron disciplines.

"The inspector job was the most dangerous. At times, enemies intercepted and arrested them soon after they left Shanghai with missions. Many

Youth Comes Gently, Leaves Too Soon...

inspectors didn't know that the local organization had been destroyed when they left. When they came back after taking the mission from their superiors, they stepped right into enemies' trap..." said the party historian.

From the early days of the founding of the party to the eve of the War of Liberation, Shanghai was not only the seat of the Central Committee of the CPC, but that of Jiangsu and Zhejiang Provincial Party Committees. At the time, transportation was underdeveloped. In order to prevent the leaking of secrets, it was the "inspectors" who delivered the party's deployment and guidance of daily affairs across the country. Especially in the three provinces of Jiangsu, Zhejiang, and Anhui, the party affairs has always been under the direct jurisdiction of the Central and Provisional Central Bureaus and the Jiangsu and Zhejiang Provincial Party Committees based in Shanghai, hence a particularly large number "inspectors" there.

And this allowed me to see the different images of other revolution-aries—

After the Nanjing April Tenth Massacre and the April Twelfth Counter-revolutionary Coup in Shanghai in 1927, the CPC's organizational work on the Shanghai-Nanjing line was extremely difficult and dangerous. The Jiangsu Provincial Party Committee and the party organization in Shanghai suffered serious destruction. At this time, a youth from Yixing was transferred to the Jiangsu Provincial Communist Youth League Committee in Shanghai. He was Shi Yanfen, capable and experienced. Prior to this, he was Secretary of Yixing County Party Committee of the Communist Youth League. And as deputy commander-in-chief, he had just organized the Yixing riot.

"Enemies have seriously wrecked the Shanghai-Nanjing front-line party and league organizations. We have therefore decided to appoint you as the new Shanghai-Nanjing line inspector and Secretary of the Nanjing Municipal Party Committee. Any questions?"

"No."

"Great. You start tomorrow. Manage this line, focus on the inspections in Shanghai and Nanjing, and meanwhile stay active in the hinterlands of the enemies in Nanjing..."

"Yes, sir."

It was simple for the superiors to appoint cadres and assign tasks, just a few words, a couple of minutes of conversation, and the work started. It might be to meet with the organization of a certain place, or to explain something to another local person in charge. In the process, one might encounter a shameless defector and end up in cold iron fetters and prison.

Shi Yanfen was a highly experienced young inspector familiar with the enemy activities on the Shanghai-Nanjing front. And in Shanghai, Suzhou, Wuxi, Changzhou, Zhenjiang, and Nanjing, he was able to speak local dialects. It was a necessary ability for inspectors doing underground work, because people in Shanghai and Nanjing were extremely cautious with foreigners who couldn't not speak local dialects—that was how local secret agents identified non-local underground party members. Once Shi Yanfen inspected Changzhou. As he was meeting with a local underground party leader in a teahouse, several secret agents suddenly broke in. They interrogated the local underground party leader about his occupation. He replied in Changzhou dialect that he was running a small local business. So they immediately stared at Shi Yanfen. With fluent Changzhou Wujin dialect, he explained that he was running a tofu business. The secret agents were at the end of their wits. They didn't know that Shi Yanfen, a Yixing native, attended Changzhou Number 5 Middle School. Once, as he was walking while reading, he tripped over a rock and knocked out a front tooth. "With the tooth gone, my Changzhou dialect sounds more authentic!"

After he became an inspector in the spring that year, he experienced many similar moments. And he was always able to emerge out of danger. Kuang Yaming, former Dean of Nanjing University, Secretary of the East Shanghai, West Shanghai, and Zhabei Communist Youth League before liberation, who once engaged in underground work alongside him, praised his young comrade-in-arms in 1945. "During my stay in Shanghai, the organization had appointed Shi Yanfen to the Jiangsu Provincial Committee of the Communist Youth League as an inspector on the Shanghai-Nanjing line. He is fearless, and had accumulated rich experience in challenging struggles."

However, on May 5, 1928, Shi Yanfen failed to escape misfortune: he attended a local Youth League branch meeting on the city wall of Jiming Temple near Nanjing Central University. There were 20 attendees scheduled for that day. "Damn. Someone is following us!" Shi Yanfen noticed a stalker, and immediately whispered to the two student group cadres accompanying him. "Try to get rid of the tail."

But it was too late. A group of police officers suddenly appeared... They were arrested.

"Interrogation" soon began. His frequent activities along the Shanghai-Nanjing line and armed riots in Yixing soon exposed his identity to the enemies. They played good cop-bad cop, trying every way to turn him.

"We know that you have been orphaned since childhood, that you have to take care of your younger siblings. Why devote yourself to the Communist Party? What have they offered you? Once you die, who will take care of your younger siblings? Will anyone remember you, a Yixing native?" Since torture turned out to be in vain, enemies played the good cop.

Shi Yanfen wiped the blood from the corner of his mouth while glaring at them. He replied: "The difference between us communists/revolutionaries and you is that we do not live for ourselves. Save your tongue. Should I fear death, I would not join the revolution, would I?"

"Another one totally brainwashed!" The secret agents shook their heads and sighed. A letter of death sentence was tossed at the young inspector.

Dear brothers and sisters:

I bid you farewell today.

I die for the society, for the country, for mankind. It is glorious and necessary. After my death, tens of millions of comrades will step on my blood, march forward, and fight. Our revolutionary cause will succeed. My body dies but the legacy survives. The reactionaries destroy my body but never my free revolutionary soul! My soul will always be with you and take care of you and my surviving comrades. Please do not be sad for the loss of me!

...

After I die, no funeral, because it is a waste. In the future, if you can continue my path, it will bring honor to our family, and I shall be glad and wish you success. If you can't, you must not side with the corrupt KMT.

Now I am calm, but I don't want to talk and write more. Although there are millions of words to say, I can't write them out.

Alright! Brothers and sisters! Farewell!

Your eldest brother, Yanfen

Revolutionaries

This was the last note this young revolutionary left to his younger siblings, a tear-jerker.

Before his execution, his cellmate He Ruilin recorded his heroic last moment in *Diary of Death*:

> *At six o'clock today, Shi Yanfen, Qi Guoqing, and Wang Chongdian were taken to Yuhuatai for execution. Yanfen left in a turquoise gown that he wore when he came to Nanjing, white cloth rubber-soled shoes and white pants that Han Qing gave him. Freshly groomed, he looked rather dashing. He was the first out, the calmest... As he walked out, he saluted us... "Farewell."*

What a last image of a revolutionary who was merely 25!

He Ruilin was younger, only 19. He started to write *Diary of Death* after he was imprisoned on September 29. Only a week later, on October 5, he had to pass it to another cellmate. Like Shi Yanfen, he walked towards Yuhuatai fearless of death...

Li Jiping was another inspector of the Jiangsu Provincial Party Committee sent to Nanjing, Zhenjiang, and Changzhou by the Shanghai underground party organization of the CPC.

Unlike Shi Yanfen, Li Jiping had been sent to study in the Communist University of the Toilers of the East in Moscow by a party organization. This gifted man, whose father was a *xiucai* in the late Qing dynasty, was particularly excellent in his studies. When he heard of the failure of the Guangzhou Uprising during his school days there, he insisted on returning to China for the revolution. Yet, the party organization had decided that he should keep studying at the Artillery School. "Learning is important, but revolution is more, not to mention the urgent need for manpower in the country." He made a firm request to the organization.

"I shall dedicate myself to the interests of the country in life and death irrespective of personal will and world." Once the request was approved, he encouraged himself to plunge into the domestic revolutionary struggle of blood and fire with the verses of an ancient sage.

Several inspectors before him had died on the job. He knew the severe situation and danger he faced. Inspectors at the time not only had to accurately grasp the basic situation and significant matters of the party

Youth Comes Gently, Leaves Too Soon...

organizations in the area they were inspecting, but also had an even more challenging mission. As required by the superiors, they went to certain places for special missions assigned by the party. For example, Li Jiping took a mission in Shanghai that he would start a riot in the hinterlands of the enemies—Nanjing.

This was a deadly mission. Inspectors had to be at the forefront to guide and lead local organizations to implement related actions, and meanwhile report the progress to higher-level organizations in a timely manner. They often disguised themselves, travelling between several cities in a short time, performing different tasks... This was their job.

"Under white terror, the party's guidance to subordinates must be timely, detailed, and accurate, otherwise it will hinder the progress." Li Jiping expressed this view in the Inspection Report to the Provincial Party Committee. He fulfilled his promise to the organization in practice. "Never a bookworm sitting idle in an empty room."

In 1930, the General Committee of the Jiangsu Provincial Party Committee of the CPC, as instructed by the Central Committee of the CPC, decided to launch an armed riot in Nanjing again. Li Jiping was recommended as secretary of its action committee for his outstanding performance.

Obviously, it was another fatal mission. But Li Jiping set out from Shanghai without hesitation to Nanjing. Under the alias of Wang Zhongbin and the cover of the local underground party, he checked into the Jiaotong Hostel as a businessman and began to prepare for the riot.

The riot was scheduled for August 1. Prior to this, Li Jiping personally travelled between Pukou, Xiaguan, and other places to check on preparations and coordinate the local underground party organizations and peripheral revolutionary forces. Everything was going smoothly. Unexpectedly, misfortune happened—on July 29, the secret service exposed the office of the riot action committee located in the Meihua Barbershop in Xiaguan. Li Jiping and five party members, who were in a meeting, were arrested on the spot by KMT's capital military police squad.

With so-called "solid evidence," they were soon shot dead at Yuhuatai.

On the second anniversary of the sacrifice of martyr Li Jiping, a frail old man staggered to the deserted Yuhuatai hillside in the south of the city.

Revolutionaries

On a pile of weeds, with trembling hands, he erected a small tablet with endless grief, and wrote down the name of his second son: Li Weixuan, dead at 22.

Li Weixuan was Li Jiping's name before joining the party. Revolution for the people and salvation for the nation were the lifelong beliefs of this young revolutionary.

Like Shi Yanfen, he stayed briefly as an inspector, as light as the wind, as exciting as a song. It was the youth of the revolutionary glowing...

I once heard a party historian describe that in special times, there were many inspectors of the CPC fighting at the forefront. They died and nobody knew where there remains were or how they were captured. Their underground work was times more perilous than underground revolutionaries with other missions, because they were always in action.

"Most of them were so young!" exclaimed the party historian.

They are the most respected heroes among revolutionaries. The names of many of them are still unknown...

CHAPTER NINE

___

My Love, Roses of Blood

A 17-YEAR-OLD FUJIAN TEENAGER, WHO WAS BORN IN A FAMILY OF theater and drama, came to study in Shanghai Pudong Middle School, then was transferred to the Naval Arsenal, and next wandered in Shanghai, unemployed... Helplessly, he moved to Beijing. Alone and lonely, he sought comfort in literature. He met a young lass who shared the interest. The spark of love was ignited and it shone brightly. But at the time, she was in deep grief for her beloved brother, who had just died. Poverty-stricken, she had to return to her hometown in Hunan. After he heard the news, he borrowed money from friends and chased after her to Hunan... When he showed up in front of her, she was deeply touched. It melted her pride and she opened the gates of love—

In autumn, they came to Shanghai together and enrolled in Shanghai University, where Qu Qiubai, Deng Zhongxia, and Yun Daiying taught. They became revolutionary literary youths and romantically got married.

Love has always been fierce and romantic while underground work was challenging and dangerous, and extremely ruthless. As young CPC members, they had just started their life together, yet they often had to stay apart to finish the revolutionary tasks–every time he was on a dangerous mission, she missed him with fear and worry. Every night and day, for thousands of times, she called out "love, my love..."

Revolutionaries

My love:

It's 11:30 at night.

The loud thunder has been roaring for forty minutes. It is the second thunderous night since you left. The sound of rain is also noisy, expect they only reflect how deadly silent the night is. All sounds have disappeared, only the endless roaring thunder and the fearful lightning. I can't sleep, but I don't feel lonelier and sadder for it, because I received a sweet letter from Qingdao before dinner. Maybe you can always guess who has this honor. I can't sleep! Half because the thunder is too loud. Even if I lie down, I won't fall asleep or I will get bored. Half because I am a little excited that someone is willing to talk to me. In such a quiet rainy night, in the tense thunderstorm, it is more fun to talk to me as if my love were beside me, isn't it? (Of course the fun is what my love calls "Interesting solitude")

The lights are out, and even if there is electricity, I cannot turn it on. So I did it the old way again. I made a small oil lamp with lard and water. It reminds me of the night in the Tongfeng Apartments five years ago. The light was dim, only illuminating the paper, and it exploded from time to time because of the water, splashing oil spots on the paper. The difficulty for me to write this letter is naturally interesting.

About my mood, how grateful I am for your love! You saved me from an extremely decadent, negative, and boring life. Only a few words of yours awakened my darkened will. They have given me immeasurable courage to fight. My love! I have to work hard, I have the strength, not for money, not for fame, even to make up for the sadness of our separation, but for you my love to never lose hope, to be happy! The past has been ruined. I have no glorious past. But from tomorrow I must live the way you hope me to.

And I hope that you will write to me every day, to encourage me, because it keeps me alive...

Women are sensitive and courageous. Their tears are crystals of love.

Suddenly one day, as if being a poet and playwright, he indignantly accused the corrupt and ugly reactionaries: "I can't tolerate it, so I stand on top of the mountains and scream..."

He, as a proud revolutionary, fearlessly walked in to the Longhua Headquarters cell, singing *The Internationale*, shouting "Down with all

My Love, Roses of Blood

reactionaries." Every hair of his, motivated by his fearlessness, stood up in the air...

And she, who had just given birth, was anxiously looking all over the city for her love – the father of their newborn child.

But she didn't know where to find him... "The wind started to howl outside. The electric light inside was on, but it was as quiet as if at a funeral. I was extremely nervous... Not sure when I dashed out of the room and ran wildly on the road." She recalled the past decades later.

Shanghai in January 1931 was extremely damp and freezing. In this kind of weather, it was tremendously challenging for a woman who had just been out of the first month of confinement after giving birth, to take care of a baby while searching for her husband. In the winter of Shanghai, it was raining with snow. "Due to poor postpartum care, her health has deteriorated. But she kept searching for him on the streets. She had frostbite on her feet, but she believed there was more hope in finding him if she kept searching... In those days, she suffered greatly," recalled the comrades.

Later, she found a lawyer in the police station, who told her that her husband had been transferred to the Public Security Bureau. So she visited the lawyer of the Public Security Bureau, who told her impatiently that he had been transferred to the KMT Songhu Garrison Headquarters.

"Lawyers of the Longhua Headquarters decisively rejected my request, saying that the case was major. Twenty to thirty captives were fettered. It only happens to felons," she said.

She and his friend Shen Congwen were worried. They consulted Xu Zhimo and Hu Shi, and made a special trip to Nanjing to find Cai Yuanpei, president of the Academia Sinica. They all confirmed that "The case was major and it would be really difficult to rescue him."

This was the story of Hu Yepin, one of the famous Twenty-four Martyrs of Longhua and his wife, Ding Ling, who later became a well-known writer.

At the time, they were young, both revolutionaries, and a couple.

On a cold day in the second half of that month, snowflakes floated in the sky. Shen Congwen accompanied the frail Ding Ling to visit Longhua Prison. She took Hu Yepin's quilt and some clothes. They waited all morning and never saw him. She recalled: "We thought for a long time, and asked to send in ten silver coins and demanded a receipt. By this time, all visitors at the iron gate had left except the two of us. The guard agreed. Soon, we heard the sound of people inside. A few people walked through the courtyard in the two-tiered iron gate. I had no clear vision of anything, but Shen Congwen saw a familiar figure. We believe that it was Yepin coming out to collect the money and sign the receipt. So we waited attentively. Eventually, I saw him. So, I shouted: "Yepin! Yepin! I am here!" He turned around, he saw me, he was about to shout back at me, except the guards took him away."

This was the last time Ding Ling saw him. Twenty days later, Hu Yepin and 23 martyrs were brutally shot to death. It was devastating to the small family that they had started. And it buried a young woman's love and marriage. It would be the lifetime pain for the child who didn't know how to speak...

In the 1920s and 30s, Western-styled weddings were particularly popular in Shanghai. Young people often chose a church for their wedding ceremony. Even if it was held in luxurious hotels, they followed the rituals of a western-style wedding. In front of God, family and friends, the bride and groom made their vows:

> ... From now until forever, through good times and bad times, in wealth and poverty, in sickness and health, in happiness and sorrow, I will always love you, cherish you, and be faithful to you.

And for young revolutionary couples, there was a particularly important additional vow engraved in their hearts:

> For the cause of the revolution, whether you survive or die, I will always be by your side until communism is realized!

This was the revolutionaries' solemn promise to love and marry, the most lofty and greatest tacit agreement and oath between revolutionary couples.

I have witnessed many other halves of the martyrs keep the promise. They have dedicated their entire lives to loving a great soul. How touching!—

First, it is the love story of a martyr named Dingxiang (meaning lilac).

My Love, Roses of Blood

We know little about her because the 22-year-old young party member was captured after less than half a year in Shanghai, when she followed the order to meet the underground party in Beijing. Then, she was escorted to Nanjing and soon shot dead at Yuhuatai. During the Qingming Festival in 2014, I visited the Yuhuatai Martyrs Memorial Hall for the first time. Having read about the story of Dingxiang, I submitted an article to *Guangming Daily* entitled *The Lilac at Yuhuatai...* Unexpectedly, it had strong repercussions across the country. Quickly, her story spread...

Is it spring rain? Or is it a trickle of tears? When I stepped into the Yuhuatai Revolutionary Martyrs' Cemetery in Nanjing, my soul and mind seemed to hallucinate... Ha, it turned out to be a piece of a flying petal that fell on my face. It was white, with delicate dew drops, and exuded a refreshing scent.

"Isn't this white lilac?" I was gladly surprised that this exquisite flower came uninvited.

"Look! There are a lot of lilac trees!" A staff member of the cemetery surnamed Sun pointed to the lilac garden ahead, where the flowers were in full bloom. She told me an even more amazing fact. "The lilac trees are to commemorate a female revolutionary martyr named Bai Dingxiang. Like you, she was also from Suzhou!"

Really? I was skeptical, but in the Exhibition Hall of the Martyrs Memorial Hall, I did find a picture of a beautiful woman named Dingxiang. In the photo, she had shoulder-length short hair, a white face, and a pair of doll eyes... Although it is an old black and white photo, I can still tell she was a charming Suzhou beauty of the 30s.

Below her portrait, there is a brief introduction:

Dingxiang (1910-1932), a native of Suzhou, Jiangsu Province, studied at Soochow University in Suzhou, joined the Chinese Communist Youth League in April 1930, and became a CPC member the following year. She later engaged in underground work in Shanghai. In September 1932, she was sent to work secretly in the Pingjin area. Tragically, she was arrested and escorted to Nanjing. In December, she was killed at Yuhuatai, only 22 years old.

"This is the only photo of the martyr Dingxiang left in the world. It was found in her husband's old house in the 1980s." Sun also told me that she and her husband were both Suzhou natives.

Revolutionaries

"What a coincidence!" I was surprised again.

"Yeah. Isn't there a Dingxiang Alley in the Pingjiang District of Suzhou? She was born in that alley..."

Ho! I had to make a soft but strong sigh inside: That is a narrow alley. Is it the place where the little sister of my grandmother was abandoned?

Nobody can confirm it for me.

But I find out that after the founding of PRC, the government renamed the alley Dingxiang Alley after a revolutionary martyr named Dingxiang who died in Yuhuatai. My grandmother passed away in the late 1970s. She believed that possibly her abandoned little sister might be the dead martyr. Her reason was that one of her sisters later followed Tan Zhenlin's New Fourth Army to fight the Japanese for many years. This Catholic lady revealed to me that when she was a child, her family was most afraid if the daughters wielded guns, so she believed in a foreign religion.

The story my grandmother told is too old. It cannot be verified that her little sister was Dingxiang. However, I often visited the Dingxiang Alley in my hometown of Suzhou, never knowing that a beautiful and passionate revolutionary martyr who died in Yuhuatai was born in that alley.

Sun is an expert on revolutionary history. She told me that Dingxiang was confirmed to be an abandoned child and adopted by the pastor of the Suzhou Christian Supervisory Council. "She's so beautiful, like a lilac!" The adopter of the baby girl was an American female priest. She loved China and the gardens with white lilacs in full bloom in Suzhou, so she gave herself the name Bai Meili. She was an intellectual lady proficient in literature, history, and music, and had a kind heart. When she adopted the baby, she gave the child a beautiful name, Bai Dingxiang. Dingxiang therefore began her beautiful life in the alley of Suzhou.

Under the endless drizzle, the light, infatuating fragrance wafted from the alleys. My baby Dingxiang, sleep tight, sleep happy. Mommy will play you To the Tune "Sand of Washing Stream"... Melodious music of classical and foreign elements came from the church in the alley: "Osmanthus, golden and with leaves as if delicately pruned, has the distinguished and admirable demeanor of Wang Yan and Yue Guang of the Jin Dynasty. Wintersweet is too focused on the appearance, thus too tacky. Lilacs huddle too tightly, thus not stretching sufficiently. The scent of osmanthus wakes me from my nostalgia.

Ruthless, isn't it?"

The alley is quiet. In the quiet alleys, mother and daughter played and read under the lilac trees. Surrounded by nightingale-like laughter and crisp recitals, the delicate bridges and narrow creeks seemed be to heaven on earth. Little Dingxiang was beautiful and smart. Bai Meili was overjoyed as she watched her daughter grow up day by day. She hired a mentor to especially teach little Dingxiang to speak English, to read the Bible and history books, and to play the piano. When Dingxiang turned 15, Bai Meili sent her to Soochow University to study biology and algebra.

The free and ideologically emancipated college campus put wings to the dreams and love of this beautiful young talented lass. When the storm of a great revolution came, the passionate and innocent little Dingxiang listened attentively to Xiao Chunü's speech on where China under the rule of the counter-revolutionary warlord was headed. She burst into tears, and since then firmly believed that the revolution was the only way out. Later, when she heard that Xiao Chunü, whom she admired, was shot dead by KMT reactionaries, regardless of the objections of her adopted mother, she ran to the spot where the revolutionary students gathered. Under the red flag of the sickle and hammer, she solemnly dedicated her ideals to a communist future—she joined the Communist Youth League and became a CPC member the following year.

After that, in that narrow and deep alley, there was always a beautiful figure running and shouting and holding a small flag that said, "Down with imperialism" and "Down with reactionary rule." One day, the gate of the church was tightly shut, and she left the American mother who raised her and embarked on the road of revolution.

"We are from the same place!" One day, a tall and handsome male schoolmate blocked her way on the campus of Soochow University.

"What? What are you talking about?" The moment she looked up, she blushed. He was so handsome!

"Well, my ancestral home was in Taicang, Suzhou. Later, my family moved to Nanjing. Nice to meet you..."

He reached out his hand, "My name is Le Yuhong, and everyone calls me Le."

"So you are Le?!" She shyly blinked her big, beautiful eyes. She often

Revolutionaries

heard people talk about a CPC member named Le, who not only marched forward at the strikes for the revolution, but played the erhu beautifully.

"Yes, that's me." Two warm hands joined together. Two young hearts ignited the spark of love.

Thereafter, on the Soochow University campus, under the Suzhou Huqiu Pagoda, a beauty of Suzhou, as exquisite as celadon ware, and a noble and handsome man-child, often nestled under a lilac tree, rhapsodizing about revolution, about love, about music, and poems of lilacs at home and abroad.

"The spring night is serene. The spring lovesickness is endless. Outside the flower shrubs, cuckoos are calling, as if begging the moon to stay. You are too far to be seen, to appear in my dreams. My lonely heart is the dim light in a gauze lantern. I hate the season of goodbyes. In the spring, lilacs bloom lushly on the stairs. Each one shaped like a true love's knot. The night mist dissipates. Dawn breaks at the horizon. Chirping cheerfully on the crossbeam are a pair of spring sparrows." Le had to drop out of school due to family financial distress. Later, he came to Shanghai to professionally engage in revolution. In those nights, he composed long and melodious music for the ancient poetry-themed lilac, and through his erhu, in the silent moonlight, he played to his love far away in Jinling.

"The dusk climbs up the tall towers. I am patiently waiting for my love who hasn't come yet. The crescent moon is a hook. Bananas have not stretched, nor have the lilacs. To the spring breeze, they whisper their sorrow. My dear, I prefer this poem by Li Shangyin. As I chant it, my heart has already flown to you," replied Dingxiang.

"Dingxiang, there are traitors in the underground party of Shanghai and the organization is compromised. The party has decided to send you... The situation is serious now. Be well prepared." Shortly after she graduated, the party organization talked to her.

"Rest assured, I fear nothing!" That day, she packed the boxes and rushed to Shanghai overnight. She snuggled up tightly in Le's arms. On the Bund wharf, they trotted hand in hand, laughing, competing against the gulls on the river over who was prettier and happier under the sunrise.

Underground tasks under the white horror were extremely challenging and dangerous.

Shanghai in early spring was cold and damp. Le went to a factory in

Zhabei District to organize a workers' strike. Unexpectedly, the reactionaries launched a sudden attack. Several workers were killed or apprehended in the fight. Luckily, Le escaped. Back at the dormitory, he played the erhu in the middle of the night with great indignation, and broke the bowstring. Dingxiang silently fixed the bowstrings for him...gazing at the graceful figure in a pink dress, Le pulled his sweetheart tightly into his embrace.

In April 1932, the organization approved their marriage. They got married secretly in a crude hut.

Every second for the newly-weds was sweet. Their marriage also brought great convenience to the young couple engaged in underground work. In the following days, they used their attic to transmit information to the party organization and convene clandestine meetings. Her piano and his erhu were their tools to convey a message of safety to their comrades. When she played Ave Maria, *the comrades would know it was safe; when he played* The Moon Over a Fountain, *they scattered vigilantly.*

One late night five months later, after she happily told her husband that she was three months pregnant, she sat in front of the piano and played Destiny *by Beethoven...*

"My dear, you are off to Beijing tomorrow. When will you come back? I am worried." Le stroked the soft long hair of his wife, deeply concerned.

She raised her beautiful face and shook her head softly: "Not sure. But I will come back as soon as possible, for you and for him..." She patted her belly gently.

That night, he shared a long kiss with her, as if to keep the scent of her lips beside him forever.

Dingxiang left and never returned.

Despicable traitors sold her out the moment she arrived in Beijing. Guns were pointed at her beautiful back—she was apprehended.

"You are so young, so beautiful, and with such a poetic name. A promising college student, why work for the Communist Party?" The enemies tried to coax her.

She replied: "Because the Communist Party serves the toiling people. They will overthrow you reactionary rulers."

"But the church raised you. I heard you have a foreigner mother!"

"But the blood of the poor runs in my veins."

Revolutionaries

"You know, one only gets to die once. When a petals falls off a flower, it doesn't get to go back."

"I am a revolutionary. I am always ready to die. A meaningful life. Do it!" She raised her head high.

The enemies gained nothing from her and had no more tricks, so had to take her to Nanjing and imprisoned her as a communist felon. Soon, she was secretly killed in Yuhuatai.

Dingxiang was only 22 and three months pregnant.

"Dingxiang! My love—!" December 3 was a devastating day for Le, who stayed in Shanghai. When a comrade engaged in underground tasks broke the awful news to him, tears ran down his face like waterfall. That day, he played erhu in the small attic all night. The sad song To Dingxiang *moved the sky to rain...*

The next day, Le risked a visit to Nanjing Yuhuatai. In a straw raincoat, he stood in the heavy rain. Then, he knelt on the bloodstained muddy ground where she was killed, clenched his fists, and vowed at the sky: "Our love will be my fuel to keep fighting. I will give every ounce of my strength until her dream is realized."

"...Is the sorrow from the lilacs that do not bloom? It is from the parting, never heard anything more from the hometown. I assume under the blossoms, in the moonlight and spring breeze, she is as lovesick as me." After losing his young and beautiful wife, Le did not collapse. Instead, he channeled his hatred for the enemies into fighting enthusiasm. Next, he was appointed to Qingdao as Head of the Propaganda Department of the Shandong Provisional Working Committee of the Communist Youth League. In 1935, the KMT arrested and imprisoned him. Two years later, on April 21, 1937, he was taken to the Capital Penitentiary in Xiaozhuang, Nanjing.

In the penitentiary, Le and the communists and revolutionaries detained there fought a special battle side by side against the enemies. In order to protest against the KMT reactionary government's non-resistance to the Japanese aggressors, Le and his cellmates held a concert during the exercise hour in the prison yard to protest against the authorities. With superb erhu skills, Le encouraged his cellmates. Like a horn of battle, the sound of erhu shook the prison. Le recalled it later. "In front of me, there seemed to be standing the soldiers who were fighting in a world of ice and snow, and the comrades who

My Love, Roses of Blood

were, heavily fettered, locked in a dark cell suffering. I lowered my head and held my tears, fully concentrated on the desolate and solemn vibrato on the strings. The mellow and sweet sound of the erhu echoed on the sunny lawn, and each note touched the heartstrings of the prisoners. After I finished the last note, I stood up and suggested that everyone sing The March of the Volunteers. *They asked me to teach them the song. Although I have never had such an experience, I still cleared my throat, waved my hands, and led the singing: "Rise up! Those who refuse to be slaves..." I taught them to sing again and again. They were excited, the more they sang, the more energetic they got. Even the 'instructors' and the staff of the penitentiary were so attracted by the majestic singing. One after another, they came out to watch us..."*

Le's performance touched many comrades in prison at that time. Among them, there was a comrade named Tong Rugong. He became the principal of a certain normal university in Shenyang after the liberation. And he composed a long poem to sing his praises:

The lad from east China stood out, his fingers had the power to inspire. His wife died tragically. He invited us to listen to the erhu sing. It had us at the first note. The more we hear the more fueled we became. No one made a sound on the spot. It was merely the melody from the erhu string. Suddenly a storm struck. Waves roared. Fish wailed. The deceased have gone too soon. As far as three thousand miles away. This is the soul of the great nation of China, about to rise up and awe the world.

Thanks to Zhou Enlai's personal intervention and care, in September 1937, the authorities finally released Le and his cellmates. Since his return to the revolutionary ranks, Le was following the Fourth Division of the New Fourth Army led by Peng Xuefeng to the south of the Yangtze River. In a rain of bullets, he had never missed his deceased wife Dingxiang any less. Instead, the more victories the liberation war won, the more he missed her. Whenever he was free, he sat alone somewhere and played his self-composed Dingxiang songs on his erhu. His love moved everything. Years went by, yet Le's love for his wife grew stronger. It moved the courageous and upright general Peng Xuefeng, who had been on the battlefield all his life, so much that he wrote a free poem, a rare move in his life: A lonely friend, lost his wife ten years ago... now, all his love is heard in the melody he plays...

In 1951, when the foundation stone laying ceremony of Yuhuatai

Revolutionaries

Revolutionary Martyrs Cemetery of Nanjing was held amidst salutes, Le was in the troops marching towards Tibet on the snow-covered plateau. By the time, he had been promoted to be Minister of Propaganda of the Eighteenth Army of the Chinese People's Liberation Army. He has remained single in memory of his deceased wife for 18 years. His comrades and supervisors were worried: is he ever going to remarry again?

No one dared rip the bandage off his scar. But something unexpected happened: One day, Le ran excitedly and yelled to some of his colleagues: "I am going to marry her! Marry her!"

"What? Are you insane?" His comrades observed his strange behavior, wondering if he had gone crazy.

"I'm fine! Really fine." Le smiled and led his colleagues to the Military Communications and Reporting Department.

He pointed to a girl and said, "See, she looks like my Dingxiang, doesn't she?"

They were surprised to notice the great resemblance.

This female soldier who looked much like Dingxiang was named Shi Zhongman. In the Eighteenth Army, everyone knew that Le had remained single for his late wife for 18 years. When Zhongman learned that her chief Le was about to propose to her, her heart skipped a beat...In May 1954, Le married Zhongman, who was 23 years younger than him.

Le was later transferred to civilian work, serving successively as Director of the Tibet Working Committee and Director of the Tibet Branch of the Xinhua News Agency. Next, as work demanded, he moved his family to Anhui and Northeast China, and had a daughter with Zhongman. When she asked him what name to give their daughter, his eyes stopped at the pot of lilacs on the table with Yuhua stones dotted around it... Finally, he advised, "Let's call her Dingxiang (lilac)!"

"Le Dingxiang. Well, my daughter will grow up to be as beautiful as lilac, and learn from her selfless and heroic dedication to the revolutionary cause." His wife Zhongman leaned affectionately on her husband's broad shoulders, taking in his noble and pure love.

"In the moonlight lilacs bloom. The fragrance attracts the groom. An ancient knot of true love is found. The spring breeze unties it now." Zhongman was always considerate and often recited to him his favorite lilac-

My Love, Roses of Blood

themed poems. On December 3rd, Dingxiang's death anniversary, she always prepared a bottle of fine wine and an erhu for her husband so that he could express his love for the deceased woman.

Year after year, he missed the deceased Dingxiang even more. Because of the special nature of underground work, he had no possession of a photo of her. So he painted a portrait of her based on his own memory and hung it on the wall of the living room. "Auntie Dingxiang looks exactly the same as mommy when she was young..." said the little girl. In fact, Le saw them both as one. His wife Zhongman greatly resembled his late wife, the martyr Dingxiang. Le loved his wife even deeper.

In 1982, on the fiftieth anniversary of Dingxiang's death, Le took his daughter to Yuhuatai, and planted a lilac tree on a narrow path next to the spot where she was killed. After that, when the cemetery staff and visitors heard about their love story, they were moved and planted more lilac trees. They have grown into the lilac forest we see today... White lilacs bloom at every turn between spring and summer, exuding waves of fragrance. After Le planted the first tree there, he brought his family to Yuhuatai to pay his respects every year on the Qingming Festival.

"Before the trip, he would have a haircut and groom himself properly," said his wife and daughter.

In 1989, Le visited Yuhuatai for the last time. He was 81 years old that year. Deeply ill, he knew the clock was ticking. Seeing how lush the tree he planted had become, he couldn't help crying. He took a moment to calm down. Sitting under the lilac tree, he took the erhu that his daughter handed over, touched the string with his left hand, and held the bow with his right hand. He adjusted his breath, lowered his head, and started to play skillfully. The instrument immediately poured out his ocean-deep love, leaving no dry eyes among the tourists who stopped by...

In 1992, Le died of illness in Shenyang. The following year, his wife Zhongman took their daughter and his ashes to Yuhuatai in the endless spring drizzle, and buried it under the lilac tree.

"The leaves of lilac are bitter, but the flowers are fragrant. As a woman, Aunt Dingxiang was happy. She sacrificed her life to build the new China, and she won the lifelong love of a man." Le Dingxiang still comes to Yuhuatai every year on Qingming Festival to mourn her father and the martyr whose

name she shares. Whenever someone asks about the love story between her father and Dingxiang, she always tells them those words.

The lilac trees in Yuhuatai have grown into a forest, and the long and fragrant lilac path has become a tourist spot. Visitors to the revolutionary martyrs' cemetery always stop there for a photo. And the revolutionary deeds of martyr Dingxiang and her love story with Le circulate widely a classic ballad...

The lasting love between Dingxiang and Le is the perfect testimony to their wedding vows:

For the cause of the revolution, whether you survive or die, I will always be by your side until communism is realized!

Now, I am sure that the scent of lilacs floating from the Bund has begun to permeate the city of Shanghai and the entire country...

Next is another magnificent love story of revolutionaries—

As I was writing it, I couldn't help bursting into tears... Because the couple died tragically: one was escorted to the KMT Songhu Garrison Headquarters prison on May 16, 1931, and half a month killed as a communist felon at Nanjing Yuhuatai; the other remained single for 42 years, and later became the first Minister of Supervision, Minister of Internal Affairs and full-time deputy secretary of the Central Supervisory Committee of the PRC. During the Cultural Revolution, she was detained in a small hospital ward of about ten square meters by the Gang of Four, with eight burly men guarding it day and night. She was tortured until she weighed only 30 kilograms. On the hospital bed, she was frail and whispered:

For the cause of the revolution, whether you survive or die, I will always be by your side until communism is realized!

July 26, 1973, was a hot day. Under the surveillance of the minions of the Gang of Four, she left the world for good...

Her name was Qian Ying. She was nicknamed Sis Qian or Sis in the revolutionary ranks. And I believe she deserved to be called the "iron sister."

Few knew who she was, but many must know the song *Honghu Lake Waves* and the movie *Honghu Red Guards*, where there is a female captain named Han Ying. The character is based on the story of Qian Ying.

Han Ying is an artistic image that lives in the hearts of the Chinese; Qian Ying, a real person, was a female warrior made of steel. I always mispronounce her name as Tie (iron) Ying.

Her husband died, gone forever.

Three months after she married him in Shanghai, she was sent to study in the Soviet Union–for over a year, the young couple fiercely loved each other from afar... For over 380 days, he wrote her more than 130 letters from tens of thousands of miles away. Back then, it took at least a month for a letter to reach Moscow from Shanghai. "One letter every three days, with a special secret signal, tell me all about the domestic revolution." At the Huangpu River Wharf, before they parted, she made this request while nestled up in his embrace.

"Sure, I promise!" He kept the promise. Whether in the difficult and dangerous nights of white terror, or on the bloody streets where the armed uprisings of workers took place, he bore in mind the promise to write a letter to her far away, with love...

Fang, I love you! Did you call me in your dream? How did you call me? You asked me how I was. Ah, I am loving you! Until forever! Don't you know? I am to console you, I am all yours! Believe me! My love!

Man, I love you too! I love you very, very much! I can't survive without you, not even for a moment. Never leave me! You, how are you? Ah, what are you doing in City C at this moment? I'm worried for you! For you!

He called her Fang, and she called him Man, more poetic than the "man" in romance.

The revolution needed him to travel to Wuhan. And he wrote to her:

Fang, my dearest Fang:
Do you know what situation I am in? Would you guess that I am reluctant

Revolutionaries

to leave the Yellow Crane Tower? If so, you are wrong. Fang, when will you return to City C? Although my body has come to the Yellow Crane Tower, my soul is always by your side. Your eyebrows may twitch slightly, your heart may beat fast. That is all me.

Fang, do you believe it? That I can feel your soul around me all the time too! I can sense your presence by my side. Every time I want to hold your hands, embrace you, kiss you, your soul vanishes! I am going crazy. It is all you, isn't it?

Do you believe it? Will you believe it?

My Fang...!

When she wrote back to him, she said: "We are expecting a baby."

He was so ecstatic that he uttered the crazy words, "I am going to board a Russian rocket and fly to you, otherwise, your Man will die!"

"Don't say that! Our lives have just begun... It is no longer just the two of us! We must stay alive for him, for a promising future, and for the revolution!"

"Yes, for him and the future, we must stay well alive until communism is realized." He was not talking crazy this time. He was going to fight another cruel battle.

Later, she gave birth to their child alone. In order to fully devote herself to the dangerous underground tasks back in China, she left the child in Moscow.

In the spring of 1931, she returned to Shanghai, to her husband... As the saying goes, a little separation is better for the newlyweds. The fact was that they parted shortly after their wedding. It was not until a year later that they reunited in Shanghai again. "Doesn't it feel like we are newly married again? Fang, my love! You are finally back. I have missed you so much."

"Comrade Qian Ying, the organization has decided to send you to the revolutionary bases in western Hunan and Hubei. You shall assist He Long's troops to open up new revolutionary battlefields and ease the pressure on the Jiangxi Revolutionary Soviet Area." Before the young couple had enough time as a couple, the organization had already assigned a new task.

"Sure. When do I leave?" she asked.

"Tomorrow. A few comrades will go with you. Safer that way."

My Love, Roses of Blood

Tomorrow? My Fang, leaving tomorrow? He held her tightly in his arms, afraid of losing her forever... "For the revolution, for our child to live in a brand new nation, I support you—my love! My Fang!"

He murmured, even when he was asleep. The next day, she left and he stood on the Waibaidu Bridge for hours, long after her ship sailed out of his sight.

The moment he turned around, the clouds above Shanghai got thicker and darker... The reactionaries made more aggressive moves to destroy the Shanghai underground party, the Central Committee of CPC, and Jiangsu Provincial Party Committee. As Secretary-general of the All-China Federation of Labor Unions, he was actively trying to resume work in the destroyed Federation of Labor Unions as instructed by the party. Suddenly one day he was betrayed and arrested. Thereafter, he lost contact with her completely...

As a communist felon, the KMT Shanghai Public Security Bureau and Songhu Garrison Headquarters interrogated him repeatedly, in an attempt to obtain confidential information of the CPC from him.

Within one month after his arrest, he suffered all sorts of cruel tortures. On May 16th alone, the KMT Public Security Bureau's investigation team hung him upside down for two hours, branded his chest and abdomen with burning iron bars. He passed out. When he woke up, they did it again and again... It lasted for nearly ten hours. However, the only thing he said to them was no. The infuriated enemies applied more vicious torture to him— they broke his fingers and ankles until he fell in a coma.

My dear Fang! Where are you now? I miss you. You give me the power to endure all tortures. You soothe my heart-drilling pain... Without you, I will give in; but as I think of you, I will never! Until I am back to you again!

In the prison, before every torture, he always called her name in his heart silently, "My Fang, my love!" and then he was fearless. Fire and whips, torture-rack and whatnot. "Bring it all on, I feel no pain as I think of her, call her name, my Fang! My love. It is only her love washing over me, driving away the fear, even the fear for death."

"Mr. Tan, time to die." The enemies called his name and escorted him

Revolutionaries

from Shanghai to Nanjing, to Yuhuatai...

"Bang!" The first round of bullets didn't knock him down.

"Bang bang..." The second round didn't knock him down, either.

The executioner drew his bayonet in panic, stabbed him in his abdomen, head, and chest, and fired another round of bullets...

Tan Shoulin, a steel fighter of the CPC, one of the leaders of Chinese labor movement, one of the founders of the CPC organization in Guangxi, and Comrade Qian Ying's husband, died in Yuhuatai on May 30, 1931, at the age of 35.

"My soul always follows you, follows our distinct flag." This was his last words to his wife, who had not yet returned from Honghu Lake, where it rained bullets. When she snuck back to Shanghai in disguise and heard that he was brutally shot dead at Yuhuatai, she really wanted to take her guerrilla team to kill all the enemies. However, the organization assigned her an urgent task: *Jiangsu Provincial Party Committee is in need of a secretary-general of the Women's Committee. You are the perfect candidate. Note that the current situation is severe. Stay particularly vigilant and safe.*

"I'm not afraid. I have dodged the rain of bullets by the Honghu Lake. I would really like to see how bullets fly on the street..." With her husband gone, her eyes were less soft but colder; she smiled less, but put a serious face more. In the next few decades, comrades misunderstood her as being born unable to smile...

Qian Ying truly became Tie (iron) Ying—Many revolutionary comrades believed so. Only those who knew her well knew that after work, she used to cry all night holding her wedding photo every day. But with revolutionary work and in front of revolutionary comrades, she never shed a tear or showed any weakness.

Enemies were afraid of her, so somewhat were her comrades. Despite her small figure and soft voice, every word and every sentence she uttered was full of hatred to the enemies, of definite obedience the principles, and of absolute loyalty to the organization.

"Don't move! You are arrested!" One day, on her way to an underground party activity, due to the betrayal of traitors, she was ambushed, guns poking into her waist before she arrived at the rendezvous—if it were in Honghu, she would take out a pistol and fire at them, but at the moment

My Love, Roses of Blood

she had no weapon. Reluctantly, she had to follow the secret agents into the Longhua Garrison Headquarters prison.

"What is your name?"

"Peng Yougu."

"Peng? Not Qian?" The enemy looked at her with doubt, trying to see through her.

She remained calm, and answered: "Peng it is!"

"Have you ever stayed in Honghu Lake?"

"What's that?"

"You!" She irritated them. They finally resorted to bringing out a traitor to confront her.

"Shame!" She slapped the traitor with all her strength, for herself, and for her dead husband. "You don't deserve to speak to me. You don't deserve to live in this world? Get out! Out! Out!"

The traitor was terrified. So were the enemies. They had never seen a tender woman unleash such fury and strength!

Indeed, she was that strong and powerful. People who knew her knew that before she joined the revolution, she opposed to an arranged marriage by slitting her wrist in front of her father... Eventually, the family caved. When opposing a wrong route within the party, she always ruthlessly and candidly pointed out the mistakes of those leaders of higher ranks.

Naturally, she was escorted to Nanjing Prison as a felon and sentenced to 15 years of imprisonment. She was not killed because the comrades in the prison had been secretly protecting her—they knew that her husband had died, and that there was a child alone in the Soviet Union thousands of miles away...

Cellmates did everything possible to protect her. Everyone shared the same goal: Big Sis had suffered enough, with her family divided in three places (her was husband dead, she was in prison, and her child was in a distant foreign country, whose safety was not guaranteed), so we must help her survive and get released.

Big Sis therefore become another nickname of hers.

In prison, as their Big Sis, she cheered up her cellmates, help them build faith and find strength. To young comrades, she read, paragraph by paragraph, the autobiographical novel *Survival of the Captives* written by

Revolutionaries

her dead husband, so that they could see that a revolutionary is affectionate and righteous, and has will and faith, directions and goals.

In prison, she and several other female communists formed a temporary party branch. It successfully organized and led four hunger strikes. They also set an example to learn foreign languages, because there was news in English newspapers about the Soviet area and the Red Army. That was the bit of hope that imprisoned communists could directly obtain.

Prison days were harsh. When they were whipped and put through rack-torture, their bodies suffered, their faith and ideals tested. Women were more vulnerable. But with her hatred towards the enemies since he was killed, she survived all the cruel tortures and temptations again and again. Even they had to give her credit for her strong endurance.

On August 18, 1937, Zhou Enlai and Ye Jianying appeared in the KMT penitentiary. Their kind words brought her to tears in front of everyone for the first time after his death...

I am free! I can devote myself to the revolution again! I will turn my hatred into actual actions! Dear Man, your Fang is taking up weapons again to kill the enemies like the old days of commanding the Red Guards in Honghu Lake!

I am going to avenge you—my dear Man!

She was released from prison, bathing in the sunlight again. She was assigned to work in Wuhan for the underground party of Hubei Provincial Party Committee with revolutionary Tao Zhu—it was a national war against Japan. The one thing that pained her was that the party required her to cooperate with KMT people, who had killed her Man. However, she promised the organization: personal pain would never get in the way of the great national struggle and she would temporarily bury her personal hatred deep in her heart.

KMT reactionaries had not sincerely cooperated. They showed no mercy to the communists. Instead, they got worse. When the Japanese planes violently bombed Wuhan, the KMT not only withdrew early, but also viciously sealed the ships on the Yangtze River. Under the leadership of Li Kenong, she had to employ a small steamer. Unfortunately, a bomb blasted it to pieces... The comrades of *Xinhua Daily*, who were evacuated later, found out that she was missing—"We can't leave her behind," the

My Love, Roses of Blood

comrades cried, fearing that she would die.

However, she survived. A boatman rescued her ashore, to the place she was familiar with—Honghu Lake.

"My life is tied with Honghu." She shed tears of gratitude.

Facing the sun is a red flag, dyed with tons of blood.
Qian Ying survives, winning a heroic reputation.

Zhang Zhiyi, an old comrade-in-arms of hers, wrote this poem for her. Once again, she survived with love for her dead husband. Her new journey was underground work in Chongqing, hence the revolutionary story of *Red Crag*. She was the person in charge of the underground party organization in Eastern Sichuan. In Chongqing, the second capital of the War of Resistance, Chiang Kai-shek's secret agents were spread all over the city. No communists were allowed to engage in any struggle against the KMT under their noses. The struggle was extremely difficult and complicated. Over 300 loyal communists were shot dead before the dawn broke—a few days before the liberation of Chongqing, the enemies slaughtered revolutionaries, including Jiang Zhujun and a three-year-old martyr, even younger than Song Zhenzhong (the little radish, 8 years old)...

They showed no mercy to us revolutionaries. Now that you are in the revolution, you will face cruel struggles and ferocious enemies. You must not have the slightest illusion. You must fight them! This is what she often said, not only to her comrades, but also to herself.

"... The International working class shall be the human race!" The voice of a soprano rose from the fire in the broken ancestral hall and soared into the night sky, echoing.

It was January 1938. The party training class that the Hubei Provincial Party Committee organized in an ancestral hall deep in the mountains of Qiliping at the border of Hubei, Henan and Anhui Provinces was about to end. Thanks to two months of classes, we, a group of youths full of enthusiasm about the War of Resistance, yet ignorant, have learned a little bit of the fundamental principles of the Chinese revolution and of the party. Comrade Ye Jianying, who has come from far to teach, dabbled in the war situation, strategy, and tactics. On a cold night, we set a blazing bonfire in the hall, and dozens of people casually sat around it. The person in charge of the training class, Comrade Fang Yi, brought in a short woman in her 30s and she was introduced as Comrade Qian Ying, Minister of Organization of the Hubei Provincial Party Committee. We were advised to call her Sis Qian. We were told she had studied in the Soviet Union and been detained a long time in KMT prisons. It had been only a few months since her release.

I no longer remember what Sis Qian had said. But I do remember her singing The Internationale to us as we applauded along. We all knew this revolutionary anthem. Although she was no professional singer, we agreed she sang well. She held her head high and her bright eyes gazed forward, so firm and affectionate, as if she were singing to the chained martyrs walking to the execution ground in Yuhuatai and Longhua. I believe that she must be thinking of the martyrs, that she must be ready to sing it in prison at any time.

Because we heard that she had been to the Soviet Union, we encouraged her to sing The Internationale in Russian. She sang the first verse, and then we all joined her. It was a passionate moment. Our voices rode the flames and flew out of the ancestral hall, floating into the night sky and to the distance:

"'Tis the final conflict;

Let each stand in his place.

The International working class

Shall be the human race! "

In the next few days, Qian Ying had private talks with many of us. This was her job as head of the organization. She also talked with me, asking what I planned for my future. Like many other youths, I yearned to fight with the guerrillas. She smiled and said: "People are needed everywhere. The organization will decide properly."

...This was written by Ma Shitu, a senior writer.

Before liberation, Comrade Ma was an important member of the Chongqing and Sichuan Underground Party. He later served as a leader of the Propaganda Department of the Provincial Party Committee, a subordinate of Qian Ying. He had an extraordinary admiration for. He once recalled:

My Love, Roses of Blood

Before the fall of Wuhan in the autumn of 1938, I was asked to mobilize some workers for guerrilla warfare on the southern section of Pinghan Railway. I was sure I would be picked. But Sis Qian wanted me and a group of comrades to retreat to Xiangfan in northern Hubei. Soon I was sent to Zaoyang rural area for development tasks. I worked there for a few months, straightened and developed a large number of party members, and established the County Party Committee. One day, Sis Qian contacted me, "Didn't you want to fight guerrilla warfare? You are selected. Come with me to Dahongshan." It turned out that she was going to serve as Secretary of the Special Committee of Central Hubei. Zaoyang County Party Committee was therefore affiliated to Central Hubei. I followed her to Dahongshan to join the Central Hubei Special Committee. I was ready for guerrilla warfare, and I was excited. But within a month, she told me again that she had been transferred to the Western Hunan and Hubei Provincial Committee and she wanted to assign me to the Enshi Special Committee of West Hubei. Frankly, I was upset with the change. Also, it was in KMT jurisdiction, thus dangerous and irritating. I was more unwilling to go. She immediately saw through me and criticized me: "A party member acts selflessly, doesn't he? Wherever he is needed, he will go there, and do as told. Even the most dangerous and harsh environment will never scare him off."

After I served as Secretary of the Special Committee in West Hubei for more than half a year, the KMT reached its second anti-communist peak. In the summer of 1940, Sis Qian was working in the Organization Department of the Southern Bureau. Regardless of distance and danger, she travelled from Chongqing to Enshi to inspect the work progress. She lived with us in a farmer's house. She and my lover wife Liu shared a bed. The bed bugs prevented them from sleeping well. I was an unemployed teacher. Every day, the meals we provided were simple. She suffered poverty with us. We felt apologetic, but she told us not to. She said: "Much better than the prison days." She told us that in the past, there were so many bed bugs that she couldn't terminate all of them. She tried to drown them in a bowl of water. Easily, they filled half the bowl. She said the rice was moldy, and there was so much sand in it that when sifted, it filled half a pocket. She took the opportunity to educate us in revolutionary integrity. She talked about the heroic martyrs who died

Revolutionaries

in Yuhuatai. These undoubtedly inspired Liu to keep fighting when she was arrested and imprisoned. Liu eventually died heroically.

Sis Qian conveyed to us at the special committee meeting the central government's policy of keeping a long-term low profile. She also announced that the newcomer He Bin would serve as Secretary of the Special Committee. Before returning to Chongqing, she had a private chat with me and Liu. And she addressed two matters: one was that I became second-in-command, not because I performed poorly in the past. It was because focus was to shift to rural areas and I was needed in southern Sichuan, Hubei and Hunan border areas to lead preparations for armed struggle. She said that communists have always accepted the appointment of the organization, regardless of personal gain of reputation and status. I have always felt that whatever she says, however simple, is powerful enough, convincing enough. The second was that she was going to transfer Liu to serve as a traffic officer between Southern Bureau and organization in the western part of Hunan, Hubei, and Hubei. She told her it was an important job yet most dangerous. One must be ready to die at any time. Liu gladly accepted it, and left for Chongqing with Sis Qian at once. It was the first time she was a traffic officer. She brought back some documents with central instructions in a confidential way.

In January 1941, the Southern Anhui Incident broke out and the anti-communist trend reached the climax. Betrayed by some defectors, He Bin and Liu were arrested and imprisoned along with the child she had just given birth to. It was the biggest loss for the Western Hubei Party. After evacuating the organization, Comrade Wang from the Special Committee and I went to report it to the Southern Bureau.

At the time, the situation in Chongqing was rather tense. Anything could happen at any time. The Southern Bureau was set up in Hongyan Village, under close encirclement and surveillance by secret agents. Sis Qian feared that I might get lost in Hongyan Village and captured by the enemies. She sent Cai down the mountain to me and guided me in detail how to get around in the village. Cai drew a route map for me, warning me not to lose direction and walk into an enemy's trap. We made a secret code to identify each other. He told me to go up after dark the next day. Sis Qian was still worried. She asked He, who had been up the mountain, to lead me to the mountain opposite Hongyan Village to check the route during the day. Her deep concern over my

278

My Love, Roses of Blood

safety and careful arrangements to guarantee it moved me to tears.

When it was dark the next day, I went up the mountain and the journey went smoothly. However, when I was approaching the gate, I was confused and walked behind the bamboo fence. I turned back anxiously and accidentally touched the bamboo fence. Immediately, the alarm bell rang upstairs. Footsteps of people running could be heard. I stepped back and found the gate at the end. I walked up the stone ladder and saw the light upstairs. I wanted to cry. I finally reached the destination.

As I just sat down in the reception room, two guards came to me. I replied to the agreed code of identification. They immediately said, "Sis Qian is waiting for you!" They told me to go in through a secret door. As soon as I reached the second floor, I saw her approaching. We shook hands and she reprimanded me: "What happened? I thought we had taught you well. We were wondering if something serious had happened." She was telling the truth. I noticed that several guards in the aisle had already loaded their pistols.

I smiled awkwardly. She didn't say anything more, but led me into her room, told me to me sit down, and poured me a glass of water without saying anything. What an embarrassing silence! It was as if I were home sitting in front of my mother. How many things did I want to say, but where should I start? Of course, I should start with the destruction of our organization. Comrade He Bin, my wife Liu, and our daughter who was not one month old fell into the enemy's hands. But before I could speak, she gestured me to stop. She looked at me sadly and spoke in a tender voice, "Needless to say, I know what happened."

I didn't go on. As I looked at her mournful and soft eyes, I couldn't stop my tears. It was not that they reminded me of the arrest of my wife and comrades-in-arms, but her eyes reminded me of my mother's loving gaze. I almost wanted to cry aloud in her embrace, but I got myself together and wiped my tears with a handkerchief. I had no right to cry in front of her, because I know that her husband was killed in Yuhuatai, Nanjing after being arrested ten years ago. Why should I use my cowardly tears to sadden her? She seemed to understand what I was doing and said calmly: "Rest early tonight! We will talk tomorrow."

The next day, she first showed me some documents before talking to me. She carefully checked with me what caused their arrest and what to do next.

He Bin, a comrade she had always adored, was arrested. She was sad, too.
But she still criticized him for not being vigilant enough about the current
white terror and making mistakes (Later, Comrade He Bin sent the last letter
to the Southern Bureau through his father, in which he also reflected on his
carelessness). When I told her that we were going back immediately after the
report is done, she severely criticized me again: "Aren't there enough of us
arrested?" She explained to me: "According to the policy of long-term low
profile of the central government, not only the Special Committee staff have to
hide, but all the core members below have to be transferred somewhere else to
set an ambush. The unexposed grassroot organizations can stay underground
as seeds. When the time is ripe, they will naturally sprout, blossom, and bear
fruit."

I nodded in agreement.

"This is her. She looks frail, but she is agile in her thoughts and behavior. She is in excellent physical health. In daily life, she is as careful and considerate as a big sister. With work, she is like an experienced big brother. In short, she is made of special materials," evaluated Ma Shitu.

After Chongqing, she returned to Shanghai.

At the time, Shanghai was the last territory where the dying regime tried to prolong its last gasp. Therefore, the reactionary authorities were more vigilant about the underground activities of the CPC, doubling their efforts to strangle any symptom of a trend. When they discovered any CPC activity, they immediately suppressed it with violence. As Minister of Organization of the Shanghai Bureau of the CPC, she assumed more arduous and heavy tasks, expanding the organization while preserving its strength. She had always been thrifty and honest, but she had to dress up as a wealthy lady every day and travel through the city to carry out party work under the nose of the enemies—she became an iron lady, wherever she was, she rarely smiled. Even in the party, she spoke and behaved that way. She heard what people talked behind her back, but she didn't care. "As long as one less comrade is killed, it doesn't matter if you hate me to the bone." She knew that in the revolutionary ranks, most comrades were married. She had tasted the pain of losing her other half. "I don't want them to go through it too..." Because of this, as Minister of Organization of the CPC,

My Love, Roses of Blood

she made stricter requirements on people and cadres than ordinary.

Shanghai was at the dawn of liberation. Many working underground were ready to disclose their true identity as soon as possible, while she went to Hong Kong alone, persuading and mobilizing household by household, so that she could take the valuable intellectuals stranded in Hong Kong back to the motherland...

When the PRC was founded, she was promoted to be the first Minister of Supervision. Premier Zhou Enlai suggested to Chairman Mao Zedong that she was the perfect candidate for the position because he believed she was a selfless person, who would let no personal interest get in the way of her work. Her husband died in Longhua, Shanghai, and her only child was never found in the Soviet Union. She was left all by herself. She said in addition to being his Fang, she had only one identity: a daughter of revolution.

Surviving, but where do I belong?
The howling storm is wreaking havoc.
Several imprisonments only made me stronger,
My loyalty is proved in thousands of battles.
As hot as the sun, as deep as the sea,
Devastated at Yuhuatai yet I carried on.
Thirty-one years since I parted with my love,
Reading his last writings brings me back to our first date.

In the Qingming Festival of 1962, holding the reprinted posthumous work *Survival of the Captive* of her Man, she composed the poem above as tears rolled down her face. The tears welled her eyes again when there was no one around...

In their three years of marriage, they spent less than 100 days together. Before they knew it, death separated them for good, already 31 years had passed. She had also aged from a young woman to a serious old lady— except that her comrades still called her Sis. Apart from her identity as the female Minister of Supervision, she was a typical old lady of the revolution.

With loyalty to her Man and dedication to the party, she never heaved a sigh until she was persecuted to death by Jiang Qing, Kang Sheng, etc.

Revolutionaries

There was only *Look Forward* that she left.

When later generations talk about this revolutionary Sis, they feel sorry for her. Her family of three were apart for the cause of the revolution. But I believe, the last words of hers, *Look Forward*, are the greatest hopes and ideals of a revolutionary.

What can be see if we look forward? Us today and our great new country!

She and her husband, as well as their child lost in a foreign country, if they could see our prosperous motherland today, would be happy...

The people of Shanghai love her, and respect her and her husband. She and her Man (Tan Shoulin), are both included in the martyrs list in the Longhua Martyrs Memorial Hall as revolutionary martyrs.

After writing the romantic yet tragic story of Qian Ying and her Man, I accidentally read 36 love letters a revolutionary martyr wrote to his wife Wen, from an old historical archive that had been sealed for seventy years. Each of them reveals his fiery love for his wife Wen...

As I carefully brushed away the dust of history, I discovered the author was Wang Yifei, one of the important leaders of the CPC and an outstanding proletarian revolutionary. I was surprised yet curious: it turns out that professional revolutionaries also love like it is the last day of the world.

His wife Lu Zhuiwen was a loyal underground party member. She came to study in Shanghai when she was under 20. She had always been at the forefront of the student movement during the May 30th Movement. Active among young female students, she was presented to join the party by the early revolutionary Xuan Zhonghua. When Luo Yinong, a leader of the CPC, became Secretary of the Shanghai District Party Committee, Lu Zhuowen served as its cryptographer. At the time, Wang Yifei was Secretary-General of the Central Military Commission. Since it had still been a complete organization, Wang Yifei often handed over some important confidential documents to her for safekeeping. It was in those days that the lad secretly "deposited" his love in this beautiful and dignified lass from south of Yangtze—on February 7, 1926, the young revolutionary couple got married in Shanghai. In the special environment of the underground struggle, their wedding ceremony was rather simple. There

My Love, Roses of Blood

was no feast, no wedding candies, no superfluous formalities. In a family letter, Wang Yifei described the marriage of these revolutionaries: "One table, one chair, one single bed that two share, that's it... The common goals brought two communists together. Nothing else is needed. In the following days, they will spend more time apart than together for the cause of revolution."

As the first military talents sent to study abroad by the party, in February 1925, Wang Yifei, Ye Ting, Nie Rongzhen, and others returned to China from the Soviet Military Academy, a famous Soviet military school. The Central Committee of the CPC kept Wang Yifei in Shanghai to prepare for the establishment of the Central Military Commission and he served as its Secretary-General. On March 18, 1926, after a warlord's bloody murder of patriotic students in Beijing, the party leader Li Dazhao could no longer make public appearances, so the central government sent him to the north. Newly married and on a honeymoon, he broke the news to his wife and asked her to pack and leave for Beijing together. But soon, he hurried back and said that the central government wanted him in Wuhan immediately.

"So, do I still go to Beijing?" she asked.

"Not for the time being. Stay in Shanghai."

Lu Zhuiwen quickly unpacked. She took out half of her belongings, tied up the other half, and called a rickshaw to send her husband to the train station...

The revolutionary newlyweds parted in too much of a hurry.

After Wang Yifei arrived at Nanjing Xiaguan Wharf, he quickly boarded a ship heading for the upper reaches of the Yangtze River. With heavy responsibility, as he rushed to Hankou to meet the leaders of the central government who had arrived there before him, he was deeply concerned about his newlywed wife alone in Shanghai. He stared at the rolling waves behind the ship, missing his wife. Knowing that he could mail a letter at the Jiujiang Wharf ahead, he wrote her the first love letter after they parted—

My love:

Today is the third day since we parted. It is truly difficult to get through these few days without you! Please let me briefly mention a few matters first, and confess my random thoughts.

Revolutionaries

1. After I leave, Chongmin will hand over a "little book" to Yinong. When you see Yinong, tell him to give it to Bishi, he will naturally explain it for me.

2. I once paid Tihua to get a driving license for me. Until today, he still hasn't got it done. Tell him, I don't want it anymore and refund us! (If he doesn't refund us, forget it.) For you personally, I suggest:

1) During your menstrual period, be cautious with your clothing, diet, and activity!

2) Still go to the hospital for regular checkups. Money is no problem. Health comes first always!

3) If you are well, go to the Shi family once a day, and visit brother Te every other day; if not well, leave all that to brother You.

4) To prevent loneliness and boredom, study English or hang out with Dezhi (only when you are in good health).

5) If you want to go to your parents' home, this is the perfect time, and prepare them with what is happening with us! But you must: A) leave the address to me, B) before 28th, return to our home, because I may have already be back by then.

6) All new fabrics can be handed over to the tailor to make new clothes. Could make them a bit bigger. Don't just leave them in the box to save money.

My love, this is what I remember to say for the time being. First, I must have forgotten many things. Second, what I said may not all be right; in short, my love, you make the final decision! Anyway, may you be well. All my love is in these words. Maybe you can feel it.

As for my random thoughts these days, the most important is that our sudden separation has caught me off guard as if I have lost something precious! Although, this time I volunteered to handle school affairs and left you behind, I can't shake away the frustration for not spending every second with you! I assume that you are missing as well, no less! Sweetheart, we have become one. One day apart is suffering enough for me, let alone weeks, months. But we live to fight. In the turbulent days, we can never sit idle and merely watch! As I think about it, I guess parting will become a usual thing for us and I intend to cherish every moment of our living together!

Every time I think about your innocence, your love, I am a hundred times more energized, so I can better work for the school. Your love gives me endless power! My love, I am dull and mediocre, yet you love me. It encourages to be

My Love, Roses of Blood

a better self! Love is magical. I can't help kissing your photo whenever I am alone.

Darling, there is still a lot to say. But I won't say it now. Let's wait until I am in Wuhan. But there is something I have to mention. To apologize again. At the banquet on the 18th and 19th, I spoke harshly to you due to my illness and trouble at work. I have apologized, and you have forgiven me. But I regret it every time I think about it, especially now that we are apart. I see how deep your love is! Darling, I am ashamed of how rude I was. I promise to never be that again!

Enough with trivialities. Next, allow me to talk about my whereabouts:

After we parted, I arrived at the station, bought a third-class ticket, and boarded the train. It was 40-50 minutes away from departure, but there were no seats left. Some passengers occupied three or four seats to lie down and sleep. The latecomers had to stand. Awful behavior. I was lucky to have brought bedding, so that I could sit on it. It was not until the trained passed Zhenjiang that I had a seat. At 7:25, it arrived in Nanjing.

I hired a rickshaw to take me to the ship terminal. On the way, an employee from the ship's ticket office picked me up. He bought me a ticket and sent me to the terminal. We waited until 12 o'clock (lunch time) before the ship pulled in (to Ruihe). It was an ordinary ship, whose business cabin was worse than economy cabin of other ships.

The ship departed from Nanjing at 10 p.m. and arrived in Wuhu at 7 a.m., in Anqing at 2 p.m. on the 21st, and in Jiujiang at 12 a.m. It is expected to reach Hankou at 10 p.m. tomorrow (the 22nd). I believe if there is no delay on this trip, I will be home about around the 27th or 28th.

It's late. The ship is about to anchor. Talk next time! Stay well, my love!!!

Your man
21-26 days of the 3rd lunar month
The first letter from a boat on the Yangtze

This is what a revolutionary wrote to his newlywed wife after their first departure. The affection is so real that reading it feels like it is bathed in love. There are many secret codes of underground work involved, which are not to be explained here.

Revolutionaries

The letter shows that Wang Yifei was a cautious man. Before leaving Shanghai, he arranged for Xi Zuoyao (martyr, a native of Jiangyin, Jiangsu, killed by the enemies in Shanghai on October 26, 1926, at the age of 29), technical secretary of the Military Commission, to be the fake husband of his wife. They rented a small house in an alley in the concession at Nanshi District. It was actually one of the secret organs of the Military Commission. After Wang Yifei left, Xi Zuoyao managed the workers' armed uprising at Nanshi District. But only a few days later, Lu Zhuowen couldn't find Xi Zuoyao. She searched everywhere, yet fearing exposing the secret organs of the Military Commission. And then she read in a newspaper that another group of communists had been arrested, including a man with a red mole on his forehead. She knew at once that it was him. In peril, she swiftly transferred the guns the military organs hid in her residence, and quickly disappeared into the vast crowd... A few days later, she saw the news that her a-couple-of-days "husband" was killed. Back then, the lives of revolutionaries were hanging on a thread at all times.

The newly married man Wang Yifei didn't stay long in Hankou this time. As he completed the tasks the central government assigned, he took a boat to Changsha and brought Ren Bishi's fiancée Chen Congying to Shanghai as entrusted. Ren Bishi and Wang Yifei joined the Communist Youth League together, went abroad together, and studied together. After returning from the Soviet Union, they both served as leaders of the Central Communist Youth League. They had a deep bond. Along the way, Wang Yifei was careful and thoughtful to Chen Congying, who felt a gratitude for decades. She said to Lu Zhuiwen, "You have married a decent man. He did not want me squeezed on the boat. So he protected me, but he didn't want to touch me either, so he just circled me around..."

Soon after they got married, Wang Yifei feared his wife might get lonely, so he moved to the same building as Qu Qiubai and his wife Yang Zhihua, and Yan Changyi and his wife Fu Fengjun. (Yan Changyi, a native of Hunan, an early CPC member. It was Deng Zhongxia who introduced him to join the party. On August 24, 1929, a traitor sold him out during a meeting with Peng Pai, Yang Yin, and Xing Shizhen at 12 Jingyuanli, Xinzha Road, Shanghai, and he was arrested. After a week of brutal torture, the enemies shot him dead. He was 31 when he died.) These three essential

My Love, Roses of Blood

CPC leaders/couples lived in the same building, helping out each other in life. For the wives especially, it helped solve many daily problems. However, when Deng Zhongxia came, he immediately ordered them to separate, on the grounds that three essential CPC figures living together would make an easy target, too exposed, and dangerous.

Deng Zhongxia was right. The three families made new housing plans at once.

The Central Committee later assigned Wang Yifei to Wuhan to manage military tasks related to the Military Commission. It was another long distance separation. He was still madly in love, writing letters to his wife in Shanghai almost every other day. Three selected letters are presented below. (Note: some of them are too long, thus there are deletions):

Wen, my precious,

I have arrived at the destination at 4 p.m. today. But I have not yet met with the manager. Probably tomorrow. I am not sure how long I have to stay. I shall write to let you know in a couple of days!

During this trip, I am more worried about you than the previous trips, because you don't take good care of yourself! I want nothing else but you to follow these suggestions:

(1) Get up early and go to be early as well to have 8-9 hours of sleep

(2) Eat more healthy food. Spend more money on buying quality food. No dirty booth food.

(3) Read but not for too long, especially avoid sad and depressing novels, because they may frustrate you and harm the fetus.

(4) When you get angry at times, try to control the anger properly instead of lashing out at your classmates, your mother, and brother. In short, remember, good mood, good health. This is important.

I am well and safe. Don't worry. That's it. Love yourself (it is another way of loving me)!

Greetings to your mother and brother, too

Yifei

August 12

Revolutionaries

My love,

I reached a new destination yesterday afternoon. I wrote a letter immediately. Please forgive the incompetent mailman that delayed the delivery.

There has been a lot of flooding here recently. Three or four days ago, the water on the streets of the concession was three to four feet deep. I was not optimistic until it was sucked out by a pump to the river. But I still encountered pools of water when trying to rent a car in the concession after I went ashore (Chinese territory) yesterday. I had to make a big detour to get to the concession (it was just in front of me). As for the heat, it is cooler than Shanghai, and not too cold in the morning and night, but there are more mosquitoes and bugs. I live in a fancy hotel, but I didn't sleep well last night! Wind started to howl and rain to pour this afternoon, no sign of ending. It has been a whole day since I arrived but I still haven't met the manager. I was alone on this journey. I only had a few reports and a boring novel to kill time. I don't feel like trying the other recreations for common travelers (singing, gambling, watching dramas...) They annoyed me more! So when I woke up at noon and the person still hadn't showed up, I thought I might as well write you...!

In the previous letter, I have stressed the idea of "good mood, good health," and I hope you will take the advice. Now I remember one more thing. It was autumn when we bought the last watermelon. Not the best timing. I advise you not to eat it! Don't harm your health because you don't want it wasted. Ha-ha, as I write these words, I am laughing at myself. By the time when you receive this letter, I assume the watermelon will have been swallowed. It is too late to advise you to discard it. But it is written, so don't laugh at me! Take better care of your diet in the future!

...Sweetheart, I love you, you are my life. I want all the best for you, more than for myself...

When I write, I am not thinking of anything else but I love you, and I want you to be safe (in all aspects)...!"

As for myself, I am naturally working hard as well...!

Babe, one last thing. You said you were overwhelmed because I love you too much. Babe, don't think that way! Accept my love, stay in a good mood,

My Love, Roses of Blood

in good health. So that I know you have accepted my love and that you love me too.

It's late. Next time, I'll write more!

Greetings to mother, brother, Shi and Yao as well!

To Lu Zhuwen

(In Wuchang, August 19, 1926)

My dearest Wen,

Today is the 19th. Ten days have passed since you mailed me a letter, and one week since I sent you the first letter. The mailman came today, but there was no letter for me. It really upset me. I miss you so. Were my five letters sent by incompetent mailmen? Are you unwell? Or is it something else I don't know of? Otherwise, why ten days without a letter from you?

Love, you know that this traveler is waiting to hear from you every day, to erase my loneliness in the journey. No matter what, write to me. Even if you are ill, tell me honestly, babe! Why don't you write?

Today I received a letter from Brother Chang, saying he couldn't return, nor could the junior college students, and asked me to go. I have not yet decided, please tell Brother Yao to inform Wenweng! You can also ask Brother Wanhe for advice!

Don't write to me at this address in case I am transferred somewhere. When I return, I will telephone you first and take a boat straight home. May mother and brother stay healthy!

Love

19th day of the eighth lunar month

Soon after his wedding, Wang Yifei travelled all the time as the revolution needed. He had to leave Shanghai often for secret missions in other cities. His wife who stayed in Shanghai was all he cared about and missed in addition to his revolutionary missions.

In July 1926, the Northern Expedition Army departed from Guangzhou with great momentum. The party sent Wang Yifei to Wuhan again to plan the assistance to the Northern Expedition Army. At the time, his wife was pregnant. Wang Yifei, who temporarily lived in the hotel, was fully

Revolutionaries

occupied with party affairs and military affairs during the day. Only at night could he look far to the east, miss his wife, and write a letter to her. He wrote: "If our love cannot encourage each other to make progress with our studies, our careers, we will be sorry. As a man, will I not rest in peace if I fail to inspire you?"

At the end of August, Ye Ting's independent regiment of the Northern Expedition Army defeated powerful enemies at Tingsi Bridge and He Shengqiao. During the attack on Wuhan, Wang Yifei crossed the line of fire, met with his old comrade-in-arms Ye Ting, and interpreted for General Gallen, Soviet military adviser to the Northern Expedition. Chiang Kai-shek also spoke highly of him and sent him a lieutenant general's uniform, saying, "We are both from Zhejiang," meaning to buy him over. Wang Yifei returned it intact to Chiang Kai-shek.

His heart was 100% loyal to the CPC.

At the moment, the revolutionary armed struggle in Shanghai entered a new stage like never before. Under the leadership of Zhou Enlai and Wang Yifei, the armed uprising was going smoothly, especially in Nanshi District, directly commanded by Wang Yifei. When they won, they turned around and attacked the Songhu Police Department at Dadongmen, forcing a legion of policemen to surrender. Next, they attacked the Gaochangmiao arsenal and seized a large quantity of weapons and ammunition. Early the next morning, when he heard that the North Station was still not breached, Wang Yifei immediately selected a group of young, strong, savvy, and capable comrades to form five combat storm troopers, including the machine gun team, the handgun team, and the rifle team. As he was ready to lead them to the north station and launch a major offensive, Commander-in-chief Zhou Enlai had someone call to report, "The battle is over!"

The workers' pickets of the armed uprising at Nanshi District chanted slogans to celebrate the first great victory of the workers' revolution in the history of Shanghai.

Amidst the cheers and excitement of his comrades-in-arms, Wang Yifei raced to Fumin Hospital to visit his wife, who had just given birth to their son...

Having been discharged from the hospital, Lu Zhuiwen went to

My Love, Roses of Blood

Hangzhou to hire a wet nurse as her postpartum health was poor and she lactated little. She lived in Xuan Zhonghua's home because his wife was her classmate in Suzhou Middle School. Because of their friendship, Xuan Zhonghua referred her to join the CPC later. At the time, the white terror permeated the country, especially in places with frequent revolutionary activities such as Shanghai and Hangzhou. One day, Xuan Zhonghua hurried home and announced to Lu Zhuiwen: "Move out immediately. It is dangerous here now."

Without asking what was going on, she immediately left Hangzhou with the baby and wet nurse. As soon as she returned to Shanghai, Wang Yifei broke to her the devastating news that after Xuan Zhonghua left Hangzhou in disguise, unfortunately he was captured by the reactionaries on his way to Shanghai, and shot dead in Longhua that night.

On August 7, 1927, the Central Committee of CPC summoned an emergency meeting in Hankou, Hubei. Wang Yifei attended it as a representative of the Central Military Commission. This was the famous August Seventh Meeting.

Once the meeting was over, in order to strengthen the leadership of the Autumn Harvest Uprising in northern Hubei, the Central Committee sent Wang Yifei there to offer guidance. In early September, he reached Xiangyang and Zaoyang. When he learned of the low ebb of the local peasant movement, he decided to halt his plan to launch a riot in northern Hubei. This decision received severe criticism from some leaders of the central government, yet he refused to defend himself. In late September, the Central Committee of the CPC summoned him back to Hankou. After the leading organs of the Central Committee of the CPC one after another moved to Shanghai, it was decided to establish the Yangtze River Bureau under the leadership of Luo Yinong in Wuhan, with Wang Yifei as its member. In early October, the Central Committee of the CPC sent a letter to the Hunan Provincial Party Committee, appointing Wang Yifei and Luo Yinong as special Commissioners of the Central Committee to Hunan to convene an emergency meeting of the provincial party committee. Consequently, the Hunan Provincial Party Committee was reorganized, and Wang Yifei was appointed as its new secretary.

Revolutionaries

From November 9–10, 1927, Qu Qiubai hosted a meeting of the Provisional Politburo of the Central Committee of the CPC in Shanghai. The Central Committee of the CPC mailed a letter to the Hunan and Hubei Provincial Party Committees requesting to launch simultaneous riots in the two provinces. On December 10, the riot broke out. Commander-in-chief Wang Yifei led dozens of armed workers in attacking the enemy's garrison headquarters. Yet, they were outnumbered and the riot failed.

It was at this time that he wrote a letter to his wife Lu Zhuowen, saying how he longed to reunite with her and their son in Changsha. However, the situation was worse than what he estimated. While the letter was still on the way, he was captured... He had never expected that the letter to ask for a family reunion would be a farewell.

In January 1928, the Hunan Provincial Party Committee and the Changsha Municipal Party Committee of the CPC were successively destroyed by the KMT Changsha reactionary authorities because of traitors within the party who informed on them. One day, Wang Yifei was arrested during a meeting with the leaders of the Hunan Provincial Party Committee. A few days later, he and several revolutionaries were killed at the Changsha Education Association.

His wife Lu Zhuiwen knew nothing about his death. She only received a letter from him asking her to go to Changsha with their child:

Dear Zhui:

I thought it through. If you come, take our child with you. As for the wet nurse, we will figure it out. This is one way. But you must come quickly. The end of the year will be too late.

Or wean the child, or replace breast milk with milk powder, or porridge and others. Come with the child in February in spring (lunar calendar). The local custom here says that it will be bad luck to build a mansion in the first and last months of the lunar calendar. This is a better and simpler way, except you have to stay another two months at home. I wonder if you can are okay with it?

When you come, travel light. Except for the essentials for you and the child, leave everything else at third brother's instead of our home. As for the travel expense, ask Sis or brother Chang for help. It will be no problem. Now

My Love, Roses of Blood

that the year is ending, it is inconvenient to travel. You must be careful along the journey. Remain calm and converse less with others. Friends made on the road are often unreliable.

Regards

Your Peng, December 24

In the early morning of December 24, Wang Yifei wrote his last letter to his wife, which means that while it was in the mail, he was shot dead. His wife was busy arranging the care of their son in Shanghai. After all, she was also an underground party member, thus aware that Changsha was no safe nest. She decided to send the child back to his hometown in Shangyu, Zhejiang. After everything was well arranged, she obtained approval from the organization and set off for Changsha at once. To reach Changsha by water had to go through Wuhan first. There were two underground party members travelling together with her, who went to Wuhan to report to the Central Committee. The three took care of each other. Upon their arrival in Wuhan, the organization sent Deng Yingchao to receive Lu Zhuiwen and hoped that she would tell her the news of her husband's death. But Deng Yingchao couldn't bear to say it to her face...

"What happened to Yifei? Tell me!" Lu Zhuiwen asked the comrades in the central organs, but nobody replied. Instead, they avoided her.

So she begged to go to Changsha. Everyone tried to talk her out of it saying the situation over there was tight. It was not the best timing.

"It means Yifei is exposed to greater danger there. I can help him when I am there, and share the danger," she pleaded.

However, no one approved her request. Some female comrades reasoned: "They are vigilant. You have short hair. Can't get ashore even if you reach Changsha."

"Why?" she was confused.

"Because there were riots in Changsha. Women who participated all had cut their hair short. The reactionaries will capture all women with short hair as revolutionaries!"

Lu Zhuiwen was skeptical, yet accepted it. She could do nothing but cry. In the end, she was persuaded to return to Shanghai.

Afterwards, she took her son back from Shangyu, and they lived at Luo

Revolutionaries

Yinong's place on Xinzha Road. She kept waiting for any news from her husband Wang Yifei... But the comrades in the party seemed to have made a pact. No one told her the truth.

Shrouded in melancholy, she came to Qu Qiubai's to try to get information. Qu Qiubai and Yang Zhihua received her with the warmest welcome, but next it was awkward silence.

"Allow me to play the flute." Qu Qiubai broke the silence, took off the flute on the wall and started a performance. She knew the mellow yet plaintive tone of the flute was how her dear comrades were missing her dead husband—Wang Yifei's sacrifice was great and noble. Before being shot dead by the enemies, he held his head high and declared proudly at the sky: "Born with nothing and die with nothing, the nature of the proletarians. May the suffering people in the world be liberated. And I will have no regrets about my death!"

Her husband died for the faith, gloriously. He will be forever remembered. In the long years that followed, Lu Zhuwen, also a revolutionary, cherished all the love letters from her husband. She lived her revolutionary life peacefully in Shanghai. She confessed affectionately: "I have never been lonely but am fulfilled because my heart is filled with love from my man."

Alas, there are many, many more... In the battles to liberate Shanghai alone, there were 7,613 heroic deaths. They were the husbands, the wives...

They sacrificed their lives in the arduous battles to found the People's Republic of China.

CHAPTER TEN

—

Family Note, Last Note and Final Cry, the Eternal Wave...

THESE DAYS, IN ORDER TO WRITE THIS BOOK, I OFTEN WALKED alone through the streets and alleys of Shanghai, visiting or paying respects to the places where the revolutionaries used to work and live. They were either the narrow and small attics or the zigzagging, damp alleys that attract little attention. There were hardly any separate and decent houses. Secretaries of the provincial party committees, of the municipal party committee and even the central leaders and cadres, with no exception, resided in the most remote and unobtrusive corners. Compared with the modern Shanghai today, full of skyscrapers and luxurious architecture, I could only sigh with emotion—

Our ancestors succeeded in the revolutionary cause under extreme difficulties!

Every time I stand in the memorial hall, sit in the archives room, gaze at the portraits, leaf through the last notes and belongings of the martyrs, my heart pounds violently and my thoughts run wild. Especially when I read the words dripping with tears and blood, it is as if there was a giant rock on my heart and I fall into a reverie...

When I think of every busy street, of every fast-moving high-speed passage in Shanghai, of the roaring Huangpu River, and of the ebb and flow of the Suzhou River, I am washed over with waves of emotions: without

Revolutionaries

them, without their struggle and sacrifice, without their struggles and uprising, without their devotion and love, what would Shanghai and China have been like? What would we all have been like?

Definitely, it would not have been as peaceful and prosperous today.

Would we still be exploring in the dark?

Would we still be in misery and sorrow?

Perhaps more miserable and darker than we could imagine... However, there is one thing that many still fail to understand: happiness is earned in struggle and effort, yet without an equal and free system that allows most people to be masters of their lives, the greatest effort cannot result in happiness. It would remain unobtainable.

A happy and wonderful life requires to the presence of an ideal and an effective system first, meaning that there must be a powerful country and an ideal social system backing us up. And the goal of the Chinese communists who fought bravely, giving their blood, was to establish such a country and such a system. Therefore, they never wavered, never hesitated, but were fully devoted, fearless, with no regrets at all...

They are the revolutionaries under my pen.

Their greatness, in my opinion, lies in all their selfless efforts, struggles, and sacrifices. They put ideals and beliefs ahead of themselves.

The blood stains on the streets of Shanghai in the past and the criminal gunfire at Yuhuatai in Nanjing constantly remind me: a true revolutionary, on the journey of life, has no boundary between living and dying but a sacred farewell ceremony—which perhaps is an exciting slogan, or a gaze up at the sky, or a glare at the enemies, or the courage to face a bullet.

Revolution is not only to eliminate all reactionary forces and enemies of the decadent world, but also an ultimate act of a believer ready to give his life at all times. It must be a thrill, a fulfillment to defeat the others; yet the real test is the courage to give one's life. Only the true revolutionaries and communists have withstood such a thorough test and become glorious martyrs whose souls and spirits live eternally despite their physical death.

In the vast materials of party history and revolutionary history, I have read the record by a survivor about the before and after of the shooting of five revolutionary martyrs. It brought me to tears, astonishing—

Family Note, Last Note and Final Cry, the Eternal Wave...

...Several cellmates who were shot dead by the enemies were lying there in silence. The guards standing next to them wept. So did everyone who heard the news.

It is 7:30 in the morning on September 19th. At 6:30, the five of them, who were locked in three prison cells, had just washed their faces. Before they started their morning chanting, the deputy warden suddenly walked to their cell gates. One prisoner asserted, "Someone is going to take a bullet (meaning execution)."

Zhu Jianguo firmly said: "I must be one on the list." Every time the deputy warden walked in early in the morning, death fell. He unlocked the gate, and the first he called was Xie Shiyan, and next Zhu Jianguo and Shi Chun. With heads held high, the three walked out without making a sound.

Ding Hang was locked in the next cell, and he was called next. He cursed: "Fuck, I haven't yet written my will." Zhao Liangzhang was in the third cell. Before his name was announced, he took off the leather jacket he was wearing, and said to the cellmates: "I must be on the list! Who wants this leather jacket? Take it." Eventually, he was called out. His cellmates were stunned and speechless. They watched him leave with great sympathy. His strong and broad back disappeared in the corridor.

As usual, before the execution, the sentence must be pronounced. They were led to an office and ordered to stand in a row. The military judge surnamed Fang read out their verdict, where there were words like "spies," "attempts to subvert the government," "confession," and "execution." Then, they were given the chance to speak their last words. Xie Shiyan raised his voice, "Kill us today, and the people across the country will avenge us!" Next, they wrote their last words. Some have already finished before and the paper was in their back pants pocket. On a table, there were two dishes, a jug of wine, and a small plate that held an opened pack of cigarettes. Xie Shiyan and Zhao Liangzhang both smoked a cigarette. After they handed over their will, they were taken to a vegetable garden outside the prison. A guard commander ordered them: "Kneel!"

Zhao Liangzhang turned his head and cursed: "Motherfucker!" It made the commander tremble. "We never kneel!" Next, they clenched their fists tightly and raised them to the sky. The gunshots echoed with their chanting "Long live the CPC."

Revolutionaries

Their death shocked the entire prison. Every heart was overwhelmed with emotion. A guard returning from the execution ground told me: "We are so frustrated. But there was nothing we could do. We only stood by and watched it happen. When they died, they held their heads high with no fear at all. When they shouted slogans, the judge's face turned pale with fright. He waved his hand to signal the execution to begin at once. When the bullets were fired, we were close and they almost hit us. We knew that they didn't break the law. They were all good citizens. Why were they sentenced to die? We don't understand. We have witnessed a lot of executions except only this time we were overwhelmed with sorrow, but we could not tell why."

As he was talking, he lowered his head. The shootings were common for them. Everyone was so emotional because we were touched by the martyrs' exemplary reactions to the difficulties.

It was no coincidence that a CPC member could exhibit such noble spirit of self-sacrifice. It resulted from the nurturing from the fine traditions of the party, the training of Marxist-Leninist theories, the correct leadership from the organization, and the experience of constant practical struggle. Therefore, one could become a fighting unit in the revolution, and the entire party the total driving force of the revolution.

...

They walked in front of us. They were our pioneers, our role models, and the giants we should look up to.

They illuminated the dark night, were the stars in the sky, forever shining on the world, in history, in our hearts.

Their spirit will never die, but live forever with us, with the future generations.

On the following day after they were shot, there was a heat wave. In the buildings, it was all stuffy and sweaty. Towards noon, a gust of wind blew open sunshade in the yard, turning it upside down, and the scattered paper on the wall shelves flew all over the room. Dark clouds thickened in the sky, gradually dimming the light. We knew a heavy thunderstorm was coming. Soon, thunder roared, and rain poured like falling cannonballs. Puddles quickly formed. Every raindrop raised ripples on them. Boom, boom, boom! It must be the roar of millions of people! It must be the tears of millions of people! This was the great tide of the revolution, the march of the revolution!

Family Note, Last Note and Final Cry, the Eternal Wave...

"Sky, it is time! Open your crack wider! Torrential rain, pour down on us! Our souls are agitated, our fists clenched. We are ready for you! Unleash your wrath upon the world!"

...

The truth is many of those who made records of the executions and death diaries were also killed later. Therefore, the few words they managed to leave to future generations are extremely precious. There were also many revolutionaries who managed to leave their last words and family letters via various ways before they died, or heroic poems. Although all these remains of the martyrs are now covered in the dust of the history, like the pieces of information sent to Yan'an by the protagonist Li Xia in the movie *The Eternal Wave*, they have been guiding those with ideals and aspirations in the revolutionary team to march forward and illuminating the path for our great nation to advance. The prototype Li Xia was created based on a revolutionary martyr named Li Bai. He was a member of the Shanghai underground party and veteran of the Red Army who participated in the Autumn Harvest Uprising and the 25,000-li Long March. For the revolution, he came to Shanghai from Yan'an, lived in a small attic of 14 square meters on the third floor of 148 Beile Road (now South Huangpi Road), and engaged in intelligence tasks under the white terror. On May 7, 1949, the enemies secretly shot him dead. It was merely 20 days away from the liberation of Shanghai. Before he died, his wife took their four-year-old son to visit him in prison. He showed them an optimistic face. "Don't be sad. Working for the revolution is my greatest joy. It is always darkest before dawn. When the revolution wins, you, our children and the people of China will live a happy and free life. How great is that!"

An experienced revolutionary, who lived in a small attic of merely a bit over ten square meters with his wife and son, fought alone almost day and night, and all he cherished was the happiness and liberation of every Chinese. One must be impressed by such a noble soul.

Today, when skyscrapers form concrete jungles, high-speed trains run in all directions, and urban life has been greatly modernized, shouldn't we take some time to listen to the last words of the martyrs, shouldn't we put down our phones and spare a moment to read their last notes, stained with tears and blood? That will inevitably be a lesson that will purify our spirit and soul.

One day when I was out for an interview, I noticed a bustling small park at the corner of the street. I looked from a distance and discovered a statue of the musician Xian Xinghai standing there. And I quickly asked the taxi driver to pull over because I wanted to pay my respect to this revolutionary musician.

Among the thousands of revolutionary martyrs in the Longhua Martyrs Memorial Hall, Xian Xinghai had a special identity. He was not killed by the enemies, nor did he die in prison but of illness when he was in the Soviet Union composing a series of symphonic numbers. He was regarded as a revolutionary martyr for his special contribution and special ties with Shanghai.

This talented revolutionary musician, whose representative works are of anti-Japanese themes, was filled with hatred for the invaders during his days in Shanghai. On the other hand, as a revolutionary musician, his job took place underground, too. He achieved his self-worth in his unique revolutionary musician way and sacrifice, thus becoming a widely respected martyr. The words he left to his children when he was alive have been branded in my mind.

In this great era, we must contribute what we can to the nation, to the party. Don't always focus on our personal happiness, because that depends on the liberation of the nation and of mankind.

The last words of this revolutionary musician are as classic as *The Yellow River Cantata* he composed for us, an awakening that can be passed on forever.

The co-creator of *The Yellow River Cantata* is Guang Weiran, whose real name is Zhang Guangnian, a senior leader of the Chinese Writers Association. Mr. Zhang personally narrated about how they created the number. "It was not long since Xinghai moved from Shanghai to Yan'an. I wrote a long poem called *Yellow River Song*. He suggested that I change it to *Yellow River Cantata*. Naturally, he put it to music. The living conditions in Yan'an were difficult. Knowing that Xinghai was from Panyu, Guangdong,

Family Note, Last Note and Final Cry, the Eternal Wave...

naturally fond of sweets, I prepared for him a kilo of white sugar while he was composing. And he really completed the music score of *The Yellow River Cantata* on the *kang* (a heated sleeping platform widely used in villages in northern China) after six days and six nights, while taking some sugar at times. It became popular across the country. *The wind is howling, the horse is neighing, and the yellow river is roaring.* The score was performed for the first time in Yan'an. It caused an immediate sensation in the audience, even Chairman Mao Zedong praised it. Back then, we had a saying in Yan'an that *The Yellow River Cantata* was a masterpiece made of Xinghai's soul and sugar."

This great battle anthem of the Chinese nation, co-created by the people's musician and writer, inspired and encouraged the people across the country to resist Japan. It became a thunderous force to defeat the enemies. Therefore, Xian Xinghai received infinite love from the people.

From Mr. Zhang, I also learned some other stories about this revolutionary musician: Xian Xinghai was born poor. His father was a poor fisherman. Before he was born, his father died at sea. So, Xian Xinghai was born without a father. His mother received little education. But she sat on the beach, looking up at the stars, and gave her son a poetic name: Xinghai (an ocean of stars).

Next, mother took him to Southeast Asia, where she made a living as a laborer, and suffered a lot. But she was optimistic, often humming some tunes or folk songs. She found joy amid hardships. Xian Xinghai always called her his music enlightenment.

Since school, teachers encouraged Xian Xinghai to pursue a musical path because he exhibited great interest in musical instruments. With musical talent, he was admitted to the High School Affiliated to Lingnan University after returning to his motherland. Later, he studied music in Beijing. After the school was closed, he was admitted to the Shanghai National Music College, and from then on began his true music career. In 1929, Xian Xinghai, with a dream to wake the country up with music, earned enough tuition as a boilerman on a sea-going vessel and financed his study in France. In Paris, he met Ma Sicong, a student of music from his hometown, who introduced him to become an apprentice of the famous violinist Paul Oberdoeffer. To learn music well, Xian Xinghai worked and

Revolutionaries

studied hard. He got up at 5 a.m. and went to bed at 12 a.m. Once he was waiting tables in a restaurant, his blacked out because of fatigue and rolled down the stairs with a tray of plates. He took some bad beatings from the boss. It was difficult to get new employment. He became a hobo on the street countless times. Thanks to the other hobos who helped him, he was not identified as a corpse and dragged away after he fainted... During seven years of a harsh life, with tenacious perseverance, he studied while working part-time, and created *Wind*, a score that perfectly depicts the joys and sorrows of the world. He submitted it to an examination by the Paris Conservatoire. It succeeded and won an award. When the chief examiner announced to him, "We have decided to give an award to you. According to our rules, you can make material requirements."

With trembling lips, he only uttered two words: "Meal tickets."

This was the path the musical genius had walked on. After that, he became a protégé of the school's world-class composer Paul Dukas.

In 1935, Xian Xinghai returned to his motherland, came to Shanghai again, and started his revolutionary musical career. When the powerful and influential in the city induced him to write music that panders to the public instead of the dangerous songs about national salvation, he retorted: "Why do I write songs with the theme of resistance to Japan? Even some peers ridiculed and disparaged me, but I am a musician with a conscience. I aspire to write about the dire peril of my motherland, and have my songs heard across China, across the world, reminding them to go against feudalism, against aggression, against imperialism, especially Japanese imperialism. I believe this means something." In the next two years, he devoted himself to creating music with the theme of resistance to Japan and national salvation. With famous musicians like Tian Han, Wu Yonggang, and Mai Xin, they co-created over 200 scores, including the famous *Military Song of National Salvation, Love of the Yellow River, Hot Blood*, and *Youth March*.

In 1937, the War of Resistance broke out into a full scale war. Xian Xinghai joined the second team of the wartime performance in Shanghai drama circles and performed on the front lines of the War of Resistance nationwide. Along the way, he had gone through the ordeal of battle, thus many juicy ideas about music creation. A number of excellent scores were written, such as *Defending Lugou Bridge, Song for the Guerillas Fighting, On the Taihang Mountains* and *Going Behind the Enemy*. Next, they became the war anthems of the anti-Japanese troops and greatly encouraged and inspired the anti-Japanese passion of the frontline soldiers and the masses.

During the difficult years, Xian Xinghai wrote to his mother with deep affection: "Reluctantly I have to leave you and stand among the people... devote my greatest love to the country, and spend the most precious time and spirit on the national struggle!... The motherland is nurturing us selflessly. In order to survive, we must unite to defend our motherland that is even greater than our mothers!" It was this kind of mind and sentiment of a revolutionary musician that inspired him to create the immortal and epic score *The Yellow River Cantata*.

"Its great imposing manner naturally cheers people up while conveying lofty emotions. This alone is a bath for one's soul," the famous writer Mao Dun commented on Xian Xinghai's great scores.

"I deeply believe in the victory of the people of my motherland, in its revolutionary strength. My most precious dream is to see the freedom and happiness of the Chinese people." These were his last words.

"His last words are etched on my memory," said Vano Muradeli, a famous Soviet musician who had been accompanying Xian Xinghai during his treatment.

So far, we have understood the reason why he could write the scores that ignite the flames of passion in people when they sing them is that he had always prioritized the happiness of his motherland and its people. As he put it before his death, he would always "Double his efforts and devote his heart and soul to the great country until the last breath."

He made it. His scores will live forever, and so will his name.

There are many more revolutionary martyrs that will live forever in our hearts. We still talk about them often today, like Mr. Taofen, a newspaperman, editor, and reporter who fought in Shanghai for decades. When he said goodbye to this world, his last message to his family contained only two words: "Fear nothing."

Fear nothing perfectly depicts the life of this revolutionary.

He was every word that Mao Zedong commented: "He loved the people, served the people, with the greatest efforts he could. This is who Mr. Taofen was, and why he moved us."

Revolutionaries

This scholar wielded his pen as a gun to fight against the ruthless enemies. Not everyone had the courage. But Taofen did. In Shanghai during the War of Resistance, with gentle and frail demeanor, he devoted himself to castigating the weak defectors and hateful invaders. He exhibited power ten times stronger than that of guns and swords, because he awakened the people and the nation.

Fear nothing is the character and basic quality of the revolutionaries, and the spiritual pillar of those with ideals and beliefs. When faced with the enemy, the difficulties, the darkness, the setbacks, and death, those who fear will waver, lose their way, and eventually become dregs. Instead, Mr. Taofen feared nothing. That was his revolutionary strength.

Forget me, also two words, was the last message of another martyr, Luo Hemin. This revolutionary martyr, who died at 35 years old, spent over 20 years in Shanghai. All major events during his life took place in Shanghai, in the revolutionary missions. Before he was beheaded by the enemies, he only uttered the two words to his family.

In fact, *forget me* is how the martyr loved his family. To his wife, he implored: "Farewell. Don't feel sad for me. Think of where I have done you wrong. Forget me! "However, he never forgot the ultimate mission of the revolutionaries—to eliminate the enemy and overthrow the reactionaries. Knowing that he could no longer continue the missions, he asked his wife to tell their underage child, "Make sure she never compromises to the people I hate!"

This was the last sustenance and all hope of the revolutionary.

Forget me, two succinct words, not only contains his affection and love for his family, but also the hope that they shall not lose their will and strength to fight due to grief, nor the determination to eliminate the enemy.

Forget me, it was with blood flowing, tears running, heart trembling, it was the last hoarse cry of the revolutionary...

Among the thousands of heroes in the two martyrs memorial halls of Longhua and Yuhuatai, there was one martyr, handsome and smiling, escorted to the execution ground with both hands tied. He was martyr Wang Xiaohe.

This martyr, who was shot dead by the enemies a year before the founding of PRC, was born in Hongkou, Shanghai in 1924. His father was

Family Note, Last Note and Final Cry, the Eternal Wave...

a furnaceman on a foreign ship. This studious boy joined the CPC at the age of 17. As a descendant of Shanghai workers, the organization arranged him to work at the Yangshupu Power Plant. In the later stage of War of Liberation, Shanghai became an important city for the final decisive battle between the KMT reactionaries and the CPC. Under the leadership of the underground party of the CPC, the labor strikes of the Yangshupu Power Plant workers attracted great attention in Shanghai. It broke out in January 1946 and lasted for nine days and eight nights, shocking the city of Shanghai. In early 1948, a major strike against KMT rule broke out again at the plant. The KMT blatantly steered armored vehicles into the plant area in an attempt to suppress it. The secret agents, who learned that Wang Xiaohe was its worker leader, visited him at home to coax him into surrender. He calmly responded: "I am a standing council member of the labor union elected by the 2,800 employees of Shanghai Power Plant. It is my duty to speak and stand up for the staff. I see no need to surrender."

As soon as the secret agents left, the family was so worried that tears welled in their eyes. They suggested that he lay low in his hometown of Ningbo. However, he refused. "It is the critical moment for the fate of my worker brothers. I can't leave them behind." He insisted on staying in Shanghai, in the power plant.

The next day, Wang Xiaohe rode his bike to work as usual. On the way, a few secret agents ambushed him and abducted him in a black police vehicle.

The enemies tried to make him surrender with brutal torture, but he would rather die. Helplessly, in order to deceive the workers, the secret agents published his "confession" in various Shanghai newspapers the next day, mentioning his referral to join the party was xxx. On the contrary, when the news came out, the workers and party organizations was certain that Wang Xiaohe had withstood the test and protected his comrades.

The arrest of Wang Xiaohe became major news in Shanghai at the time. The secret agents imposed torture on him again and again, hoping he would talk, but after a few months they gained nothing. The irritated enemies eventually sentenced him to death.

The scheduled execution date was September 27. When the news came out, workers from the power plant raced to the execution ground. Their

Revolutionaries

angry shouts terrified the KMT reactionary authorities. They hurriedly changed the date.

Wang Xiaohe left three precious "last notes." The followings are excerpts of three last notes to his parents, pregnant wife, and cellmates respectively:

Mom and Dad:

Thank you for raising me up. When I saw the injustices in this society, I did not forget to be an honest man as you have taught me to be. Today, my life comes to an end! I hope you will not grieve for me. I have suffered injustice but my death is glorious, way much more than that of the traitors, the corrupt officials. Ying has suffered enough. I hope you will treat her as your own daughter and find her a good man. I only hope that she will not forget me, and I shall be eternally grateful in the netherworld. Please explain to Qinnü and the future child, Pei Min, how and why I leave them behind. My death is major as an individual but to the society, it is too insignificant? Millions of righteous and honest people are still alive. They will avenge me. Mom and dad, take care. Open your eyes and wait to see: This tyrannical government is about to collapse! My injustice will be redressed. Don't forget to punish my murderers.

After I die, everything should go as simple as possible. Fortunately, there are two younger brothers. I hope that they will also remember me, treat Ying as their own sister and the two children as their own flesh and blood, teach them well, redress my injustice, and avenge me.

...

> *Your unfilial son, Wang Xiaohe, with tears*
> *Noon of September 27, the 37th year of the Republic of China*

Dear Ying,

My lovely wife, I am eternally grateful to you, and apologetic to you. You did your best for me. Although today's result is not the best, there is something gained. I have suffered injustice. The unreasonable Special Criminal Court decided my destiny. But I hope you don't grieve excessively. In this unreasonable world, thousands of people die for justice, leave their wife and children for justice, don't they? Don't be sad! Take care of yourself, of our two

Family Note, Last Note and Final Cry, the Eternal Wave...

children! Tell them who killed their father and not to forget! See my parents as your own parents. If you meet a nice man, be with him. I will never blame you. Instead, knowing that you are loved, I can rest in peace! I hope your upcoming childbirth goes smoothly! Name him/her Peimin! Again, take care. Soon I will be avenged! Send my regards to our friends and relatives, and thank them for their kindness.

The special criminal court violates the law, illegally sentences the death penalty, and holds court secretly. Let's see how long it will last...

Your husband, Wang Xiao

Two o'clock, September 27, the 37th year of the Republic of China

Righteous men! I wish you good health! Keep fighting for justice! The future is bright, waving at us! Work hard and we shall get there!

Wang Xiaohe

It hurts to read these last words of a revolutionary. What is a noble soul? What is unshaken faith? What is firm loyalty? What is deep love? What is deep hate? The last notes of the martyrs offer a detailed explanation. The courage and fearlessness they exhibited when faced with slaughter by the enemy is truly touching.

When he was sentenced to die, the enemies attempted to humiliate the communist by summoning in over 20 reporters to watch. Unexpectedly, after the "judge" read the verdict, Wang Xiaohe remained calm and requested to speak in front of the reporters. "I'd like to say a few words to the reporters present..." He talked about the crimes of KMT reactionaries, their violation of the law, their killings of innocents, and suppression of workers, etc. The speech earned loud applause from the reporters present in the court. A foreign reporter asked him in English. Wang Xiaohe was merely a labor union cadre at the power plant, but he had studied at Shanghai Inspirational English College. He answered several questions in English fluently, which embarrassed the reactionary judge. In a panic, the judge hurriedly announced: "No more questions! The prisoner is to be executed immediately!"

As usual, several reactionary bailiffs came in with a bowl of liquor mixed with narcotic drugs for Wang Xiaohe to drink.

Revolutionaries

"I'm no coward. I won't need this!" He knocked the liquor bowl to the ground. The reactionary bailiffs had to leap forward, grab his arms, and escort him to the execution ground.

Wang Xiaohe cursed as he walked. In the face of the ugly atrocities of the reactionaries, he laughed... These moments were captured by the *Ta Kung Pao* photographer Ma Gengbo, so that now, we can see a set of extremely precious photos of a revolutionary before his execution.

His bright smile in front of death leaves an eternal impression on us. He could smile at death with great calm, perhaps because, as he suggested in his last words to the cellmates, the light was waving at us. One should be happy to know that.

This is the mind and sentiment of the revolutionaries, absolutely admirable.

The name of the martyr Ye Tiandi is known to few. But when I finished reading the last note he wrote to his brother before his death, I was overwhelmed with strong emotions...

The last note said: *I have no chance to survive. I will not die of disease, but at the hands of my enemies. A revolutionary never fears death... The blood of the martyrs, the flower of communism... I would rather stand to die than kneel to live.*

What dauntless mettle!

Ye Tiandi came from Shangyu, Zhejiang Province, also the hometown of many revolutionaries in Shanghai.

He was formerly called Ye Linwei. And he spent the most important days of his revolutionary career in Shanghai. In 1920, at the recommendation of Chen Wangdao, he proofread the manuscript of *New Youth* at a printing factory in Shanghai, which gave him the opportunity to meet early communists, including Chen Wangdao, at a young age. One day, when Chen Wangdao, also a Zhejiang native, saw the *Bamboo and Rock Painting* that Ye Linwei collected, he left an inscription on it. *"Rock on the bamboo shoots, they grow from the side. Rock no longer on the bamboo shoots, they grow straight."* Ye Linwei was overjoyed and changed his name to Ye Tiandi–to be a man like bamboo shoots under a rock, he vowed. He used this as his motto and hung the paintings on the wall of his study.

In this way, the road of revolution widened. Ye Tiandi also became one

Family Note, Last Note and Final Cry, the Eternal Wave...

of the founders of the Chinese Socialist Youth League (the predecessor of the Communist Youth League).

In the spring of 1921, Chen Duxiu sent him to study in the Soviet Union. Unluckily, he suffered a sudden case of typhoid fever and failed to go. After Yu Xiusong, former Secretary of the Shanghai Socialist Youth League, went instead, Ye was actually in charge of his work in Shanghai. As the typhoid had not been cured and the workload was great, in addition to his weak constitution, Ye had to leave Shanghai for his hometown for convalescence. Concerned with the revolutionary missions in Shanghai, he wrote to his comrades-in-arms: "Depravity means a dead heart. My heart will never die before my body does! My heart cares about nothing but the revolution..."

In the days of recovery, he never forgot his responsibilities. He took the opportunity to be a substitute teacher at Shangyu Chunhui Middle School in his hometown to promote Marxism and revolutionary principles to the students, planting the seeds. This school later became a local Red Revolution base, and many young students from the school participated in the revolution in Shanghai. Decades later, at one of school anniversary celebrations, the famous scholar Hu Yuzhi gave a speech. "There was a revolutionary youth, one of the most respectable heros, who lived frugally, worked without asking for credit, sowed the earliest seeds of communist revolution, and sacrificed his precious life. This man was Ye Tiandi, an early CPC member. Now the seeds he planted have bloomed beautifully and borne juicy fruits."

Ye Tiandi was not only a propagator of revolutionary fire, but also an accomplished man in literature. He published *Enlightenment, Autumn Night,* and documentary writings *The Great Japan Earthquake* and *Nights at the Yellow Sea.* He returned to Shanghai in 1923 and engaged in literary theory research at the Shanghai Oriental Art Research Association. In those days, he also became an auditor at the revolution crucible—Shanghai University. He befriended Qu Qiubai, Luo Yinong, Yun Daiying, and joined the CPC under their introduction. Soon, the organization appointed him as a teacher at the Suzhou Leyi Girls' Middle School, under the leadership of Hou Shaoqiu, to establish the party branches in Suzhou.

The frail Ye Tiandi fell ill again because of overwork... He had to leave

Revolutionaries

Shanghai again and return to his hometown of Shangyu to recover. At the beginning of the Northern Expedition, he accepted the order of the Shanghai Party Organization of the CPC to actively organize revolutionary forces in Shangyu and Shaoxing and cultivate peasant armed forces. With his unremitting efforts, the revolutionary armed uprising was a success and they seized the county seat. However, the Chiang Kai-shek reactionary group launched a coup and slaughtered the communists on a large scale. Ye Tiandi, who was sent from Shanghai, was arrested and escorted to Hangzhou.

"As a senior member of the CPC from Shanghai, you have a great influence. Our superior thinks highly of you. Sign this to turn yourself in and you are free to go." Many senior KMT officials were also Zhejiang natives, so when they came to induce him to surrender, they always made a promise, "Just nod and side with us, and you will get an official position!"

Ye Tiandi sneered: "Sign? You must not know me well! I would rather die."

The scheming KMT Zhejiang Provincial Party Headquarters resorted to a different trick–allowing him to "see a doctor outside prison," and meanwhile sending a few "Zhengjiang natives" from Shanghai to persuade him. He never wavered and repeatedly expressed: "Since I joined the CPC, I have always believed in communism. Now I am arrested due to illness. My only regret is that I haven't done much for the party. Death is coming and I am ready. It is an honor to die for communism. Be aware, any attempt to make me surrender is an insult to me."

The "Zhengjiang natives" all sighed and left.

The frail revolutionary turned out to have bones harder than steel. In the face of powerful enemies, he declared proudly and fearlessly to the sinful world that was about to destroy him: "I – would rather than stand to die than kneel to live!"

He would never kneel to survive before reactionary and dark forces, but would rather stand to die for the sake of communist faith and the noble interests of the country and the people. This is our proletarian revolutionary.

Family Note, Last Note and Final Cry, the Eternal Wave...

Longhua has been admiring the lofty morals for ages. The heroes die yet the dreams continue.
The peach blossoms outside pop inside the walls, beautiful and bright-red.

A broken halberd is buried at Yuhuatai. There is no ripples in the Mochou lake.
Missing Sun Yat-sen and his followers, yet they are gone, where the river and the horizon meet, I sing aloud.

Of the two poems above, the first one was the work by a revolutionary imprisoned in Longhua carved on a cell wall. Lu Hsun was the author of the second.

In the two memorial spots for revolutionary martyrs, Longhua in Shanghai and Yuhuatai in Nanjing, a female martyr left a deep impression. She was Huang Li. Before she died, she was Minister of Organization of the Jiangsu Provincial Party Committee of the CPC. On April 25, 1933, she was arrested by reactionary military police and the French concession police at her residence on Xiai Xiansi Road (now Yongjia Road) in Shanghai. It was her secretary Zhou Guangya who betrayed her. The enemies searched every corner of her apartment and only found a silver coin, six pennies, a handkerchief, a steel watch, and a pair of glasses. The reactionary military police found it hard to believe that a high-ranking CPC cadre had only a few simple possessions.

After her arrest, Deng Zhongxia, her direct supervisor and one of the important leaders of the CPC, concluded with immense regret: "She shouldn't have fallen into the hands of the enemy." Huang Li had been fighting side by side with Deng Zhongxia. This outstanding female cadre, who lived in the Soviet Union for six years, was arrested soon after her transfer to Shanghai as Director and Party Secretary of the Chinese Revolutionary Mutual Aid Association. Huang Li was one of the few female communists who joined the party during the May Thirtieth Movement in 1925. Afterwards, she was sent as a core member to study at Sun Yat-sen University in Moscow. In 1926, she fell in love with Yang Fangzhi, a classmate, and got married. In 1928, she accompanied Qu Qiubai to Berlin to attend the Congress of the World Anti-Imperialist League. In 1929, she

Revolutionaries

and her husband Yang Fangzhi accompanied Deng Zhongxia to Vladivostok to attend the Second Pan Pacific Labor Conference, and then stayed there to engage in the Far East International Labor Movement. Seeing the drastic changes in the domestic revolution, she requested to the organization to return to China. It was approved and she came to Shanghai.

Back in China, she, with her extraordinary leadership, rescued a large number of revolutionaries that the enemies had imprisoned, and handled most of the consolation and compensation to the families of the martyrs, thus her fine reputation. Later, because the Jiangsu Provincial Party Committee of the CPC in Shanghai suffered repeated damage, the Central Committee decided to appoint her as its Minister of Organization. At the time, the work of the underground party was in dire peril. The central government was also concerned about her safety and decided to transfer her to the Soviet area. But before she could leave, she was betrayed and fell into the hands of the enemy.

The KMT authorities had high expectations for her, hoping that this essential female communist would surrender and switch allegiances. They spared no effort and exhausted all tricks, but failed to shake her revolutionary beliefs. With no more tricks, they escorted her from Shanghai prison to Nanjing. What the reactionaries never expected was that in the Nanjing Military Prison, she charmed a prison chief with her communist personality and he switched allegiance. As a result, information regarding the enemy's next move to suppress the revolutionaries was fed to the underground party of the CPC, thus effectively protecting a group of revolutionaries. When the enemies found out, the leader of the Nanjing reactionary authorities, Gu Zhenglun, was furious and immediately ordered the execution of Huang Li and the prison chief.

When she learned about her death penalty, she calmly talked to her cellmates: "I'm going to Yuhuatai soon." Then, she pointed her fingers to the temple, gestured trigger pulling, and smiled. She was ready to give her life. She took a small knife, cut off a strand of her dark hair, and handed it to Qian Ying, a cellmate, and implored: "Please give it to my husband. He is also imprisoned, suffering torture yet still fighting..." This was her last words to her family and friends.

On the day of the execution, Huang Li stood on the prison vehicle and

Family Note, Last Note and Final Cry, the Eternal Wave...

still tried to fulfill the final mission of a revolutionary—propagandizing to the KMT officers and soldiers escorting her: "You are also born poor like me. I believe you love this country, too. For the love for our nation, we strive to regain the lost land in the northeast and oppose the KMT's surrender policy. The reactionaries are hunting us, but you cannot kill us all. A government that rules by murder will never last. The KMT is about to die. Fight, everyone! We will surely build a new China, prosperous and powerful, where there is no oppression..."

"Long live the Communist Party of China!"

"A new China will definitely be built!"

The 28-year-old female communist made a last cry at the criminal bullet that pierced through her body.

She fell, but the revolutionary prophecy came true. On October 1, 1949, Mao Zedong solemnly announced to the world at the Tiananmen Gate Tower in Beijing:

The Central People's Government of the People's Republic of China is established today!

From the establishment of the CPC in 1921 to 1949, the revolutionaries have achieved the greatest feat of the Chinese nation after 28 years of bloody struggles. Along the way, how many revolutionaries have sacrificed their lives in Shanghai, Nanjing, and all over the country? Who were they? What were their names? Like the roaring Huangpu River and the Yangtze River rolling eastward, they had countless stories and quantities. Those who have been included in the Revolutionary Martyrs Commemorative Album are only a fraction, and there are many more, whose names remain unknown. We don't know where their families are...

The spirit of the revolutionaries is the most precious legacy of a nation. Inheriting and promoting their spirit is the essence of "Staying true to the Party's original aspiration and the founding mission."

Let us always remember the revolutionary martyrs who fought and sacrificed their lives for the founding of the People's Republic of China.

This book is complete. However, my heart could not calm down—that deep emotions for the revolutionaries keep washing over me... Let's sing the *Song for the Prisoners* written by Lin Jilu, a martyr who died in 1943 again—

Revolutionaries

I cried tears for the nation's history,
Dynasty after dynasty, generation after generation,
Seeing the patriots,
Ambitious and indignant, yet taken to the execution ground;
The cruel and evil with a mouth full of fangs,
Always domineering and arrogant.
Oh! My nation, our mother who suffered,
In your five thousand years, countless heroes have died.
For your billions of years of a great cause, how many more to sacrifice their
lives.
The prison walls killed the lofty ambition to serve the country,
Darkness devoured the promising bodies,
The fetters locked and broke the wings of freedom.
The iron gates have imprisoned too many patriots.
Civil war benefited the foreign invaders.
Those who commit infinite sins would reap what they sow.
The stench of blood would be washed away with the blood of the murderers.
Prisoners, new prisoners, with firm convictions and a loyal stand.
Beheaded, shot, yet their souls returned home;
Severe torture was nothing rare.
Prisoners, new prisoners, with firm convictions and a loyal stand.
Dedicate our lives to build a pyramid of freedom,
Shed our blood to dye the flags red, and they would fly forever!

Spring 2014 to Summer 2019
In Beijing, Shanghai, and Nanjing

ABOUT THE AUTHOR

HE JIANMING, a well-known author of reportage literature, has been awarded the *Lu Xun Literature Prize* three times, the *National Excellent Reportage Prize* seven times, and the *Xu Chi Reportage Prize* four times. His main works include *The Country, Fidelity and Betrayal, Fundamental Interests,* and *Falling Tears are Gold.* He is additionally the author of the filmscripts *Westbound Convict Train* and *Folksong Xintianyou,* and the TV series *Founders* and *National Action.* He has published over 50 works of literature, including over 30 works of literary reportage, which have been translated into dozens of languages. He is vice president of the China Writers' Association.